# THE RISE AND FALL OF CAPITALISM

# THE RISE AND FALL OF CAPITALISM

*Y.S. Brenner*

*Professor of Economics*
*University of Utrecht*

Edward Elgar

Published by
Edward Elgar Publishing Limited
Gower House
Croft Road
Aldershot
Hants GU11 3HR
England

Edward Elgar Publishing Company
Old Post Road
Brookfield
Vermont 05036
USA

A CIP catalogue record for this book is available from the British Library

A CIP catalogue record for this book is available from the US Library of Congress

ISBN 1 85278 527 6

Printed and bound in Great Britain by
Billing and Sons Ltd, Worcester

# Contents

# Preface and Acknowledgements

Adam Smith believed that an 'invisible hand' naturally, or rather necessarily, leads people to prefer that employment of their resources which is most advantageous to society. The author of this book is more inclined to agree with the assertion that no principle of distribution is either self-validating or self-enforcing. I believe that the materially improved living standards of most people in the capitalist societies must be regarded as a 'special case' – the product of a fortuitous concatenation of new economic opportunities with particular patterns of culture which imposed legality, rationality, even a degree of humanity, upon the quest for riches.

Against the background of a synoptic historical analysis, I try to explain why and how rapacity and exploitation were confined within legal boundaries, and ingenuity rather than brute force became the source of wealth. I explore the interaction of economic with social and cultural developments, and arrive at the conclusion that 'deregulation' will 'kill the goose that laid the golden eggs'. I suggest that by an inner logic deregulated capitalism must lead to social polarisation and to the waning of elements in bourgeois culture which are necessary to sustain the proper functioning of a technologically advanced, complex and interdependent industrial economy.

The book arose out of my lecture notes for a course in Social Economics at the University of Utrecht. In the first part an attempt is made to explain how capitalism replaced feudalism (chapters 1-7); the second part focuses attention on labour's challenge to the capitalist system (chapters 8-13); and the third part deals with the recent drift toward neo-feudalism, and the threat deregulation poses to the compromise between capital and labour and therefore to the reasonably equitable distribution of the fruits of industrialization and perhaps to industrial society itself (chapters 14-16). Much of the material was collected from my earlier work, particularly for *Looking into the Seeds of Time* (Van Gorcum, Assen, 1979) and *Capitalism, Competition and Economic Crisis* (Wheatsheaf, Brighton, 1984). Inevitably readers familiar with these books may recognize some of the arguments. This cannot be helped. But the questions raised in the present book are different, and so is the focus of attention.

Finally it remains for me to express gratitude to my wife Drs Nancy Brenner–Golomb, and my friend and colleague Dr Antoon Spithoven, for the many hours they spent helping me to improve the manuscript. I also want to take this opportunity to thank the students of the Social Economics seminar of 1990 for their comments and the secretaries for the work they did putting this manuscript into its final shape.

Y.S. Brenner
Bilthoven

# Introduction: Economic Progress

*Economic progress* normally means a sustained rise in the product of labour per unit of time; an increase in the yield of produce per unit of land and materials; and the exploitation of previously unrecognized resources or the utilization of resources which for technological, economic, or other reasons had remained unexploited. The effect of economic progress is that it gives societies the opportunity, but no more than the opportunity, to become more affluent and to augment their freedom of choice.

Reduced labour-time enables them to choose between working less hours to satisfy customary wants or, by continuing to work as long as before, to satisfy additional wants. Increased yields from land and materials provide them with resources for sustaining a growing population, and with a combination of choices, such as increasing the wealth of a few or spreading affluence to a greater number of people; or enjoying directly the fruits of the new surplus or investing it in bigger future advantages.

In short, at least in theory, *economic progress* provides people with greater freedom because it reduces the constraint imposed on them by the need to satisfy basic wants. The augmentation of freedom is only theoretical because economic progress does not depend on the availability of land and labour alone but also on capital and incentives. The instinct for survival may well suffice to explain fruit gathering and hunting, but the creation of economic capital is more complicated. Land and labour are 'given', but capital, the wealth used in the more efficient production of further wealth, needs to be 'created'. Whether it takes the form of mechanical equipment, of inputs in land amelioration, or of

1

learning, it can only be obtained at the cost of forgoing something else which holds direct satisfaction. Consequently the provision of a crucial factor for the promotion of economic progress requires not only the *ability* to produce an output which exceeds what is needed to sustain its producers, but also foresight and incentives.

Persons who can produce no more than the goods and services required to assure their immediate survival have as a rule neither the time nor the ability to produce the means by which future wants can be satisfied more effectively. They are trapped in the vicious circle of poverty. But even if the necessary surplus of resources is available it alone is not enough. The incentive – the *wish* to utilize it for the satisfaction of future wants must also be present. No economic progress is likely to ensue when people do not recognize the possibility of improving their future by refraining from consumption and transforming their savings into productive investment; nor when they believe the eventual advantages are too small or remote to make their effort worthwhile. Neither will economic progress materialize when people do not feel the need for improvements, nor if those who are able to save have no confidence that their savings, and the expected fruits of their investment, will remain in their control.

It follows that given the level of available technology, the parameters determining the limits within which an economy can grow are delineated by both the *ability* to save, which depends upon the size of the difference between the volume of output produced and the minimum of the output necessary for current consumption; and the people's *wish* or propensity to save and invest, which depends on the cultural, social and political environment. Consequently, next to technology, the *ability* to invest determines the upper limit of potential growth and the *wish* to invest its actual pace and path.

As even primitive societies normally support a number of people who do not directly contribute to their material output, for example priests and kings; and as they often produce surpluses which are lavishly consumed on festive occasions or stored in treasure hoards or expended on the construction of pyramids, pagodas and similar economically unproductive edifices, it may not be unreasonable to assume that the lack of *ability* to invest cannot always be regarded as the major cause of economic retardation. This assumption is borne out by the historical record of the ancient civilizations of Mesopotamia, Egypt and Rome, which despite their impressive achievements in construction, trade and manufacturing, neither gave birth to a mode of production capable of increasing labour productivity sufficiently to engender a striking expansion of the *total* volume of their social product nor to a *general* rise in living standards.

While each of these civilizations produced a measure of advancement in the utilization of land and other resources, and very considerable improvements in living standards for parts of their populations, the latter were mainly the result of a *redistribution* of the economic surplus and not of an appreciable rise in labour productivity. They were obtained by skimming off the surplus produced by thousands of people and concentrating it in the hands of few. The rulers of Mesopotamia achieved this by claiming a share of the harvest along the Tigris and Euphrates, and the Pharaohs of Egypt by the exploitation of slave labour and appropriating the surplus from the fertile Nile delta. Their riches rested upon power, i.e. on the rulers' ability to force the cultivators of the land to hand over a good share of their produce, and upon their ability to organize and administer the collection and transportation of this share and its distribution among those whom they needed for these purposes. Except for wars of conquest the enlargement of their fortunes hinged upon the measure to which they could prevent floods and drought by controlling the steady flow of the rivers. And indeed, they showed great initiative and ingenuity in this. To obtain labour they resorted to force. They imposed corvees on peasants without too much loss to output, because labour requirements in agriculture are not evenly distributed over all seasons, and they kept slaves to perform the tasks which required extra effort or skills.

The system was brought to near perfection in ancient Rome. The high living standards of many Romans by the end of the Republic were sustained by the collection of surpluses from the entire Mediterranean Empire and by the stream of slaves the wars provided. Only after the wars of conquest ceased, when slave labour was no longer as cheaply available as before, Rome's prosperity began to subside. It may therefore be said that neither the rulers of Mesopotamia nor of Egypt nor of Rome were lacking the *ability* and the *wish* to invest, but the character of their investments were determined by their specific political and cultural environment. Their powerful position enabled them to obtain the goods and services they wanted without much economic ingenuity, and the ready supply of slaves discouraged a search for important labour saving innovations. The rulers had simply no reason to allocate such additional produce as did materialize for raising the living standard of the majority of the population; and there was no inherent mechanism in the system to compel them to do so. Their patterns of culture, which separated them and their dependents from all other strata of society, hardly encouraged the distribution of wealth beyond what was deemed necessary to maintain their power base.

In recent times a similar situation has evolved in several of the countries which euphemistically are called developing. In almost all these countries a modest rise in productivity was accompanied by a deterioration in the living standard of the majority of the population and an increase in the affluence of a minority. Usually the rise in productivity was 'disguised' by a simultaneous fall in *per capita* income due to population growth. While few students of this problem will deny the coexistence of abject poverty with great riches in the Third World, they all too often tend to regard the falling living standard of the majority of people as a kind of transitory, perhaps necessary, phase in the development process which eventually leads to greater affluence for all. Like S. Kuznets [1955:18-20; 1959:1-100; 1963:12], they regard the growing gap between rich and poor as part of a long-run trade-off between the rise in the level of income and its equality of distribution. They believe that growth and equality of distribution are negatively correlated in the early stage of development and positively correlated in the later stage. In the absence of foreign investment this seems logical because domestic capital can only be obtained by concentrating the available surplus in the hands of those who are not encouraged by poverty to expend them on current consumption. Later, when the accumulated savings have become productive investments and cause the total volume of output to increase, it is assumed that the mechanisms of the market will take care of the more equitable distribution of the surplus. Recent examinations of this hypothesis provided no statistical evidence to support the existence of such a long-run trade-off [Lee and Koo, 1988:175-177]. They indicated that the degree of imbalance in economic growth has no significant long-run influence on equality.

The upshot of all this is that *a measure* of economic progress can be attained which yields advantages to one part of a population without providing any to the rest. This implies that Adam Smith's statement that an *invisible hand* naturally, or rather necessarily, leads people to prefer that employment of their resources which is most advantageous to society [Smith, 1776:423], cannot be held generally valid. It must be regarded as a special case – as a proposition which is only true for a society where economic relations are not governed by power but by exchange.

The point was succinctly made by Ernest Gellner who argued that

> the emergence of a society without poverty, a society blessed with perpetual economic and cognitive growth, an egalitarian and/or fraternal society which incorporates everyone in a shared moral citizenship and a high culture, a society without oppression or arbitrariness... is not inscribed into any historical plan. On the contrary,... A stored surplus needs to be guarded and its distribution enforced. No principle of distribution is either self-validating or self-enforcing. Conflict is inevitable, and victors have no interest in permitting a return match. They have every reason to prevent it by pre-emptive action. Herein lies... the root cause of political coercion [Gellner, 1988:3].

It may therefore be concluded that the *ability* to save – the availability of a surplus – is a necessary condition but not a sufficient condition for *economic progress*. Incentives – the *wish* to turn savings into *economically productive* assets – are equally required. This observation does not deny the well known identity of saving and investment. It does not suggest that there is an alternative to the trite proposition that everything produced can only either be consumed or not consumed and therefore saved (if goods wasted are also regarded as consumed). But it does suggest that in the process of economic growth the catalytic effect of saving is not a foregone conclusion. It suggests that the catalytic effect of saving only materializes under specific circumstances, namely under the pressure of brisk market competition, when the controllers of productive assets are fearful of losing their market share to competitors unless they constantly invest and innovate.

In a way Lenin's and Stalin's attempts to accelerate the pace of economic growth in Soviet Russia by forced saving and state directed investment may be regarded as a special variant of the Kuznetsian theme. Recognizing the catalytic role of savings, and the need for investing to effectuate it, Lenin believed that Russia's economic progress could be expedited by apportioning to the state the role of the autonomous investor and by using the power of the state to impose a regime of forced saving to provide the necessary resources for the investments in assets which produce economic growth. The state was to invest as large a share of the national income as was reasonable, and under Stalin even more than was reasonable, to provide the productive capital assets necessary 'to overtake and outstrip the advanced countries economically' [Lenin, 1917:XXI,216]. As the only resources available for this purpose were the 'internal resources created by the labour of the workers, peasants and intellectuals,' Lenin acknowledged that 'certain sacrifices, difficulties and privations' had to be expected, especially in the early stages of industrialization [Lenin, 1917:XXXII,434]. Under Stalin, the development of large-scale industry, and primarily heavy industry, came to be regarded as the key to the reorganization of the entire national economy [Dutt, 1964:559]. Industrial investment was to increase with the progress of technology regardless of actual market demand. In the words of the Russian textbook on the fundamentals of Marxism–Leninism: 'Industrialisation requires huge material and financial outlays... The share of the national income previously devoted to the parasitic consumption of the exploiting classes must therefore be used for socialist accumulation.' The revenue from the state enterprises, from foreign and domestic trade, and from banks must be used for industrialization; and the peasantry (released from paying mortgage debts and land rents) must provide the financial assistance of the countryside for the industrial development [Dutt, 1964:571-2]. In addition, Stalin prescribed maximum taxation and price fixing to obtain the difference between *potential* and *actual* savings and the extra surplus from the economies of scale which were expected from the replacement of small agricultural units by large-scale farming. Agriculture itself was to progress through the application of technologically improved equipment and the lower prices of industrial products. It was taken for granted that 'accounting and control is the main thing required for arranging the smooth working, the correct functioning, of the first phase of communist society' [Lenin, 1917a:243].

It is probably no exaggeration to say that while the human sacrifices associated with Stalin's attempt to implement these policies were enormous, their results in promoting economic progress were no better than those of other countries, with a similar level of economic performance on the eve of World War I, whose economic progress was mainly advanced by market forces [Brenner, 1966:246]. Still it would be rash to draw conclusions from this comparison without taking into account the immense devastation of the Soviet economic potential in the course of World War II. The salient point is that a dedicated leadership is not sufficient to sustain for long an accelerated pace of economic progress even if it is as capable as the Pharaohs of skimming off the economic surplus of a nation and as ruthless as the Roman Emperors in trying to make people work. The problem of incentives and distribution cannot be avoided. In theory it seems simple enough to turn an economic surplus into accelerated growth-promoting industrial capital; in practice both the size of the surplus and the efficiency of its utilization depend on the measure of identity between the *short-term* desires and expectations of millions of individuals and the *long-term* objectives of the planners.

Returning from the battlefields of World War I, and the Civil War that followed, the Russian peasants and workers expected things to be better than they had been before. Each had personal hopes and dreams which were expected to come true now that things were to be different in Russia. But what was the reality? The country's economy was in utter chaos and the government, committed to its plan of accelerated industrialization, had little to offer but promises for a brighter future and a further 'tightening of belts' for the present. For the people who expected to reap the fruit of their revolution, and found their living standards sagging, the vague hope of plenty in a distant future was not enough. They became alienated from the leadership and obliged the state to exact by force the surplus it required for industrialisation. Before long a huge bureaucratic apparatus collected and administered the economic surplus and suppressed any real or imaginary outbreaks of popular discontent. In time the farmers (who provided the major share of the country's output), and not only the farmers, lost confidence in the government's promise of the good things to come. Fearful of being forced to surrender increasingly more of their produce to the state and being left with less and less for their own use, many people learned to hide as much as they could of their economic capacity.

The paradox of current wants and future perspectives not only affected the size of the 'investment fund' – the *ability* to invest – but also obstructed the optimal utilization of the 'savings'. The absence of a mechanism by which the contribution by individual enterprises to the economy could be assessed, and the imposition of a system of accounting by which the losses of individual units of production were hidden behind general aggregates, hardly promoted a high level of efficiency. A high degree of *social* supervision might have helped but social supervision requires social consensus – not a society in which a kind of 'class' of state and party officials enjoys privileges denied to the rest of the people. In addition, a community in which people feel better served by cultivating personal contacts than by strenuous and diligent work is hardly a good environment for innovation [Brenner, 1984:18].

There were of course short periods in the history of many societies during which, in spite of large differences in incomes and status, a wide constructive consensus did prevail. Britain during World War II, and several other European countries during the early period of post-war reconstruction, may serve as fairly recent examples. But common to all was that they were either fuelled by an external threat to the entire community or by the hope of imminent and palpable improvements. The constructive consensus invariably waned once the external threat was gone, or when people realized that after all their personal dividend did not measure up to expectations.

The conclusion from the preceding is that in the pursuit of economic progress two kinds of rationality are in conflict: a concrete rationality relating to individuals, and an abstract rationality relating to large aggregates. The fact that the fruits of investment need not accrue to those who save, makes people who consume all they earn act no less rationally than others who act upon the proposition that restricted consumption may in the long run be more beneficial to them because it provides the savings which can be turned into economic growth-producing assets. The point is that this paradox, or inconsistency, cannot be resolved outside its social and cultural context.

For a while the *free market system* did in fact resolve this paradox. The *competitive* element in this system introduced a mechanism which simultaneously wielded the whip of fear of unemployment – even starvation – over the heads of those unwilling to compete, and at the same time raised the hope that effort and ingenuity may in the fullness of time be personally well rewarded. The free market introduced the illusion of *voluntary* exchange; an exchange which, from time to time, enables not only individuals but entire groups of people – for example craftsmen with special skills – to raise their living standards [Brenner, 1969:145-94]. The system did not work smoothly; over the years its ups and downs took a terrible toll of human misery, but it produced results. It not only raised per capita production to unprecedented heights but allowed a greater proportion of people than ever before to benefit from the achievements. So much even Karl Marx admitted [Marx, 1848:5]. Therefore, if it could be taken as a 'psychological datum' that individuals' constantly pursue their own economic advantage, it may be concluded that a system in which the allocation of resources and production take place on the basis of prices generated by *voluntary* exchanges between producers, consumers, workers and owners of factors of production, sets in motion a mechanism which distributes the fruits of economic growth in a manner which allocates to all contributors a reasonable share. A *Markov chain*, or other processes, may cause the shares not to be equal but this is of secondary importance. For as long as everybody's situation is improving the system's economic growth will be sustained. Leon Walras wanted to know if such a system would also provide social justice. According to W. Jaffe [1979:386], whose view is not shared by everyone [Walker, 1984:445-69], he neither purported to describe nor analyse a real world system, nor to suggest that such a system actually exists. All he intended to do was 'to formulate (invent?) an economic system in conformity with an idea of social justice' [Chase, 1979:84]. His idealized model suggests that *voluntary* exchange leads to equitable distribution. But, how long can such a system survive before it falls prey to its dynamic mechanism, before competition eliminates itself? How soon will the freedom of exchange be reduced by some new form of coercion and will what Gellner called 'the dreadful regime of kings and priests' [Gellner, 1988:3-4] be reinstated in the form of the rule of bureaucrats and captains of monopoly?

From the point of view of economic efficiency it is probably true that the closer an economic system comes to *perfect competition* the more likely the problem of incentives – of the *wish* to work conscientiously and to invest – approaches a solution. Similarly, the closer the system comes to monopoly the more likely the problem of savings – of the *ability* to invest – will be solved by accumulation and concentration of capital and by increasing economies of scale. However, both 'ideal images', the Walrasian model of *perfect competition* and *monopoly*, have little realistic content. They are 'timeless', static, while society is always undergoing change. Therefore it is usually futile to rely for the solution of other than short-run micro-economic problems on such theories which are oblivious of the dynamic character of societies' cultural, social and political environment.

Economists assume that at least in the sphere of production and exchange people act rationally to maximize their utility. They ignore that what seems rational at one time to members of one society may appear the summit of irrationality in another cultural environment. Thai peasants are no less rational than European farmers if they 'invest' their savings in the construction of new pagodas rather than in procuring agricultural implements. They *know* that the gods determine which plant will grow and which will not. Given this *knowledge* they would still be acting rationally even if they had hothouses, a good supply of natural gas, and the capital and technological competence of modern Dutch farmers. Their choice only becomes irrational if they begin to separate what *we* call ceremonial from functional activities. As long as they remain convinced that both are equally important their choice remains rational. The same is of course true for modern business managers and political leaders recruited from amidst their ranks. As long as they cannot distinguish between *price effects* and *income effects* they cannot hope to walk the tightrope between long-term mass unemployment and inflation.

A similar question as to what constitutes rational behaviour and what does not, also arises with regard to the assumption of *maximization of utility*. Though seldom explicitly, most economists use the term *utility* as if it were synonymous with economic advantage or profit. Non-material advantages are taken into account (for example, the advantages of a pleasant location of a work-place is weighed against higher wages in a less favourable environment) but on the whole the tendency is to assume that people offered the choice will prefer higher to lower wages. The desire for power, the craving for acclaim, the impulse to serve the common good, or just the urge to action, are also acknowledged but subordinate to profit making because in a certain phase of capitalism, by virtue of an inner necessity, they cannot be attained without economic success [Sombart, 1953:III,195-208]. But, this does not make the pursuit of profit a psychological 'given' – a psychological axiom of universal applicability. Christians in the Middle Ages always weighed the *opportunity cost* of worldly gains against what they believed to be 'the wages of sin' in the world hereafter. In their estimation of what constitutes *utility*, their adherence to the *fair price* was no less compelling than 'what the market will offer' is to the profit maximizers in the free market system.

The dilemma with the concept of *utility* is that given a narrow interpretation it has no relevance outside the stock exchange, and in a wider sense it is too vague to serve a useful scientific purpose. In modern economic literature it usually stands for 'the power or ability to satisfy a human want'. Some economists construe it as 'that aspect of welfare which can be expressed in monetary terms'. Others think of it as Pareto's 'ophelimity', which has no objective standard of judgment and therefore is not measurable. Altogether it is in all probability a circular concept [Robinson, 1964:48] – a concept which 'has to be defined in terms of itself' [Robinson & Eatwell, 1973:36]. Whatever its interpretation, utility depends on one individual's appraisal. This appraisal may vary with identical units of the good, and in different times and situations. People who perform voluntary work for their communities; who take care of members of their family; who may even be prepared to lay down their lives to uphold some ideas or to protect comrades in battle, all reveal their preferences and feel that they are maximizing their utility. Unless they felt like this they wouldn't do any of these things. Thus, the statement that people are always seeking to maximize their utility is true but hardly helpful. It follows that given its wider meaning the concept has a psychological dimension which can neither satisfy economists' scientific longing for quantification or elegance, nor serve as a reliable basis for prediction outside a very narrowly circumscribed social and cultural environment. But if utility is the power to satisfy a human want, the question arises how all but the most basic wants receive their order of priorities. Subject to physical constraints they must receive it from the social and cultural environment. And this, in turn, begs the question how the social and cultural environment comes into being; how economic conditions determine people's beliefs and people's beliefs their economic reality; how precisely the connection between economic and non-economic influences should be conceived.

The measure of geographical coincidence between the regions in which Protestantism was first to spread with the regions which first underwent the transformation toward capitalism may just as well be explained by the suggestion that the coming of Protestantism provided the necessary mental conditions for an economic transformation as by the notion that the slowly progressing economic transformation provided Protestantism with its influence because it could ideologically legitimize the new practices. Even Max Weber insisted on 'the fundamental importance of the economic factor' [Weber, 1930:26] and did not claim a psychological determination of economic events. R.H. Tawney evades giving a clear answer to the question by restricting his narrative to the description of the process of transformation without attempting to settle the question of causality.

> When the age of the Reformation begins, economics is still a branch of ethics, and ethics of theology;... the appeal of theorists is to natural law, not to utility; the legitimacy of economic transactions is tried by reference, less to the movements of the market, than to moral standards derived from the traditional teachings of the Christian Church....

By the time of the Restoration, religion in England

> has been converted from the keystone which holds together the social edifice into one department within it, and the idea of a rule of right is replaced by economic expediency as the arbiter of policy and the criterion of conduct. From a spiritual being, who, in order to survive, must devote a reasonable attention to economic interests, man seems sometimes to have become an economic animal, who will be prudent, nevertheless, if he takes due precautions to assure his spiritual well-being [Tawney, 1926:272-3].

For Marx and Engels the connection seemed obvious, though toward the end of his life, Engels somewhat reduced the impact of his former statements on this matter [Engels, 1890]. In Marx's own words:

> The mode of production in material life determines the general character of the social, political and spiritual process of life. It is not the consciousness of men that determines their existence, but on the

contrary, it is their social existence which determines their consciousness... In the social production which men carry on they enter into definite relations which are indispensable and independent of their will. The sum total of these relations of production constitutes the economic structure of society – the real basis, on which rises a legal and political superstructure and to which correspond definite forms of social consciousness [Marx, 1859].

But in the end the answer to the question whence the particular combination of the *ability* and the *wish* to invest originated – where the mechanism sprang from by which capitalism succeeded in creating 'more massive and more colossal productive forces than have all the preceding generations together' [Marx & Engels, 1848:15] – remains elusive.

# 1. The Origins of Modern Economic Progress

By the last quarter of the eleventh century, if not earlier, the accretion of population in Europe was accompanied by notable improvements in agricultural practices, spreading of commerce, and the growth of urban trading communities [Slicher van Bath, 1963; Postan, 1952:119-256; 1944; Pirenne, 1936:332-62; 1925; 1956; Dobb, 1937]. On the one hand the accretion of population led to the settlement and conversion to tillage of 'new' land east of the Rhine and to the conquest of new *feuda* in the eastern Mediterranean [Runciman, 1951, 1952, 1954; Prawer, 1965]. On the other hand it stimulated more intensive use of land in the traditionally settled parts of Europe and set in motion a trickle of people who could no longer find adequate employment on the land into the incipient towns. Throughout the two-and-a-half centuries during which these processes were gradually gaining impetus they did not essentially differ from other growth sequels in earlier periods and in other parts of the world [Elvin, 1988:101-12]. The historical details, in as far as they could be reconstructed, have been elaborated by Marc Bloch [1962] and a host of other scholars. Here only their relevance for explaining the developments which followed the demographic catastrophes of the middle of the fourteenth century receive special attention.

In the first place, it is fairly certain that the 'technological know-how' built up before the 'Black Death' survived and continued to increase during the fifteenth century [Slicher van Bath, 1963; Singer et al., 1956; White, 1962]. There is no reason to believe that the diminution of population eradicated the agricultural improvements which had gradually raised the per acre yield of

15

land under the pressure of the land shortage in the preceding era. Together with this it is probable that as a result of the reduced volume of labour, wherever this was possible, cultivation was restricted to the relatively most fertile holdings while the least fertile land was abandoned. Consequently per capita yields of land and labour presumably increased and with this the material *ability* to save and invest in improvements. Secondly, the *wish* to invest increased because the per capita rise in yields went together with a more equitable distribution of the fruits of production. This was not only reflected in the free and copy-holders' higher real incomes, but also in the fact that wages rose more steeply than rents, and both wages and rents rose more sharply than the prices of manufactured goods [Brenner, 1961:225-39]. For an entire century farmers and workers were able to maintain these economic advantages [Phelps Brown & Hopkins, 1956; Hirshleifer, 1966]. Competition among landlords for tenants and for the relatively diminished labour force; and the disarray of the central political power structure, together with the end of the supremacy of the heavy cavalry and its replacement by auxiliary peasant forces – the 'combined training bowmen' [Oman, 1936:646-59] – put many farmers and workers in parts of northern Europe in a perhaps unprecedented position *vis-à-vis* the mighty. The uniqueness of their position was that *they were not only able to increase their* income [Bridbury, 1973] *but also to resist their 'betters' attempts to deprive them of it by force.* Perhaps this is the answer to the question how Europe escaped what Gellner called the 'agricultural trap'.

At the same time, and probably stimulated by the higher real incomes of the working population, the towns were beginning to undergo a transformation. With relatively minor reversals most urban markets survived the demographic catastrophes and gradually adapted production to a new type of demand. In the thirteenth century their impressive growth had mainly been founded on foreign trade and domestic demand for certain high-priced goods or luxuries. After the Black Death the relatively greater affluence of the working population added a new market for everyday commodities. Slowly foreign trade and the manufacture and sale of several expensive products, and money lending, were supplemented as a source of wealth by the production and trade in goods for common use. The new type of demand, and the response to it, gradually transformed the structure of production in northern European trading centres and precipitated the development of an entirely new range of products and of a new 'production philosophy'. The 'fair price' and quality continued to rule supreme in the old established trades, but in the new trades profit began to play an increasingly important role. As James Steuart [1767:153] had already observed every person will make a demand but 'every such demand will not be answered and will consequently have no effect. The demander must have an equivalent to give, it is the equivalent, the *effectual demand* which counts.' From the middle of the fourteenth century the demand for the goods used by the common people which could be best produced in towns began to be *effectual*. Notions like 'ere shall the camel pass through the needle's eye than the rich man into heaven' were waning, and the people in the new trades devised all kinds of stratagems to evade the economic edicts of the Church. The rules against usury were not abolished but the interest was added in advance to the loans in the debt books. The idea of the 'fair price' was not abandoned but profit was added to labour cost as a kind of legitimate entrepreneurial reward. In time the higher income of the rural population not only influenced the towns but the transformation of the towns also effected changes in the countryside. The new type of productive activity in the towns required more labour and as more labour came and the towns' economic activities proliferated the number of people grew who could no longer produce their own food and became dependent on others for their victuals. In the vicinity of trading centres cash crops replaced traditional subsistence crops and farmers began to specialize in producing what suited their soils best. Where access to urban markets could be arranged *prices*, instead of *subsistence requirements*, were gradually becoming the crucial determinant of production decisions. Within two centuries the rural maps of the affected regions changed. In the Low Countries, in the vicinity of cities, land was almost entirely allocated to the production of vegetables, while more remote regions produced fruit and, often at the expense of cereals, raw materials for the urban manufacturing enterprises. By the sixteenth century the Netherlands had in fact become dependent on the Baltic trade for their supply of cereals. In England the spreading of enclosures and Thomas More's tale of the sheep 'devouring' men (which is true as far as some chalk lands were concerned) provide further evidence of a similar movement toward 'industrial crops' in the early sixteenth century. But renewed population pressure during this period caused farmers to invest more money in the amelioration of their land to find employment for the increasing size of their families. The soil was dug more deeply and manured, livestock was kept in greater numbers, and transportation was improved to convey compost and ash from the towns to the country and to bring farm produce from the country to the towns. Part of the rural population whose tenure could not be terminated continued to be affluent and maintained the level of domestic demand for urban manufactures; the rest became increasingly dependent on wage work. But the accretion of population in the early sixteenth century also caused *real* wages to fall even before the *great inflation*. Thus, while the growth of domestic demand for manufactures was tempered by the fall in *real* incomes the low production costs stimulated exports and these more than compensated for the loss of growth in domestic demand and gave rise to a high rate of capital accumulation. It was at this juncture that the *ability* and the *wish* to invest came together and that, to use Marx's formulation, commodities ceased to be exchanged for money in order to obtain other commodities but money began to be exchanged for commodities in order to obtain more money.

This alone, however, could not have produced the changes. The cultural environment, in which certain norms of conduct from the Middle Ages still exerted a restraining influence on social and economic relations, together with the slowly growing domestic market and a rapidly expanding foreign trade gave rise to Weber's *rational restlessness* [1925] and imposed it on Durkheim's *normative regulation* [1893]. It made *ingenuity* rather than *force* the new source of wealth and gave wealth a new social status but subjected its acquisition to strict rules of conduct. These rules, though sometimes better documented by transgression than by compliance, were part of the cultural heritage of the Middle Ages. They reflected the essential virtues in the teachings of the Church, which inspired *moderation* and *trustworthiness*. This is of paramount importance because without the moderation and trustworthiness which engender *confidence* business cannot develop.

There were of course also privateers and buccaneers in the sixteenth century, figures like Drake and Hawkins and others who made their fortunes pillaging settlements on the Spanish American coast or selling African slaves in Spanish ports, and shared their profits with the Crown in exchange for free pardons. But in the end most entrepreneurs preferred the *indirect* route to riches and distinction by way of business, to the *direct* avenue of piracy and highway robbery. They wanted to be *accepted*, to create room within the ruling patterns of culture for their needs, not to be placed outside them. As a result it created moderating forces (elaborated in chapter 5) which prevented greed from 'killing the geese that laid the golden eggs'.

Norms are imparted to the young by their parents and teachers, that is by the preceding generations. They therefore reflect the real needs or aspired values of an earlier period. This delays adaptation to change in the material environment but provides society with a degree of continuity and stability. For more than a millennium people had seen the universe as a system of regularities, as a hierarchy striving toward order. This unity and regularity was taken as evidence for a divine design. People lived in a world built upon authority in which 'prestige and social worth sprang less from the free disposal of property than from the free disposal of human forces' [Bloch, 1953:203-10]; a world in which, though not always freely assumed and never ceasing to contain a great deal of constraint, violence and abuse, individuals granted protection and divers material advantages to other individuals. This directly or indirectly assured their subsistence in return for their pledge to render various prestations or services and a general obligation to aid. It was also a world of resignation in which, since the decline of ancient Rome, instability and uncertainty had created a discrepancy between material aspirations and the possibility for satisfying them which was too wide to be bridged by rational endeavours. It was a world in which change through functional human effort was unthinkable, but in which life was made bearable by hope of salvation – by hope springing from a belief in a merciful God who can be reached by prayer in humility. As a result the rational elements inherent in notions of *good* or *right* were replaced by idealized ones – by mystical notions according to which right conduct, the correct manner of obtaining good, was postulated upon an imaginary world of gods and demons.

It was this world, in which forces beyond human control such as the weather determined all members' fate, which for more than a thousand years gave meaning to concepts like good and bad, true and false, virtuous and vicious, and provided criteria for selection in action, judgment, preference and choice. It was this value system which the Middle Ages bequeathed to subsequent generations in a body of stated and implicit social theory. Its formal teaching was derived from the Bible, the works of the Fathers and schoolmen, the canon law and its commentators. It had been popularized in sermons and religious manuals and its informal assumptions were implicit in law, custom, and social institutions [Tawney, 1926:28]. Unconsciously and consciously this value system was transmitted from one generation to the next well into modern times. Though gradually adapting to changing circumstances, and losing in compulsion, its main tenets proved very pertinacious. Consciously, it was transmitted by the pervasive sanction of religion, involving supernatural rewards and punishment. Unconsciously it was communicated by emotional and verbal contamination to successive generations of children by elders who imparted their wishes in a moralizing setting of rules variously rationalized. *As these emotions became overladen with habitual rules the rules themselves appeared to be intuitive and inevitable.*

Thus while reason was gradually taking the place of revelation and religion was ceasing to be the master-interest of mankind, faith continued for a very long time to be a department of life with boundaries which it was extravagant to overstep [Tawney, 1926:272]. Long after the circumstances which had given rise to them were waning, and men's economic environment had changed, the mediaeval concepts of good, right and true continued to affect social behaviour. When the realistic opportunities for material advancement arose, together with the feeling that one could never be sure whether there is retribution in a life hereafter, these social conventions bequeathed to Western Europe a social climate which confined utilitarian notions within limits consistent with economically rational behaviour.

Lutheranism was still rural in character and theologically mediaeval in outlook. Luther's and his English contemporaries' background was rural rather than of a money economy. Their conceptions of the stratification of society and of the market were agrarian, consisting of the petty dealings of peasants and craftsmen in the small market town where industry is carried on for the subsistence of the household and the consumption of wealth follows hard upon its production. Here commerce and finance are occasional incidents rather than the forces which keep the whole system in motion. 'When they criticise economic abuses, it is precisely against departure from that natural state of things – against the enterprise, the greed of gain, the restless competition, which disturb the stability of the existing order with clamorous economic appetites – that their criticism is directed' [Tawney, 1926:111]. Calvinism was different. It was active and radical. It was an urban movement that spread among men engaged in commerce, finance and manufacturing who were hardly disposed to idealize the patriarchal virtues of the peasant community. It was a movement espoused by precisely those social groups that had become estranged from rural society and whose occupations had long since become irreconcilable with the traditional scheme of rural ethics. Calvinism did not reject the old tenets of religion, not even its claim to moralize on economic matters, but it broke with the predominantly rural aspects of belief, especially those which reflected the mediaeval inability of individuals to improve their material conditions. In its variety of forms, Calvinism adjusted the rural ethical tenets of Christianity to the new needs of urban societies. It laid down rules of conduct in economic matters that were no less rigorous than those of earlier times but abandoned the belief that the riches of the world are strictly limited so that the enrichment of one person implies the deprivation of another. It did not look upon the accumulation of wealth as inherently sinful. Not wealth but its misuse for self-indulgence or ostentation became cause for disapprobation. Calvinism no longer reflected the mediaeval social and technological impotence of people in mediaeval society to improve people's material conditions, but mirrored a society consisting of people seeking actively to improve their lot with the sober gravity of men who are conscious of disciplining their own characters by patient labour, and devoting themselves to a service acceptable to God [Tawney, 1926:114]. Without touching the fundamentals of religious belief it reflected the new social and economic reality that was emerging in the cities. When the gap between desired material improvement and its attainment was no longer unbridgeable and when as a result of this irrational and ceremonial efforts to achieve success were beginning to give way to more rational and functional activities, Calvinism became the ideal of people, at least of some people, who were able to change their social and economic position by their own efforts. Again, it did not touch the fundamentals of morality but rejected some formalistic manifestations which had become dogma and lost their ethical content in the new material environment.

Lending for profit may serve as an example to illustrate this point. For centuries it had been thought morally objectionable – usury – because of its exploitative character. The opprobrium which clung to it never applied to loans granted to kings and other mighty personages. This was so because the objection was not to lending as such but against the spoiling of the needy. The good Christian was expected to share his worldly goods with his brother in adversity – to help the needy, not turn their misfortune to his advantage. In the rural surroundings of the Middle Ages none but those in direst need, and therefore in no position to refuse paying usurious interest rates, were borrowing. Therefore the moral conflict inherent in lending did not lie in the provision of loans but in the collecting of interest from the poor and defenceless. But such conflict had little to do with the borrowing of city merchants. They were neither in dire need nor at the lenders' mercy. They borrowed to increase their fortunes, not to survive when floods or drought destroyed their harvest. Why then should the lender not have his share in the wealth to which his loan has contributed? There were no ethical grounds for not demanding a reward from the traders and craft-masters for the use of borrowed funds. Such a reward hardly differed from a landlord's right to rent from peasants for the use of his land. In other words, moral values did not change – to take advantage of the poor remained as censurable as it had been before – but the formalistic aspects of religion, the dogmatic perceptions, adjusted to the new social and economic reality. Christians were given the opportunity to seek both attainment and salvation in action. Calvinism had little compassion for poverty;

> but it distrusted wealth, as it distrusted all influences that distract the aim or relax the fibers of the soul, and, in the first flush of its youthful austerity, it did its best to make life unbearable for the rich. Before the Paradise of earthly comfort it hung a flaming brand, waved by the implacable shades of Moses and Aaron [Tawney, 1926:139].

The belief that salvation comes by grace – not work – continued; but it was bestowed upon those who lead an active strenuous life serving the glory of God. Work became a means of serving God and of proving one's own state of grace through ascetic self-discipline. Slothfulness became the deadliest of sins and fear of self-indulgence made the Calvinist a small consumer and a large saver. In Geneva this resulted in an extraordinary system of church discipline and, after worldly success came to be recognized as a token of grace, the change of emphasis from church to self-discipline powerfully furthered the development of individual capitalistic acquisition [Parson, 1953].

Lutherans and Anglicans wished to reform the Church – not to abolish it. Never intentionally radical and clinging to traditional ideas, modes of conduct and organizational patterns, they brought them closer to the new material reality. In doctrinal matters they invoked temporal power to enforce religious and moral conformity. Their toleration was little more than a tribute to expediency, the manifestation of a compromise with Catholicism or secularism where this was politically unavoidable. Unlike mediaeval Christianity, which abhorred financial dealings and commercial activities, Protestantism was content to impose upon them its code of conduct and its own religious and moral control.

In the Catholic parts of Europe in which the bourgeoisie gained political power it was not long before Catholicism underwent a similar transformation. In practice, though not theologically, it also compromised with the new reality. The geographical, social and historical coincidence of the religious and economic movements is too obvious not to indicate a relationship. Both economic and religious factors were causally connected and mutually stimulating, but the real difference between Lutheran and Anglican Protestantism on the one hand, and Calvinism on the other, was that the former was only gradually yielding to the needs of the rising middle class, in the wake of the shift in political power, while Calvinism 'was not only interested in preserving moral and social control of the economic life but was more aggressive in promoting direct political measures for the exercise of that control' [Niebuhr, 1953:vol.XII,571-5]. Gradually Christianity was lifting its inhibitions on the pursuit of wealth and where this process was most forcefully advanced it was accompanied by another set of inhibitions restraining the utilization of wealth for self-indulgence. This then provided the compromise which led the pursuit of wealth away from the socially self-destructive path and onto the avenue leading to economic progress.

In summary: the accretion of population in Europe during the two-and-a-half centuries prior to the Black Death led to an increasingly intensive use of land in the traditionally settled parts of Europe, and to a trickle into the incipient towns of people who could no longer find adequate employment on the land.

The demographic catastrophe in the middle of the fourteenth century, and the repeated outbreaks of plague that followed, turned the abundance of labour into shortage. But the improvements in land use survived. Wherever possible cultivation was restricted to the relatively most fertile holdings while the least fertile land was abandoned. Per capita yields of land and labour increased and with this the *ability* to save and to invest. The *wish* to invest also increased because the *per capita* rise in yields went together with a more equitable distribution of the fruits of production. Competition among landlords for tenants and for the diminished work force, and the disarray of the central political power structure, gave many farmers an opportunity to retain a larger share of their produce than had previously been the case, and gave several categories of workers the chance to obtain high wages. At the same time it became difficult for people of rank and landlords to appropriate for themselves by force what could no longer be obtained by other means. Their attempt to do this would have met with strong resistance. Claiming their legitimate ancient rights, the men of the auxiliary peasant forces, who had been organized in an earlier age to assist their masters in the feudal wars, would have turned their arms against them. This concatenation of circumstances gave rise to, and sustained, economic conditions in parts of Europe which created opportunities for some individuals, who did not belong to the traditionally privileged classes, to improve their position. Gradually the social stagnation characteristic of feudal society gave way to a new kind of economic and social mobility. In the sixteenth century recognition of these changes was almost ferociously forced upon the Church. Its moral tenets began to be reformulated to suit a changing conception of the world, but its fundamental ethics continued to influence the social modes of conduct. It imposed upon society a measure of stability, legality and confidence, without which the increasingly more complex new economic system could have hardly been sustained.

# 2.   Estates and Classes: The Changing Universe

Throughout ancient history slavery was a constant factor in the social and economic life of Europe. It was an accepted fact of life and involved no moral problem. In antiquity, perhaps only the Hittites and Hebrews regarded slaves as human beings and not chattel. Greek political philosophy discussed whether slavery was a human institution or founded in natural law. In Roman times, when many Italian farmers were engaged in military service during the long wars of Roman conquest, the labour shortage was made good on the latifundia by slave gangs made up of enemies sold into slavery; slavery was considerably brutalized by this system of slave-gang farming. It was then when slaves became 'speaking instruments'. During the Empire, and with the establishment of the Pax Romana, the supply of cheap slaves diminished and gradually tenantry and share-cropping returned. The end of the wars and the decline in the supply of captured enemies led to the encouragement of slave marriages and the rearing of house-born slaves, which somewhat humanized the treatment of slaves again. Yet neither stoicism nor Christianity was opposed to the institution of slavery as such. They accepted the social and economic order. To be sure, Christians advocated humane treatment of slaves, but did not oppose the institution itself. But on the land, except for the two centuries of Roman wars of conquest, there was little difference between free and slave labour. Both slaves and free workers laboured side by side and were treated similarly by their 'betters'. There was also little difference in their living standards. Between the tenth and the fourteenth century slavery almost disappeared from Western Europe. It was replaced by serfdom, which economically better suited the non-commercial type of agriculture of the period. Towards the end of the Middle Ages slavery revived in Europe probably due to the new flood of captives and refugees from Eastern wars. But the new slaves were mainly 'heathens' - 'Foes of Christ'. The serfdom which then replaced free and slave labour was actually a type of combined hereditary half-free existence and peasant tenure. Particularly where feudalism was imposed by conquest this tended to 'simplify' the social and legal position of the peasants at the expense of the more privileged members of society. For example in England, where the Normans practically eliminated the allodium and reduced most free villeins to serfdom, it gave the manorial lord a firm grip on local justice. However, the lords' exactions were usually customary and less arbitrary than one may be inclined to think, though they did sometimes infringe on peasants' rights. What remained of the old differences was that those with a status above serf were exempted from certain particularly servile dues, such as the duty to obtain the lord's consent before giving a daughter in marriage. In certain cases, in theory, a free peasant could also take his lord to court, which was a right not granted to a serf, but in practice few free peasants would have taken advantage of this right. Firstly, because he rarely had the funds and opportunity to do so, and secondly, because he stood little chance of receiving fair justice. It can therefore be said that the assimilation of the slaves to free labour somewhat raised the former's status and reduced a little the latter's. Altogether, it reduced all those engaged in manual work to something less than people with full human capabilities in the eyes of the upper strata of society. This attitude was reinforced by the way of life into which the economic conditions forced the working people, and which visibly distinguished them from their 'betters'.

For a long time the Guilds' urban oligarchy set standards of behaviour in the towns which encouraged emulation by those wishing to acquire social status. This caused the *nouveaux riches* to modify their greed for profit and present it in a socially acceptable form. They achieved this by making their actions appear to be consistent with some higher public good and with the salvation of their souls. In this way the quasi-feudal oligarchic structure and urban culture of the ancient Guilds left their mark on the new would-be rich by imposing on them a measure of conformity with the traditional modes of conduct.

What both the Guilds and the post-Renaissance capitalists had in common was the 'love of gain'; but unlike post-Renaissance manufacturers and traders, the Guilds tried to prevent their members from gaining riches at the expense of other members of the Guild. They imposed strict rules to prevent price competition among their members but tried to protect them from competition from *other* cities and from 'new' people wishing to enter the established trades. They imposed uniform techniques of production and restrictions on the length and number of working days. They enforced equal wage rates and prices and fixed the number of workers in each workshop and the tools that could be used. They prohibited advertising and appointed inspectors and supervisors to assure compliance with their rules, and applied social and economic pressure to safeguard the quality of their members' products; and they reinforced the old religious and moral taboos in restraint of fraud with legal regulations.

From the fourteenth century onward Guild membership in many cities tended to become increasingly feudal and restricted to the families of established masters. The length of apprenticeship increased and competence tests for membership became more and more difficult. The 'class' of masters became exclusive and the position of journeymen gradually deteriorated to the level of wage workers. In some places masters insisted that journeymen and apprentices must swear an oath before they were taken on, never to set themselves up as independent craftsmen without their consent. At the same time rich merchants bought land outside the city limits and entered into business partnerships with members of the aristocracy. They, or their children, married into aristocratic families, obtained titles and feudal court offices, and emulated practically every aristocratic mode of conduct which did not interfere with their economic activities [Dobb, 1937:83-122]. Alone in one respect the urban elite was of course unable to assimilate to the landed aristocracy. It could not regard work as demeaning;

but in common with the Guilds it *could* stress the quality of workmanship rather than the pecuniary aspect of labour, and make *this* the hallmark of its status. In this way workmanship became its source of pride and the status symbol which separated it from other strata of society. Feudalism had disguised its economic characteristics by ignoring the money value of the services rendered by the lower members of the hierarchy to those above them; the early bourgeoisie endeavoured to conceal its pursuit of earthly goods by stressing excellence of skills. In this way the urban elite reconciled feudal aristocratic traditions, and the moral sentiments of the mediaeval Church, with its status. Although its status rested upon economic achievement, the urban elite gradually related it to descent, modes of conduct, professional excellence and other attributes not attainable by wealth alone. By this it managed to convey the impression that its status reflected more than wealth, that it held something others were lacking. In time this became the status image which left its imprint on the cultural milieu of the economically ascending bourgeoisie. For the landed aristocracy money-making continued to be 'vulgar', but in the urban environment it ceased to be derogatory as long as those engaged in it kept to the rules.

It was this milieu and conception of status which influenced the aspirations of the new middle class on its way to economic and political power outside the sphere of activities monopolized by the Guilds. The search for status within this milieu imposed upon the early bourgeoisie the new ethics that bridged the gap between the ancient mediaeval conception of descent and the new middle class conception of personal endeavour and attainment.

Having extricated themselves from a way of life imposed by poverty, the members of the bourgeoisie were ill disposed to change the order of the world. Their affluence enabled them to adopt an almost aristocratic life-style, and furnished proof for them that social and economic advancement was possible. The 'best' people took advantage of this opportunity; those who did not could not be considered worthy of it and did not deserve to be among them. The 'best' were the people who 'mattered' and the rest did not matter. The former were expected to live by a set of both inherited and self-imposed rules, which met the needs of a trading community, and placed them socially somewhere between the aristocracy and the common people, and the latter continued to live by the rules of religion and mediaeval custom. The former were encouraged to economic activity by the promise of good profits and the latter by the cold fear of starvation; the former saved and invested, and though they were not aware of it created the material basis for industrial society; and the latter paid the bill by the low standard of living which the system imposed on them.

Almost unperceived by contemporaries the society which for generations had been dominated by *vertical* hierarchical social links was becoming *horizontally* aligned. Throughout the Middle Ages everyone found his place within the feudal hierarchy. The lord of the manor at the top of the pyramid relied on his retainers for political and armed support, and both he and his vassals depended on the tenants for their economic status. The tenants, at the bottom of the pyramid, relied on those above them for legal support and their protection. There was therefore a community of interest between all strata in the structure – a bond which held the system together. A strong lord, who did not too flagrantly abuse his power, provided good protection for his tenants, and affluent tenants provided a firm economic basis for all those hierarchically above them. The rise of the bourgeoisie made these hierarchical relations antagonistic. Although employers continued for a very long time to regard themselves 'responsible' for their employees, their wealth became more obviously linked to the distribution of the fruits of production. The money value of work could no longer be ignored under the new employer–employee relationship where, at least to a degree, profits and wages stand in a directly antagonistic relationship. Gradually the need for protection waned and the feudal customs with their rural background lost their rationale in the urban setting, and new *horizontal*, i.e. class, identities of interest increased in relevance. Craftsmen, journeymen and workers slowly found that they had more in common with each other than with their various employers. Here and there they formed 'crafts', 'mysteries', or other forms of semi-religious organizations to defend their trades' particular interests against encroachments by employers.

The growth of towns and the rise of the bourgeoisie also engendered rising living standards for the emerging middle classes. This was reflected in dietary improvements and greater utilization of new clothing materials. New food crops were introduced or imported such as potatoes, maize, rice, oil seed and cane sugar, tobacco, tea, coffee and cocoa. Wool fabrics and linen and silk textiles came into wider use. In time innovations were made in printing and in the mechanization of the metallurgical industry, and the utilization of coal was spreading wider than it did before. All this left an indelible mark on the bourgeoisie's life-style for centuries to come.

The greater affluence and the shifting emphasis in the conception of the universe also left an impression on the arts. Paintings which throughout much of the Middle Ages had mainly reflected the idea of things – not their realistic visual perception – became increasingly true to nature. For example, the pre-Renaissance pictures of the crucifixion usually show little more than a symbol – a man on a cross. Later Christ is depicted as a man whose face expresses an emotion: bliss, acknowledging his sacrifice for the salvation of humanity, or pain, the convulsions of a tortured body. The themes portrayed also change. The pictures assume a distinctly bourgeois character. They exhibit property – the wealth of the person who commissioned them. Nudes take on facial expressions and postures suggesting submission to the spectator–owner of the painting; and the background becomes richly decorated, a room, a palace or a park indicating the owner's other properties – his affluence. Perspective is added so that the eye of the viewer becomes the centre of all that is visible in the painting. 'The visible world is arranged for the spectator as the universe was once thought to be arranged for God' [Berger, 1972:83-90].

Though not entirely immobile, feudal society left little room for individuals' social advancement. The new significance which the rise of the bourgeoisie gave to personal endeavour and which reduced the climate of social immobility was also reflected in the changing scientific perception of the universe. 'Men reason by analogy from the condition of their lives to the condition of the universe' [Lewontin, 1968:208], and a static society could not believe in a dynamic cosmos while a changing society saw everything in motion.

There is a complex relationship between science and society and it is difficult to explain the processes by which scientific perceptions are modified or changed. On the one hand science serves as the basis for the technological innovations which also stimulate changes in the social structures, and on the other, the 'scientific outlook' tends to reflect the character of the societies it influences. Scientists' image of the universe is tainted by the things they know from their social environment. Consequently, the relatively static society of the Middle Ages impressed upon science a static conception of the universe. The new era with its greater social mobility impressed on it the image of a harmoniously changing universe. The one conception could not, and the other could, accommodate Galileo's earth in motion. Einstein claimed that scientific concepts are free creations of the mind. With increasing knowledge they become simpler and better capable of explaining a wider range of sensuous impressions [Einstein, 1938:31]. But 'free creations of the mind' can hardly be far removed from human experience. Phenomena may well be related to things outside man's sensuous experience, but their impact on reality – their material manifestation – is almost always presented in recognizable forms such as fields, waves and particles.

In the mediaeval world, when people were born into their social status by divine providence, and social mobility and economic advancement were practically unthinkable, immutability was man's conception of the order of the world. With the rise of the bourgeoisie society began revising its static conception of the world gradually replacing it by a perception pervaded by mobility – by 'uniformitarian change'. For the bourgeoisie change *per se* was moral quality. It not only saw change as the nature of existence but attributed direction to it. 'A world in which a man could rise from humble origins must have seemed, to him at least, a good world' [Lewontin, 1968:208]. The world of the Almagest – Ptolemy's perception of a finite world contained in the sphere of the fixed stars, with the earth stationary at its centre, and the sun and other heavenly bodies revolving about it in their orbs like 'jewels in their fixed mountings' – gave way to a new perception of the universe, one more akin to man's new social reality. Questions concerning the mechanisms responsible for change crept in. The world became a mechanism of causes and events, of things ordered, and of events following a steady sequence. The entire Aristotelian perception crumbled and was replaced by a world of motion. There was of course also motion in the earlier conception, but force was needed in order to produce it. In the Galilean–Newtonian view motion in straight line and constant velocity was natural without external stimuli. Society in motion was beginning to see a world in motion, just as the immobile society of the Middle Ages had seen a world at rest. The world continued to be orderly: its regularity, as Johannes Kepler showed, was even better expressed in mathematical terms than that of the world at rest, but this regularity was regularity in motion and motion seemed to be a sequence of events before and after – of causes and effects. But events were no longer self-evident. They required new types of explanations. If man could no longer trust the evidence of his eyes, and what seemed firmly stationary like the earth he stood on proved to be in perpetual motion, and what seemed in motion, like the sun, was stationary, explanations needed to be found. When they were given reality was placed beyond man's immediate sensory perception and the universe became a sequence of causes and events [Koyre and Taton, 1964:65-8].

When events ceased to be self-evident reality could only be observed from the 'outside'. Not only had it to be explained by reason, but the explanation had also to be proven true to reason. To reason, not to authority. The world of authority and of scholastic logic was challenged by the world of facts, and in the world of facts truth could only be established by experimentation. Try as they may to reconcile their views with those of old, neither

Luther nor Galileo could in the end avoid the confrontation with authority. *'Hier stehe ich, ich kann nicht anders'*; *'E pur si mouve.'*

The need to verify the explanations led to the linking of rationality with empiricism. The traditional conception of unity and order in nature, and the success of Copernicus, Kepler and others in formulating this unity and order in neat mathematical propositions was in the next century to lead people like Descartes and Newton to believe in the universal power of mathematics. Gradually the world of hierarchies, of order and of things endowed with inert 'wills', became a world of mechanisms in which the idea of sequence assumed a central place. The world became a machine and the sequence became the God within the machine [Bronowski, 1951:41-3].

For centuries man had found regularity in nature. He had known the unerring movements of the planets from which he could calculate the eclipse of the sun and the moon. He had watched days follow nights and nights follow days and seen nature's ever-recurring life-cycle. He had learned that seeds grow into trees; that the wind moves sailingships; that rubbing stones together produces fire; and all confirmed his belief in God's grand orderly design. In the new perception of the universe, man found his explanations in this sequence of 'before' and 'after' and made it into a mechanism of causes and events. Thus *time* begins to play a more and more important role. Ancient and mediaeval farming societies had little need for very precise measurements of time. For them 'time' related to events – to the cosmic cycle of the alternation of seasons, and to the human cycle of the life of man. There was 'a time to be born, and a time to die, a time to plant, and a time to pluck up that which is planted...' [*Ecclesiastes* III] but for urban man time had to be a system of references, an abstract division, a measurement which could be consciously applied [Goody, 1968:31-41]. Urban society in Western Europe developed the mechanical device which precisely met this new requirement, namely the mechanical clock.

The first known mechanical clocks date from the thirteenth century; they were 'weight-driven', i.e. designed for controlling the force of a falling weight [Lloyd, 1957:648-58]. By the middle of the fourteenth century it became usual to divide hours into 60 minutes and minutes into 60 seconds. In the fifteenth century (and possibly earlier) a recoil spring mechanism was incorporated in clocks. Springs had of course been in use for a very long time. Primitive people already used springs to build animal-traps, and later to make catapults and bows, but their incorporation in mechanical equipment – in processes of production – probably dates from the thirteenth century, when their significance as stored energy came to light in lathes, for making the shaft revolve in the restoring direction. But the introduction of the spring mechanism in clocks and watches had a far greater implication for society than all its earlier applications. It not only permitted a more detailed organization of time without which an industrial society could hardly have developed but it provided something like a mechanical model for the operation of the universe [Goody, 1968:30-41]. It turned the universe from what appeared to be a pattern into a clockwork moved by a single spring [Bronowski, 1951:41-3]. Gradually, becoming as regular as clockwork became the bourgeois ideal, and to own a watch a symbol of achievement. The desire for precision found its way into the bourgeois heritage and reinforced the earlier mentioned pattern of culture which put store by productive responsibility.

How did all this affect the value system of society? Religion and the old philosophies continued to maintain their hold upon the fundamental conceptions of Western European societies but their tenets were re-examined in the light of rationality and social cost. The disintegration of the unified Christian Commonwealth and its replacement by nation states as the prime sources of earthly power deprived Rome of her traditional position as sole interpreter of social values. In the place of religious authority as the *raison d'être* of these values came *reason*; and before long this *reason* began identifying knowledge with good. Nature had been shown to be rational, hence all things rational could be conceived according to nature and therefore good. Theology began to be permeated by reason and rationalism and Deism were slowly taking the place of traditional religion.

Although this raised many questions about the formalistic aspects of tradition and religion it hardly touched the basic tenets of morality. It cleansed them of some of their dogmatic distortions, but far from shattering the old moral tenets, it reinforced them with new arguments congruent with the newly evolving social and economic reality. Newton's law of inverse squares – his mathematical model of the world's uniform order – did not discredit the belief in God's design but confirmed it. What better proof could there be for the divine hand than a perfectly systematic universe and the universality of the law of gravitation? The new outlook liberated the old values, good, right, true, etc., from their static 'backward-looking' disposition and delivered them from their quest for legitimization in authorities. It gave them a dynamic character which for generations allowed and even stimulated modification in the light of reason. Gradually reason rather than revelation became the arbiter of social values.

All this was also reflected in the economic philosophies of the sixteenth and seventeenth centuries. Though several centuries were still to elapse before the gap was to close which separated scientists' *explanation* of natural phenomena from their practical technological application, the bourgeoisie was increasingly becoming aware that the understanding of nature bestows powers to control its forces. In the beginning the link was only established in navigation and industrial chemistry. In the sixteenth and seventeenth centuries progress in all other fields remained piecemeal – the achievement of ingenious craftsmen. Human and animal efforts, and occasionally wind and water, remained the sources of energy; and hand tools and a very limited utilization of metals continued to be characteristic of production. Where the power of the Guilds diminished before new industries arose, and where their control over quality and the modes of conduct in general was waning, their supervisory functions were taken over by the state which by this time was, to further its political purposes, increasingly concerned with the economy [Brenner, 1966:11-20].

# 3.   The Age of Mercantilism

The various measures that together made up the system which later came to be known as *mercantilism* were initially little more 'than efforts to increase the political power of the emergent nation state by strengthening its economic base. The objective was not individuals' welfare but the power of the state. In essence mercantilism remained well within the mediaeval tradition of the harmonious society. What was new was only that harmony extended the feudal affinities to a wider social formation – the nation state. In the preceding era the personal nexuses dominated social and economic relations. With the coming of mercantilism the nation became the focal point. Henceforth groups and individuals were judged by the measure to which they contributed to the political power of the state or were deemed to do so. Where the pursuit of private gain was thought to be in line with this objective it was encouraged, and where not, it was prohibited. Taking man's actions to be ruled by some kind of universal egoism, mercantilists looked upon governments as corrective agents channelling self-interest to serve the 'public good' as they conceived it.

With Luther moral values were still divine commandments suiting a human nature corrupted by original sin. Unlike mediaeval thinkers, he recognized man as an individual, but an individual inherently corrupted by desires which were eternally subversive to the will of God. Also for Calvin moral values were divine commands, but they were separated from the secular rules which regulated man's economic relations. But as the feudal vertical ties of society were breaking down and the new horizontal class ties began developing and hereditary obligations yielded their place to contractual agreements, individuals' relationship with their creator also began to change.

Weakened by Wyclifite, Hussite and even earlier rebellions, blemished by the Babylonian Captivity and the Great Schism, its prestige marred by corruption and worldliness and shaken by the critical scholarship of Erasmus and others, Rome's hegemony over the minds and morals of men crumbled in the sixteenth century. It succumbed to the onslaught of the rising nation states and to the growing economic power of the middle class. In the seventeenth century

> what men craved to know was what they were to believe, and what they were not to believe. Was tradition still to command their allegiance, or was it to go by the board? Were they to continue plodding along the same old road, trusting in the same old guides, or were they to obey new leaders who bade them turn their backs on all those outworn things, and follow them to other lands of promise? [Bayle, 1935:9].

For generations the Church had held out the promise that goodwill, justice and brotherly love should also reign on earth – it never happened. Now that men, at least some men, found that by their own effort they could make life on earth less unpleasant, or even pleasant, for themselves, old happiness-promising credos were losing their attraction and new beliefs took their place. God was banished to remote heaven and man alone became the standard by which all things were measured – he became his own *raison d'être*.

Men's desires or impulses continued to be regarded as corrupt, but whether an individual succumbs to them or not became a matter of his choice. Entrepreneurs, men accustomed to forge their own worldly fortunes by making choices in their secular transactions, weighing the chances to gain profit or suffer loss, also began to make their choices in their relationship with God. Morals ceased to be imposed from 'above' and 'outside' and were subjected instead to individuals' decisions in the light of their expected consequences. Step by step the world of predestination became a world of causes and predictable effects.

With the passage of time the old basis of Europe's social value system, the Eternal Spirit, is increasingly challenged by Reason. The old dogmas continue to maintain their hold on society but they are re-examined from a rationalist point of view and assailed by a new secular ethic. A life firmly based on dogmatic principle founded in the laws of God is challenged by a system based upon 'laws of nature'. Confidence in God's laws, the ancient guide of human action that suited rural societies in which forces beyond human control (such as the weather) determined the destinies of men, is shaken. An urban society, of people aware of their propensity to influence their fate by rational endeavours, is asking questions about what man is to believe and how he should conduct himself. The answer the urban society came up with was reason. Acting according to reason became acting virtuously. Having abolished providence, seventeenth century man is thrown back upon himself. Growth of mind becomes growth of good. Values previously conceived in terms of Eternal Spirit become values conceived in terms of earthly power. Power itself was related to the discovery of new truth; and new truth was the result of applying reason to the analysis of phenomena. Differences of opinion were recognized, but they were not believed to spring from one person's greater ability to reason than another's. Differences were the result of conducting thoughts along different lines or not examining the same things [Descartes, 1637:41]. To apply one's mind well, was

> never to accept anything as true that is not known to be evidently so...[because] everything which can be encompassed by man's knowledge is linked in the same way, and, provided only that one abstains from accepting any for true which is not true, and that one always keeps the right order for one thing to be deduced from that which precedes it, there can be nothing so distant that one does not reach it eventually, or so hidden that one cannot discover it [Descartes, 1637:41].

The universe is a single whole – a unity analogous to the absolute state – which in the minds of men can be reconstructed by the ordered logic of geometry. From sixteenth century skepticism the seventeenth century inherited the belief that nothing must be taken as truth unless it is patently self-evident to human understanding, and from the absolute structure of the contemporary mode of government, and Galileo's systematic order of the movements of the heavenly bodies, it borrows the conception of the relationship between the central power and the complexity of individual drives. Descartes recognized in this relationship the inescapable ordering principle by which truth is always rational and mathematical. Like an axiom in mathematics, he establishes *man* as an absolute fact – 'I think, therefore I am' – and arrives at an ontological proof for the existence of God and definitions for the existence of the material world and the laws of nature that govern it [Descartes, 1637:65].

In the beginning mercantilism had taken the form of a scramble for precious metals. True to the belief that gold and silver are the 'sinews of war,' mercantilists were convinced that the power of the state hinged upon the country's stock of precious metals. Where no specie could be mined domestically, or brought from colonies, it was to be attracted by the clever juggling of exchange rates and by a favourable balance of trade with other countries [Heckscher, 1955:231-7; Supple, 1957]. Here the rulers' desires to obtain power and the bourgeoisie's pursuit of wealth combined and solved the problem of incentives. *For almost two centuries rulers' desires for power practically hinged upon individuals' wishes to enrich themselves. Consequently the state not only legitimized the bourgeoisie's pursuit of wealth but actively assisted it.* It improved land and water transport and promulgated and enforced Navigation Acts as well as other commercial legislation. It extended protection to colonial ventures, granted protective patents and foreign trade monopolies, created suitable financial institutions, and eventually also joint stock company legislation. It did of course also take its share in profits by imposing custom duties, and it restricted the importation of manufactured goods and exportation of raw materials, but these were limitations the bourgeoisie could live with. Even austerity measures were not unpalatable for the rising middle class. The state wanted austerity to stimulate saving because it was thought that saving engenders low interest rates, borrowing, and production. The bourgeoisie was able to accept this too. Austerity was neither alien to the mould of thought it was accustomed to, nor did it conflict with its practical requirements – to accumulate investment funds. In its search for status, it also liberated it from the need to emulate much of the wasteful life-style of the aristocracy. Thus, by bringing together the desires of those controlling the state's political means of coercion with the self-interested wishes of an important section of the population, mercantilism provided the link between the *ability* and the *wish* to invest and innovate which earlier social and economic orders had been missing.

As yet unable to distinguish between aggregate and per capita output early mercantilists for a long time held on to the assumption that the 'public good' or the 'powerful state' hinged upon population accretion and low wages. Mercantilist writers' believing that the power of the state depends upon its treasure of precious metals, i.e. on its ability to pay for soldiers and munitions, argued that a positive balance of trade which brought foreign specie into the country and deprived other countries of their treasure, must be the state's political objective. Following this line of thought they took it for granted that high profits enhance and good wages diminish the 'Public Good'. Profits encourage economic enterprise and poor wages increase the volume of employment and restrict domestic consumption. Entrepreneurs' 'love of gain' was therefore meritorious – it encouraged trade which increased 'the Wealth of the World,' and made the difference as to rich and poor nations, 'nourished Industry, begot more Trade; and dispensed the natural Wealth of the World,' (Defoe, 1728) while *high wages* diminish the volume of exportable goods, reduce labourers' compulsion to work hard and long for their sustenance and deprives the nation of the labour of women and children who would not be obliged to seek employment without the need for household incomes to be supplemented. Consequently that which was desirable in the one stratum of society – the 'love of gain' – was evil, nay sinful, in the other. There was little new in this dichotomy. It retained the mediaeval notion of a hierarchical division of duties between the strata of

society and continued to ignore the money value of labour
services.

The new feature was the *nation state*, which replaced the feudal
lord as the focus of social identity, and afforded the rising
bourgeoisie the opportunity to find a separate place in the social
hierarchy. The nation state adopted the acquisition of wealth as a
service to the public good and as a symbol of social distinction. At
the same time *it also restricted individuals' rapacity within limits
which prevented it from 'killing the geese which laid the golden eggs'*.
In the place of the restraining influence of the teachings of the
Church it put social pressure and the law of the land. The
aristocracy was still dominating the social scene and the
bourgeoisie could hardly ignore this if it wished to gain status and
respectability. Therefore it could not shed all aspects of the
traditional value system and had to cloak its practices in some
socially acceptable guise, or had to adapt the social value system
to conform with its purposes. This explains why the rapacious
exploits of the merchants venturing to distant lands, and the
terrible atrocities committed by them there, were often given a
veneer of respectability by the pretence of service to the public
good or missions to spread civilization and Christianity among the
heathen. Very gradually old practices and traditional institutions
were receiving a new content and being modified to suit the new
mood, and these modifications ushered in the ascent of the
bourgeoisie and the waning of the feudal social structure.

The transformation of *compassion* into *charity* illustrates this
process. The former implies a *unity* of men – brotherly love – and
the latter, a division of humanity into those able to give and those
obliged to accept charity. Whether from deeper human drives or
for fear of restitution in a world hereafter, or simply out of the
wish to assimilate to the traditional modes of conduct, the
bourgeoisie did not abandon the tradition of giving alms to the
poor, but invested it with a new meaning. It denuded it of its early
Christian *egalitarian* connotation, and of its feudal paternalistic
*raison d'être*, and gave it a new content, a content which deepened
the distinction between the bourgeoisie and the lower strata of
society. Unlike compassion, charity stressed a difference where

feudal society had emphasized unity. A similar duplicity developed with regard to the remuneration of work. Feudalism regarded labour services as a legitimate right of the lord derived from his position of protector or landlord. The bourgeoisie had no such claims; it paid wages and felt little other obligation toward the labour it employed, yet it continued to ignore the money value of work.

Only by the middle of the eighteenth century did the mercantilist conception of the role of labour undergo appreciable changes. Partly this was due to the relative labour shortage in the first half of the eighteenth century, which made low wages untenable for certain types of work, and partly it was due to the technological progress which was probably itself the result of this labour shortage. The early technological improvements increased the distinction between skilled and unskilled workers. The more the number of skilled workers increased the more they began to 'matter' as consumers and also as members of society. The growth of their income stimulated the production of cheap consumer goods for the domestic market. There were of course efforts to mitigate the effects of the skilled-labour shortage. Skilled workers were attracted from other countries and some of the 'poor' were trained for the new types of employment where this was possible, i.e. in the new trades which were not controlled by the Guilds. But on the whole neither of these remedies solved the problem. In various periods skilled labour remained scarce in some trades and was well remunerated. In retrospect it was probably this – the rising income of sections of the labour force – which allowed the growth of English manufacturing to continue at the time when other European nations were beginning to compete with England for her export markets [Brenner, 1969:147-59].

A similar process of transformation adjusted the political institutions to the requirements of the rising bourgeoisie. From the end of the fifteenth century the multiplicity of mediaeval feudal political formations was yielding to the sovereignty of kings – to an absolutism which seemed to provide stability and order where there had been none before. In the seventeenth century this absolutism acquired new foundations. Adjusting to the worldly conceptions of the rising merchant class, stripped of much of its mediaeval heritage of supernatural attributes and divine rights, it became a rational system for the protection of the individual and property. It became an order which imposed upon people

> the abstaining from that which is another's, the restoration to another of anything of his ... together with any gain which may have been received from it, the obligation to fulfill promises, the making good of a loss incurred to one by another's fault, and the inflicting of penalties upon men according to their deserts [Grotius, 1625:Sect.VI].

In other words, the absolute state adjusted to the bourgeoisie's required supremacy of the rule of law over and against individual arbitrariness – to the *law* taking the place of the religious dogmas as the standard for correct behaviour. The new basis for the determination of right conduct became *the law of nature*, a law founded on reason without mystical attributes and containing some fundamental tenets such as the right to self-preservation, which included the right to the preservation of one's property. Not this alone; the expansive nature of the bourgeoisie and its widening economic sphere of interest also required the safeguarding of certain collective interests. It required a harmonization of individual with public needs and an understanding of the complex relationship between individuals' rights and those of the state. It required, for example, the determination of individual merchants' interests and the interest of the state in their ability to trade in foreign lands. Gradually the state not only became the instrument of public order but was invested with the dynamic function of promoting the collective interest in the light of that which was conceived to be the public good. As the validity of laws was increasingly subjected to the test of reason and examined with an eye to whether they did or did not conform with the supposedly self-evident natural right to self-preservation, the society which had trusted in the laws of God turned more and more to the laws of nature for authority. Whereas formerly people had lived in a world composed of unequal social grades, they now became absorbed in a dream of social advancement, and self-interest became the centre of their social conception. 'Disdainful of history and even of a patient study of the contemporary world, they too easily believed that they had ascertained *a priori* absolute laws, to which they ascribed a universality of application matched only by the simplicity of the underlying principles' [Wenlersse, 1937:348-51].

Descartes (1596-1650) believed that by starting from 'first causes of everything which is, or which may be,' namely from God who has created all, and from 'certain seeds of truth which are naturally in our minds', man can explain everything by logical deduction of causes and effects. He was certain that the world is everywhere alike, a unity reflected in the universal applicability of mathematics, and could therefore be grasped by general rules. Like several other great men of his time, Descartes identified harmony in nature with moral quality. In the seventeenth century these men were still a minority and society at large continued to hold on to the traditional ideas, but for all practical purposes the distance separating their outlook from the traditionals' was narrowing. Most things concerning men's everyday existence, the 'thou shalts' and 'thou shalt nots' in social intercourse, remained as they had been before but their rationale received a new interpretation. God's law still stood but man could understand its reason. The notions indicating what is good and right or bad and wrong remained almost identical but their *legitimization* changed. What previously had been divine commands became the dictates of good reason. What had been modes of conduct prescribed by divine law became modes of conduct based upon individuals' or societies' needs for self-preservation. *The mind of man did not replace the will of God* but God's will could be fathomed by reason. By this self-evidence, the written law and established custom became the starting point for the determination of what is right and what is wrong – the guides to correct conduct. As already argued, by giving the value system this new foundation, by making man's mind its source, a door was opened through which new values would enter, namely a set of values more subservient to the pressures of expediency. In the seventeenth century the relativistic value system lay still in the distant future, *good* continued to be what it had 'always' been and so did *bad*. The moral notions with which the young were contaminated by their elders and teachers continued to be 'self-evident'.

Hobbes (1588-1679) too had a mechanical conception of nature and a mathematical method of reasoning. Bodies were the sole existents and their motions the only cause of diversity and *truth* a matter of correct definitions and valid deductive (geometrical) reasoning. To reason philosophically was 'either to demonstrate the effects of a phenomenon from its known causes or to demonstrate its causes from its known effects.' But unlike later generations of scientists who shared his notion about 'causes and effects' as a *sequence* of *before* and *after*, Hobbes remained scholastic in his way of reasoning, relying on correct logical deduction alone and dispensing with experimental verification. If society imposed upon itself rules and laws to restrain individuals' impulses it did so to assure its self-preservation. Hence the causes of these rules must have been intrinsic to the conditions of humanity before it imposed them upon itself. Therefore, before succumbing to these rules society must have been in 'continual fear and danger of violent death' and life must have been 'solitary, poor, nasty, brutish, and short' [Hobbes, 1651:I,xiii] a 'war of everyone against everyone' [Hobbes, 1651:I,iv]. In other words, the new legitimization of the rules of conduct has no need for divine revelation, for a Moses bringing to mankind the Ten Commandments from a cloud-shrouded Mount Sinai. Man himself can reach the will of God by logical deduction. Truth has no need for 'revelation'; definition and correct logical deduction are enough to ascertain it. To be sure, only possible causes can be ascertained because no one can really grasp the mind of the creator and be certain that there are no alternative causes which can provide equally satisfactory explanations, but with this reservation in mind, man does become the maker of his own morality. This is *not* the approach of Machiavelli whose prince is above the law because he is its originator. It is the law given by God, the Creator's morality revealed to man by his interpretation in the light of everyone's requirement for 'self-preservation'. Unlike the mediaeval conception Hobbes's is individualistic. It is human nature to seek security, not the tribal or feudal collective requirement but the intrinsic nature of the individual, his personal quest for self-preservation, which determines the social characteristics of his values and determines both his own and his society's rules of conduct. Here is a reflection of the new world. Here is no longer the world of the Middle Ages in which man is born into his social position and subjected to forces wholly outside his control for his livelihood; here is the beginning of a socially more mobile world in which men, at least some men, are making their own fortunes. The *sinful* desires of the past which are part of human nature have still to be fought and suppressed but the rationale behind the need to suppress them has shifted. They have no longer to be fought because they are subversive of a mysteriously revealed will of God, but because they are in conflict with the needs of man, of man as God created him with his desire for self-preservation and for the protection of the amenities civilized society can offer. Hobbes's image of man unable to 'assure the power and means to live well, which he hath present, without the acquisition of more' [Hobbes, 1651:I,xi] is therefore a true reflection of what Max Weber was to call the 'rational restlessness of western civilization,' and Karl Marx the dynamic and 'progressive element in Capitalism'. It was the reflection of the world of the rising bourgeoisie, namely a society in which self-centred men impose upon themselves collective arrangements to preserve themselves and their property. In this society whatever is done according to reason in the pursuit of the earlier mentioned objective is right, but not all that is right is naturally binding upon men. In the words of Hobbes, 'The bonds of words are too weak to bridle men's ambition, avarice, anger, and other passions, without the fear of some coercive power' [Hobbes, 1651:I,xiv]. Hence what is right needs to be defined by positive law and to be attended by the power to enforce it. Certainly, this power has to be limited by the basic precepts of self-preservation, but given this, positive law becomes the legitimization of what may and what may not be done – the basis for morality in the emerging constitutional state (*Rechtsstaat*).

Where Hobbes saw self-preservation as the source of the rules of conduct, Spinoza (1632-1677) saw the greater happiness of man, namely freedom, reason and the love of truth. Spinoza extends into formal rhetoric the Cartesian effort to mathematicize thinking and expression, and he owes to Hobbes its formulations on causality and necessity. But he departs from both by uniting God and nature – mind and matter – into one, and this pantheism gives nature an ethical value in his system. By understanding nature man reaches truth, and if truth is the highest pleasure attainable, then all the lesser pleasures such as love, lust, and the desire for gain, can no longer tempt men's minds [Colie, 1968:XV,134-6]. With this, *understanding* becomes the height of pleasure; and moral and intellectual confusion the essential cause of pain. The pursuit of understanding keeps man's mind active, and passions remain the fruits of a lack of understanding. Consequently the development of the human intellect is the object of morality. In this way morality is extricated from the mediaeval system of prohibitions and commandments and the penalties and rewards associated with them, and enters into a new framework relating means to the satisfaction of worldly desires. Morality is released from the conception of attainment in a world hereafter, and is placed in the context of the search for rational arrangements to obtain a more satisfactory existence here on earth. The eternal laws and inner harmony of all things and thought – the harmony which before long was also to intrigue and delight Newton – is in the oneness of nature and of mind and nature, and in the singularity in which the multiplicity of things and events are manifestations of a single whole. Passions are part of man's being which cannot be exorcized from human nature, but they are rendered harmless by a more powerful passion, namely by the passion for knowledge by which man's mind approaches and is eventually united with the sole unchanging thing among all the mutable. This is so because knowledge brings man to where mind and matter are one – where mind of man becomes one with God.

Thus at one and the same time Spinoza is both thoroughly materialistic and yet 'obsessed with God'. Wholeness, uniformity, order, is the key to his conception of the universe, and the striving towards knowledge, i.e. towards the understanding of this harmony in order to conform with it, the avenue to the proper way of living. With him morality is good reason – good reason on the assumption that the world is orderly and therefore comprehensible. God is still there but he is no longer 'instructing' a passive humanity how and by what rules to live. He is the essence of all being but not a 'personal' God. The rules by which man must live man must actively discover for himself. Not simple expediency but expediency restricted by nature's laws determines man's morality. Social values and the distinction between right and wrong are not relative – they continue to be absolute – but they are the product of man's mind in search of understanding.

Spinoza found order and unity in the wholeness of nature, Leibniz (1646-1716) discovered them in all things being but different combinations of identical fundamental 'particles' – monads. Where Spinoza proceeded from the whole to the particular, Leibniz went from the particular to the whole. Spinoza's views, not unlike Hobbes's, reflect the era of political authority; Leibniz's and Locke's (1632-1704) reflect the new and coming type of individuality and independence. Descartes, Hobbes and Spinoza had given to the material relationships in nature a strictly mechanical interpretation and had turned nature into a kind of machine or clockwork; Leibniz gave it a moral purpose – a God or ghost in the machine. The order and regularity in nature became the final proof of divine providence. By this he reconciled the new materialistic tendencies in society, and the mechanistic conception of nature which accompanied them, with the traditional essentially teleological moral outlook. Scientific discoveries were the manifestations of a higher moral force and of an ethical purpose. In spite of all the changes that were taking place man could continue to believe in divine salvation; and society could with only very gradually accumulating amendments continue to hold on to its traditional set of values. In Leibniz's *Petit Discours de Métaphysique* (1685) force, not motion, is constant and force is identical with substance – 'being and working' is the same. Leibniz assumes an identity of individuality of events and uniformity of existence. However, unlike modern scientists, he saw in this the combination of a godly purpose with the individual character of the monads, i.e. with an individual character which could be conceived of as what with men would be the soul. Every individual is a little world of its own developing according to its own laws and by its own force, as a special emanation of the divine force. The cause of the development is the common origin of all things, the harmony of the development of all other beings. Herein is a reinstatement of God into contemporary scientific outlook and a reconciliation of Christian morality and ethics with the increasingly materialistic conception of science and with the individualistic tendencies of the bourgeoisie's social reality. The mystery of God is retained. Provident men will still be wise to hold on to the old moral heritage 'just in case' and not succumb too readily to the logic of bare-faced expediency; even hierarchy is retained but in a new form. The world is an infinite number of *monads* of spiritual force or matter which are substance. They cannot interact because each is reflecting a universe in itself, yet they can be graded from the lower to the highest, which is God who allows freedom of will but still shapes the world to be the best of all possible worlds. But here the reflection of the mediaeval heritage in Leibniz's conception ends, for unlike mediaeval religion his is natural rather than positive. 'I am at a loss to understand,' he wrote to Bouruet in 1714, 'how they can deduce Spinozism from my doctrine. It is precisely by the monads that Spinozism is undone. For there are just as many true substances as...there are monads; while according to Spinoza there is only one single substance.' There is universal harmony, but within this harmony there is the individuality of a multiplicity of independent self-dependent beings which must be considered as 'little gods'. Each monad acts by its own inherent urges but God directs them all to general harmony, so that each trader follows his own interest in harmony with the general objectives of the mercantilist state or trading town. In Leibniz's own words, 'God alone brings about the union of interconnection of substances, and through Him alone do the phenomena of one man coincide and agree with those of other men' [Leibniz, 1685:Ch.32]. This is the same idea that less than a century later Adam Smith would formulate when he claimed that it is the consideration of his own private profit (that) is the sole motive which determines the owner of any capital to employ it either in agriculture, manufactures or some particular branch of trade, but the study of this, his own advantage, leads him to the employment which is most beneficial to all [Smith, 1776:IV,ii].

What separated Leibniz's conception from that of Adam Smith was that the former accepted the harmonization of individual drives and general ends as a fact, whereas the latter concerned himself with the mechanism, with the laws by which the 'invisible hand' maintains this harmony.

The genius in whose perception of the universe the difference between the old socially almost static world of the Middle Ages, and the new dynamic society of the rising bourgeoisie is best reflected is of course Newton (1642-1727). Copernicus, Kepler and Galileo saw a universe in *motion*. Descartes, Hobbes, Spinoza and Leibniz saw that it was *orderly* and *rationally comprehensible*. But Newton discovered a *mechanism* by which the motion is regulated. With Newton 'the mechanical conception of Nature founded by Kepler, Galileo and Descartes received confirmation and became more comprehensive. The world became a huge machine. Man had for sometime entertained a suspicion that this was so, now it was revealed how the machine was held together' [Hoffding, 1900:I,409]. What his predecessors had regarded as the identity of God and nature, Newton saw as the unity expressed in the likeness between the apple falling from the tree and the rotation of the moon in its orbit round the earth. God was there, but he was no longer directly involved with the observable events. The world of His will was a world of mechanisms; a world of hierarchies, of particles contained in systems governed by simple laws. His law of inertia (the tendency of a body to persevere in its state of rest or uniform motion in a straight line) and his law of gravitation (every particle in the universe attracts every other particle with a force which is directly proportional to the product of the masses of the particles and inversely proportional to the square of the distance between them) reflect both the individualism and the urge to action of the rising bourgeoisie.

Even Newton did not abandon the belief in the existence of something never changing, stable, absolute and permanent, in this eternally mobile world, namely *time* and *space*. To be sure, in practical matters man cannot go beyond his sensuous perception of space and time, but in *rebus philosophicus* man can be aware of the absolute that he cannot sensuously grasp. Before inertia, there must be absolute time and space, not *relative* but *absolute* motion, just as there must be an absolute good and bad and right and wrong at the roots of the moral value system. The source of the absolute is God, and Newton proves his existence by pointing to the purposive and harmonious arrangement of the world. 'He starts a theme which received a thousand variations in the course of the eighteenth century' [Hoffding, 1900:I,412]. Newton discovered the dynamics in cosmology, and by introducing the notion of mass frees mechanics from its non-mathematical qualities. But he retains the aether hypothesis for all that could not be reduced to mass. His contemporaries, by introducing the notion of natural law, liberated their moral value system from its religious dogmatism, but they retained the basic tenets by holding on to the idea of the just and compassionate God. Newton's world 'was presided over by an omniscient and omnipresent God, whom man can come to know only by the most excellent contrivances of things and final causes.' Moreover, infinite space is turned into a *sensorium* in which God perceives and understands all things at once. 'The harmony in the universe stems from God's deliberate choice, and not from chance. For no natural cause could have sufficed to establish it' [Koyre & Taton, 1964:II,259].

In conclusion, while the mystical interpretation of life which eroded in the Renaissance left man with the need to find a new purpose in his existence and new sources of security and stability, the dissipation of the old hierarchies made him aware of the multiplicity of things and imposed upon him the search for other types of order – for new uniformities consistent with his new-found purposeful rationality. The demise of the static hierarchical society and its replacement by a society in motion directed this search toward laws of dynamic causation. These took the form of sequences of events. The death of scholasticism led to the rebirth of mathematical logic and the linking of rational empirical thought engendered the observation of facts and eventually practical experimentation.

Thus while the sixteenth century had been a century of doubt and rediscovery of man and nature, the seventeenth century became a period of systematization of the newly discovered. It became a century in which the ideas which had previously only vaguely preyed on men's minds received deliberate conscious formulations upon which systems could be and were constructed which were claimed to do away with scholasticism, but in fact only gave to it a new form by an unceasing search for an absolute principle of knowledge. Descartes was the first of the great system-builders who endeavoured to find constructive thought through analysis. Hobbes and Spinoza followed, but they were less analytical and more disposed towards construction. With Leibniz the analytical tendency begins once more to assert itself, and with this begins the transition to the era in which the problem of knowledge and of worth were to become of predominant importance [Hoffding, 1900:I,210].

In the late sixteenth and early seventeenth century people discovered a world that was both orderly and comprehensible, a world in which God played the role of an architect or constructor who by a single act of creation had made a universe according to some orderly principle and then abandoned it to run its course. The orderly principle was comprehensible through mathematics and happiness meant living in harmony with the laws of nature which revealed themselves to man through mathematics. To live a rational life was to live a life based upon self-evident and universal principles because the same law that provided stability and confidence in nature also provided stability and security in society. The old moral dicta continued to be valid but they could be reinterpreted by man. What had been bad continued to be bad but it was so because of reasons that could be fathomed by the human mind. In the seventeenth century the human mind does not yet determine what is good or bad; the old rules still apply but man can try to explain them by reason. Man is not yet making his reason the source of the rules society is to live by but he has opened the door through which this change would gradually slip in.

# 4.    Saving the Goose that laid the Golden Eggs

If, as Gellner claims, a society without oppression or arbitrariness is not inscribed into any historical plan [Gellner, 1988:3], the question needs to be asked why in the era in which the bourgeoisie was gaining power, and individualism was becoming more and more pronounced, rapacity and exploitation were confined within legal boundaries, and ingenuity rather than brute force became the source of wealth. The answer to this question is crucial to explain why the new social climate stopped short of causing instability; why the new mighty did not resort to force rather than production and exchange to obtain their ends, and therefore did not slaughter 'the goose that laid the golden eggs'. Essentially the response is the spiritual legacy of the Middle Ages. For generations it gave the would-be rich in Western Europe a feeling of discomfort which tempered their profit-seeking with a measure of legality, rationality. It circumscribed their pursuit of wealth by social conventions and by the notion or fear of divine retribution. But for these, capitalism would never have attained its great economic success. In the words of R.H. Tawney, man became an 'economic animal', but an 'economic animal who found it nevertheless prudent to take due precautions to assure his spiritual well-being.' [Tawney, 1922:273].

It is of course true that human feelings were only allowed to enter into the interstices left by profitability but they are there. Defoe's (1660-1731) little Moor, without whom Crusoe could not have escaped from slavery and whom Crusoe had decided 'to love ever after,' is all the same sold into slavery by him for sixty pieces of eight, but with a promise from the purchaser to free the slave after ten years if by that time he has been converted to Christianity. The wives of the colonists in the *Further Adventures of Robinson Crusoe* are assessed wholly in economic terms. As Moll Flanders puts it: 'with money in the pocket one is at home anywhere'. Jonathan Swift's (1667-1745) cynical essay 'Modest Proposal for Preventing the Children of Ireland from being a Burden to their Parents or Country and for making them beneficial to the Pubick' [Swift, 1729:84-92] makes the moral dilemma of the bourgeoisie even more obvious. Employing Cartesian logic and writing in the style of contemporary rationalism, Swift presents his readers with a perfectly logical but preposterous scheme for dealing with poverty in Ireland. With mock humanism, claiming that it is the virtue of compassion that compels him to make his 'Proposal', Swift says:

> I have been assured by a very knowing American of my acquaintance in London, that a young Child well Nursed is, at a year Old, a most delicious nourishing and wholesome Food, whether Stewed, Roasted, Baked, or Boiled; and I make no doubt that it will equally serve in a Fricasie, or a Ragoust... to Persons of Quality and Fortune, through the Kingdom.

He grants that 'this Food will be somewhat dear, and therefore very proper for Landlords; who, as they have already devoured most of the Parents seem to have best Title to the Children.' But, 'it would greatly lessen the Number of Papists' give 'the poorer Tenants... something valuable of their own... help to pay their rents to the Landlords,' and increase the nation's stock of capital because 'the goods' are entirely the produce of domestic manufacture. In addition, 'all Gentlemen of Fortune in the Kingdom, who have any Refinement in Taste' will be provided with 'a new Dish,' for their enjoyment.

The author who most succinctly drove home the cultural dichotomy between the self-centred rationalism of the bourgeoisie and its Christian ethic legacy was Bernard Mandeville (1680-1733). He discovered the *mechanism* by which society is moving, namely greed. The bourgeoisie did not forgive him this indiscretion even in the twentieth century [Sorley, 1912:IX,279-304]. In the fable *'The Grumbling Hive: or Knaves Turned Honest'* (1705), and again, in *'The Fable of the Bees: Or Private Vices, Publick Benefits'* (1714), Mandeville shows that it is precisely the culturally *unacceptable* which makes a people powerful and wealthy, and the morally desirable which is its undoing. His message is simple: civilization thrives on vices. Luxury, pride, greed, envy and self-interest are the mechanisms, the driving force, by which men are made to exert themselves and make a nation great. Vices are the social corollary to Newton's Law of Gravitation in the natural sciences. Make man virtuous, take away his self-centred gravitation, and society reverts to poverty. Man is a self-seeking egoist but good government can keep his egoism in check and direct it so that it serves to make the entire nation prosperous. Those who claim that virtue and altruism are the springs of prosperity are hypocrites. Mandeville does not deny that the self-centred efforts to obtain private 'pleasures, comforts, and ease' make also 'the very poor live better than the rich before,' but he claims that this has hardly anything to do with their intentions. His attack was directed against Shaftesbury, but the real 'father' of the 'reconciliation,' the one who did most to reconcile traditional ethics with bourgeois reality, and who provided the bourgeoisie with an ideological alibi to counter the lingering morality, was of course John Locke.

For centuries society believed that resignation to one's lot was the essence of morality and wisdom; that man's life on earth was cast in the shadow of original sin; that the meek shall inherit the earth; and that self-interest and the pursuit of wealth, luxury and worldly pleasures, were all evil. For generations parents, teachers and priests had inculcated these beliefs into the minds of the young by verbal admonitions and moralizing demeanour until they appeared to be self-evident and true. And indeed, as long as the social and economic reality gave little opportunity for successfully pursuing wealth and luxury, and a lack of 'meekness', at least in the poor, drew painful retribution, there was truly no point in reexamining these 'self-evident' guides to good behaviour. But on the threshold of the eighteenth century, when it was not the meek but the self-seeking who were inheriting the earth as long as they kept within the rules of positive law, doubts steadily crept in. However, positive law, even if founded in the laws of nature, was more flexible than the written dictum of the word of God. It was interpretable in the light of common sense, and the common sense in light of which it was interpreted was that which suited the immediate needs of the rising bourgeoisie.

People do not cast off age-old beliefs they were brought up with lightly. It took scientists ages to abandon the Ptolemaic image of the constellation. They thought up the most complex and ingenious ideas to explain away the inconsistencies between the received theory and the observations which contradicted them. They held on to the Ptolemaic system even after Copernicus had shown his much more plausible and simple alternative explanation. The same is true of the erosion of the old dicta of morality. Renaissance sceptics, like Montaigne and Pico, were well aware of the contradiction between the dictates of reason and religion. But they avoided the choice between them and relegated religion to the sphere of the incomprehensible and reason to the sphere of things observable and understandable by human rationality. Making religion the arbiter of 'final truth' they regarded Christian asceticism – the subjugation of worldly desires to religious rules – not contrary to reason but due to human nature corrupted by original sin. For Pierre Bayle (1647-1706), religion was incompatible with both reason and human nature, but it did not lead him to reject religion. Instead, he precluded the one from the sphere of the other. Deists were able to maintain that the world is ordered by natural law and that its functioning is open to human understanding by observation and experience, but it did not prevent them from believing that the origins of ethics are divine and that there is a 'final' truth which can be arrived at by the search for the will of God. By identifying the laws of nature with the will of God their conception retained a firm element in an otherwise almost entirely relativistic utilitarian outlook. In this way a basis was provided for a legality and social stability which legitimated greed but did not put in jeopardy the steady growth of manufacturing and trade. Without such restraints the pursuit of wealth would have led to violence and instability and not to production and exchange. The point is that the new conception was relativistic but retained a sufficient measure of the old tenets of ethical and moral absolutism to serve the economic requirements of the new class. In this way the empirical movement from Bacon to Locke prepared the reconciliation between relativism and absolute truth and virtue, which liberated the bourgeoisie from what would have been a debilitating moral dilemma. Truth and virtue were of divine origin and the laws of nature had a rationality which man could reach by observation and experiment.

A special place in the process of ethical adjustment must be given to John Locke (1632-1704). His works did more than reconcile traditional ethics with the covetous practices of the bourgeoisie they provided them with a moral legitimization. By substituting for Hobbes's 'wolfish' state of nature one in which reasonable, almost benevolent, people improve their life by mutual agreement, Locke gave the bourgeoisie precisely the self-portrait it wanted for easing its troubled conscience. It made the pursuit of wealth, and the life of luxury that wealth could buy, respectable. It transformed the Shylocks into the new-fangled aristocrats immortalized by Molière in *Tartufe* (1664) and *Le Bourgeois Gentilhomme* (1670). Locke was neither a man of great logical consistency, nor was he gifted with outstanding analytical powers of reasoning, but his empiricism combined the new scientific conception of the universe with the social and economic reality of contemporary society in a manner exactly fitting the tenor of the times. That his conception of human motivation, unlike Hobbes's, rested upon ill defined and unexplained 'intrinsic' human characteristics bothered neither him nor his admirers. Nor was anyone disturbed by the absence of proof for his convenient assumption that the pursuit of private advantage will of necessity lead to the greatest public good. Locke saw society in his own image and being an amicable person he found it rational and liberal, and describing it as such he gave the bourgeoisie the sympathetic face it wanted.

Locke's conception of natural law also differed from earlier conceptions: it emphasized man's *rights* where earlier conceptions stressed only duties. It went even further than that; its precursors knew only the right to life, which they regarded as the right to self-preservation. Locke's natural law upheld a 'trinity' of rights: to *life, liberty* and *property*. These rights he claimed to be 'inherent', given to man from birth. What then of the right to property, and to property acquired by the labour of one's servants? The right to property in Locke's scheme is created by labour. Labouring a man extends *his self* into the objects he produces. 'By expending his internal energy upon them he makes them part of himself'. Consequently their protection becomes part of his right to self-preservation. But the fact that a man's servant expends his 'internal energy' to create property which then is alienated from him by his master and becomes the master's property, did not merit Locke's attention. He was living in a world where the lower strata of society simply did not matter. His natural law determines his morality, but his natural law is always *self-evident*. On the one hand his moral values are divine, 'external;' on the other hand they are 'intrinsic', namely what man 'feels' or 'knows' to be right. If the bourgeoisie felt it self-evident that it had a right to the fruits of their servants' labour, how then could it be otherwise? In his *Essay Concerning Human Understanding* (1690) Locke argues that things 'self-evident cannot be taken as reliable guides to truth because any time honoured custom or habit seems self-evident.' However, at the same time his entire political theory (1690a) is based upon the proposition that all individuals 'are endowed by their creator with a right to life, liberty and estate,' *because these rights are self-evident*. He denied the right of anyone to force upon people speculative opinions (1689), and claims that 'he that examines and upon examination embraces an error for a truth has done his duty more than he who embraces the profession of the truth... without having examined whether it be true or not' [Bourne, 1876], but he denied the right 'to differ' from all who do not accept 'natural religion' as the common ground for their belief. Like Hobbes he grants man individual rights, but transforms them into something different. With him Hobbes's *self-preservation* becomes *self-interest* – the psychological dimension out of which a 'calculus' of pleasure and pain was to develop. By his 'social contract' he made society the guardian of rights that antedated it. By emphasizing a right to property he converts the earlier conception of natural law from the preserver of the common good into a guardian of individual rights by implying that because there is 'harmony in nature' private advantage and the general good are identical.

It was the *transformation*, instead of the *negation* of the old established views, which appealed to the bourgeoisie and gave Locke his popularity. It reconciled the old values with the freedoms the bourgeoisie required. *Property* was part of a man's 'self,' and therefore included in man's right to self-preservation. The common good was identified with private gain and thereby the pursuit of self-interest was made respectable – almost a virtue. Deriving the right to make laws from some inalienable rights of man (including the right to property) and founding *law* on public consent (or tacit endorsement by the absence of effective resistance) provided a moral justification for economic inequality which was to last for generations.

Calvin had made the love of gain 'respectable,' though not the worldly pleasures that gain could buy. Hobbes had added the mechanism by which the love of gain was satisfied, namely the eternal struggle – the 'war of everyone against everyone' [Hobbes, 1651:i,iv]. Locke reconciled the pursuit of gain with traditional conceptions of morality by endowing man with a rationality which gave it moral quality.

Shaftesbury by the end of the seventeenth century, and Hutcheson in the first half of the eighteenth, made this more explicit by giving man an innate gravitation towards goodness. With them the love of gain becomes the love of prestige or happiness [Hutcheson, 1725], and the opprobrium is lifted from both the pursuit of wealth and from its enjoyment. Granting man innate powers to distinguish right from wrong and making him good by nature, they turn ethics into a kind of aesthetics. There is no more need to give a rational explanation for moral judgments. Virtue is what people feel it to be. In Butler's sermons on human nature [1726], the old Biblical standards of morality have not yet vanished; at least unconsciously they continue to influence what people feel, but their power to determine man's course of action is steadily receding.

Hutcheson's work is permeated with the optimism of the late seventeenth and early eighteenth century. In it man is driven by a mixture of egoism and desire to please others. Reason is the indispensable instrument for satisfying both. Man's moral sense is neither educated nor habitual but instinctive. It is the gift of God, part of His universal harmony which leads man by promoting his own desires to advance the good of others. To be virtuous is to harmonize one's inclinations with one's fellow creatures, to offend against this rule is to offend against oneself. Butler's work is lacking the optimism of Leibniz, Locke, Shaftesbury and Hutcheson. He believes in man's innate sense of moral judgment, which he calls *conscience*, but he does not deny man's tendency to follow other earthly egoistic drives. What places the one above the other is that the 'pleasures' of the conscience are direct or immediate, whereas egoistic pleasures are always preceded by desire and self-centred efforts which cannot satisfy. 'There is a superior principle of reflection or conscience in every man, which distinguishes between the internal principles of his heart, as well as his external actions.' In other words, Butler's only criterion of distinction between good and bad is that one *feels* them to be one or the other. It is a belief in God's good intention upon earth which makes intuition the only true guide to valid judgments.

In the first half of the eighteenth century the deterministic conception of the world and the trust in natural harmony, as well as the empiricism which stressed generalizations based upon observation alone (and denied all innate ideas and *a priori* truth), were still dominating European thought. But the buds of a new kind of scepticism were beginning to sprout and found an early expression in the work of David Hume.

Hume (1711-1776) separated *moral judgment* from *judgment by reason*. Rejecting the possibility of obtaining *certain* knowledge from observation he fell back upon common sense and faith. Moral judgment, he maintained, can never be judgment by reason. Reason must always be concerned with facts or with the relations between ideas, while passions relate to the prospects of pleasure or pain. Reason can inform about such prospects and indicate the best ways to attain pleasure and to avoid pain, but it is the servant and not the master of man's passions. In Hume's words: 'The objects of human reason or inquiry may naturally be divided into two kinds, to wit, *Relations of Ideas*, and *Matters of Fact*' [Hume, 1748]. Among the first kind he counts 'the sciences of Geometry, Algebra, and Arithmetic; in short, every affirmation which is either intuitively or demonstratively certain...'. Among the second kind he numbers 'matters of fact.' These cannot be ascertained in the same manner as the former; 'nor is our evidence of their truth, however great, of like nature with the foregoing.' That 'the sun will *not* rise tomorrow is no less intelligible a proposition, and implies no more contradiction than the affirmation that it *will* rise.'

Reasoning concerning 'matters of fact' is with Hume a question of *cause and effect*. He believes that by means of this relation people can go beyond the evidence of their memory and senses. But to arrive at the knowledge of causes and effects, they depend entirely on experience with no *a priori* reasoning. However,

such is the influence of custom, that, where it is strongest, it not only covers our natural ignorance, but even conceals itself, and seems not to take place, merely because it is found in the highest degree. But to convince us that all the laws of nature, and all the operations of bodies without exception, are known only by experience,... may, perhaps, suffice. [The] ultimate springs and principles are totally shut up from human curiosity and inquiry... The most perfect philosophy of the natural kind only staves off our ignorance a little longer: as perhaps the most perfect philosophy of the moral or metaphysical kind serves only to discover larger portions of it...

Hence there is also no need for an understanding in order to embrace a religion because it may well arise out of the unintelligible, namely the feelings of hope and fear, suspense and uncertainty. Hume believes that it is in fact impossible to ascertain the causes of man's moral judgments by reason. The sapling destroying the parent oak is judged by other standards than the son destroying his father; the former is simply not subjected to man's judgment, it is neither morally approved or disapproved, it is alone taken as a fact. Patricide can therefore hardly be the reason for opprobrium because factually there is little difference between one and the other – the sapling and the son. Yet men do make a distinction. They feel that the one leaves them unconcerned and the other arouses their strongest disapprobation. Consequently, in Hume's own words, 'morality is more properly felt than judged of' [Hume, 1739:II,3,3]. 'To have the sense of virtue is nothing but to feel a satisfaction of a particular kind from the contemplation of a character. The very feeling constitutes our praise or admiration' [Hume, 1740:III,1,2,]. Thus Hume's work reflects simultaneously both tendencies in his society, the utilitarian–rational and the traditional–conservative. By founding moral values in man's innate power of judgment he reflected the tendency (which was spreading with the growing affluence) toward an assimilation of morality with expediency; by claiming that it is a vain attempt to discover 'the cause of all causes' (because the 'ultimate springs and principles are totally shut up from human curiosity and inquiry') he confirmed the existence of God and the continued authority of revealed religion for those who from 'hope, fear, suspense and uncertainty' wish to hold on to them, though, for himself, he denied as an unproven proposition the relevance of God and the authority of religion for the formation of moral judgments.

Hume's criteria of morality are *utility* and *sympathy*. But his opinion of mankind is less optimistic than Locke's, Shaftesbury's, Hutcheson's, and even that of his friend Adam Smith. He did not believe that *by nature* man will prefer that which is best for the 'public good' over his own interests. What he did believe was that in order to serve his self-interest, to protect himself and his property, man has devised *artificial virtues* in customs and rules of law which constitute the mechanism by which society's long-term collective interest is protected against individuals' short-term impulses. In spite of later less pessimistic ideas he really never abandoned this view. Perhaps it is symptomatic of the era's growing self-centred rationalism in spite of the lingering influence of the traditional values, that Hume combined in his personal life and in his work a moral conservatism with a strong atheistic scepticism. Missing a sense of evolution, and although he was a historian a sense of history, he looked upon human nature as well as on morality as 'given' and eternal. For him the rules of morality are immutable because they are common sense – because he *feels* them to be self-evident. The possibility that things self-evident can one day no longer be self-evident simply did not occur to him.

In France reasoning on the nature of man's moral values (with the important exception of Rousseau's) went little further than in England. Its presentation was sharper, more aggressive, reflecting that the old order was still deeply entrenched in eighteenth century France while its disintegration in England had already advanced much further. Montesquieu (1689-1755), for example, questioned the trust in the utilitarian individualism on which much of the contemporary speculation about morals and human nature was based by indicating the complexity of the relationship between individuals and society. Unlike Hume, he did not believe that human values are innate and eternal, but that they are functionally related to man's natural and social environment. He did not accept the view that there must be only one set of values which is valid for all times and in all places. However, a prisoner of his own environment, he too was searching for an absolute standard, for some 'revealed' truth. Consequently, his theory also becomes inconsistent. Explaining the foundations of various types of government he names *fear* for despotism, *honour* for monarchy and *civic virtue* for the republican system. Doing so he does in fact list the different, and sometimes contrasting, assumptions about human nature which were current in his time. *Fear* is of course the same as what in the English literature appears as the wish to avoid pain; *honour* the same as the wish to gain the appreciation of others; and *civic virtue* is altruism. Montesquieu achieves the reconciliation between the contradictory assumptions concerning human nature by granting each a greater or lesser degree of importance depending on the specific social and political circumstances.

Helvetius's (1715-1771) ideas are not unlike Hobbes's but the emphasis is different. In tune with the cultural climate of the mid-eighteenth century, the *pursuit of pleasure* replaces *avoidance of pain*. With few exceptions, such as Rousseau, contemporary thinkers were not concerned with those socially and economically below their class. Helvetius's human nature is therefore almost unmitigatedly pleasure-seeking and egoistic. But he believes in the power of education to redirect this pleasure-seeking egoism toward 'self-evidently' *socially* desirable ends. He is convinced that man can be taught to enjoy benevolence so that his egoism is satisfied by altruism. This is not Locke's altruism nor Hutcheson's; it is no innate passion but an acquired taste generated by a self-seeking desire for a pleasure inculcated into the social mind by education.

An almost contrary view was held by Diderot (1713-1784). In so far as 'eternal values' were concerned, Diderot continued to uphold the traditional ideas, but he believed that these eternal values, or rather the actions they prescribe to men, could be subverted by bad government. Evil deeds, in spite of man's better nature, have their causes, but they can hardly be ascribed to 'man's fall' and 'original sin'. In his early writings Diderot still assumes that the knowledge of good and right is innate, part of human nature, a moral sense with which man is endowed by birth. However, in his later work he comes to the conclusion that there is no such innate moral sense, and that what gives the impression of being innate is really no more than the result of an infinite number of separately insignificant experiences which from their earliest childhood and throughout their entire life are internalized by men. Unconsciously these experiences influence man's sense of values and determine his concrete judgment. As he wrote to Mlle Voland: 'All is experience though we may not be consciously aware of it.'

The 'odd man out' among the French great thinkers of the eighteenth century was undoubtedly Jean-Jacques Rousseau (1712-1778). 'Rousseau differed from his contemporaries in everything; even when using the same words he meant something else. His character, his outlook, his scale of values, his instinctive reactions, all differed from what the Enlightenment regarded admirable' [Sabine, 1961:575]. Where the Enlightenment believed 'the growth of knowledge' to be 'the growth of good', he held that man, good by nature or at least neither good nor bad at birth, was corrupted by civilization. Where the Enlightenment spoke of equality and meant equality before the law – the freedom for the bourgeoisie to protect its business interests against claims founded upon aristocratic privileges and the freedom of the intelligentsia to evolve and voice opinions contrary to state and Church – he spoke of social and economic equality embracing all strata of society including the plebeian 'rabble.' Where the Enlightenment looked upon the pursuit of wealth with favour, making it an inalienable birthright – part of the trinity 'life, liberty, and property' – he turned it into the 'original sin', the source of all corruption, the fountain-head of all oppressive political and social orders which serve no other purpose but to preserve inequity and to protect those who wrongfully appropriated man's common heritage for themselves.

Rousseau rejected both the traditional doctrine and the new philosophy which arose in opposition to it and which, in the wake of the social changes, reflected the bourgeoisie's need for greater moral flexibility. He regarded those who upheld the old beliefs as irrational dogmatics who were trying to maintain their hold on society by superstition; and he looked upon the protagonists of the new ideas as 'vain and futile declaimers' who are out 'to sap the foundations of our faith, and nullify virtue.' He saw them as people who 'consecrate their talents and philosophy to the destruction and defamation of all that men hold sacred.' As Sabine [1961:578] pointed out: Rousseau believed that 'intelligence is dangerous because it undermines reverence; science is destructive because it takes away faith; reason is bad because it sets prudence against moral intuition.' All this 'the Enlightenment could not easily understand – unless it were a covert defence of revelation and the Church,' which it was not. It was in fact the reflection of his growing fear that the demolition of the traditional dogmas of religion might engender the extinction of the other moral values which were worthy of retention. He shared neither Hobbes's individualism, which turned society into the guardian of individuals' right to self-preservation, nor Locke's individualism that made it the guardian of individual property; nor did he agree with Hume's predilection for enlightened self-interest. What he believed in were the redeeming powers of good government and education. He

simply did not conceive of man *outside* society. Society itself was
the source of human values. The test of good government was not
the satisfaction of individuals' self-interest but the adherence to
values of which society was the final arbiter. Natural man was
neither good nor evil; his values were moulded by society. Man's
fall began with the institution of private property. When some
men first appropriated for themselves part of the common wealth
and created private property, and to preserve their ill-gotten gains
imposed upon society their rules and laws and originated
inequality, the true character of society was distorted and
government became the tool of its corruption. The good society is
one which controls the corrupting influences of property-perverted
social institutions. It is the society in which government and
education serve 'the common people who compose the human
race', and serve the great majority of men, for 'man is the same
in all ranks and.... the ranks which are most numerous deserve
most respect' [Rousseau, 1762:II,226].

The idea that man is the same in all ranks was hardly one the
bourgeoisie was prepared to embrace. The eighteenth century did
not consider 'the common people' equal partners in the 'human
race'. The rising bourgeoisie was ready to commiserate with the
poor in their ill plight, to pity them, to deplore their ignorance,
but its attitude was always condescending, and in England it would
remain so well into the late nineteenth century. The lower class's
way of life, its disregard for bourgeois virtues, simply did not fit
the bourgeoisie's image of equal members in the human race. The
difference is even now still reflected in the use of words: people
who 'matter' perspire, the workers and the poor sweat; people
who 'matter' become intoxicated, the others get drunk; people who
'matter' are frugal – they save and invest, the 'rabble' squander
the little money they come by on sordid pleasures. In the eyes of
the bourgeoisie the poor represented the very opposite of its
aspired image of what constitutes 'society'. They were uneducated,
immoderate, improvident and sinful – their very life-style placed
the poor outside the 'human race'. In an era which regarded
*'causes and effects'* as *the* principle of science, it was easy to see
the poor's conduct as the cause of their poverty. The idea that

poverty may be the *cause*, and the behaviour of the poor the *effect*, was not only inconvenient to consider, but contrary to what had been accepted as 'true' for centuries. The Church had always placed misfortune at the sinners' doors.

No wonder that Rousseau's ideas were unpalatable to a bourgeoisie still struggling to establish its own norms of conduct. His biographers write that after the publication of the *Discours sur l'origine de l'inégalité* (1755) he felt increasingly unhappy in Paris. After the publication of *Emile* (1762) and its condemnation by the Paris *Parlement* he was in fact forced to flee from France. His *lettres écrites de la montagne* so much provoked the Genevan bourgeoisie that he had to seek refuge in England as a guest of David Hume (1766). He does not remain there for long. After a quarrel with Hume he returns to France in 1767 and spends the rest of his life moving from one place to another. His biographers put this down to 'his oppressed thought of universal persecution.' Perhaps it was not only the 'thought' of persecution he had to contend with. Ideas such as that people are 'the same in all ranks,' and that 'the right which each individual has to his own estate is always subordinate to the right which the community has over all,' and that 'the first man, who, having enclosed a piece of land, bethought himself of saying "this is mine", and found people simple enough to believe him was the real founder of civil government' and of all evil, were certainly not ideas suited to endear him to contemporary 'society'. This went too far even for Diderot who admitted that Rousseau's ideas 'disturbed' but did not convert him.

The eighteenth century was more an era of consolidation of earlier achievements than of revolutionary innovations. It was the era in which the bourgeoisie established and confirmed its position *vis-à-vis* the upper class and began to fortify it against new pressures from below. Most historians of Western culture use the term 'Age of Reason' to designate the seventeenth and eighteenth century together, and reserve the term 'Enlightenment' for the eighteenth century when *rationalism* had spread from the small group of advanced thinkers to a relatively much larger educated public. 'The eighteenth-century public acquired its Enlightenment less through direct contact with the work of "philosophers" than through what we should now call "popularisers" – journalists, men of letters, the bright young talkers of the *salons*' [Brinton, 1967:II,519]. The major themes absorbed in this way by the educated public were the *social contract* (developed from Hobbes through Locke to Rousseau), and the *theory of knowledge* (developed from Locke through Berkeley and Hume eventually to Kant). At the same time the increasing prestige of the natural sciences convinced the educated that

> human beings, using their 'natural' reasoning powers in a fairly obvious and teachable way, could not only understand the way things really are in the universe; they could understand what human beings are really like, and by combining this knowledge of nature and human nature, learn how to live better and happier lives [Brinton, 1967:II,519].

Apart from Rousseau, whose thoughts foreshadowed the ideas which were to gain ground only later, when the bourgeoisie's newly acquired economic hegemony was beginning to be challenged by the working class, the ethics of the great thinkers of the 'Age of Reason' was essentially a compromise between the norms and values of the Church (which through the ages had become 'self-evident' by cultural contamination) and the practical need of men who were learning to determine their earthly fate by their own efforts. It was this combination of cultural inhibitions inherited from the past, and the opportunities to gain riches and social esteem within the gradually adjusting confines of these inhibitions, which confined the pursuit of wealth to ingenuity, rather than force, that saved the 'goose that laid the golden eggs.'

# 5. New Paradigms in Science and Society

'Men reason by analogy from the condition of their lives to the condition of the universe, and a static society could hardly believe in a dynamic cosmos' [Lewontin, 1968:208]. In the Middle Ages, when man was born into his social status by divine providence and social mobility and economic advancement were almost unthinkable, static stability was man's conception of the order of the world. In the 'Age of Reason' when social mobility increased, the old conceptions in the natural sciences lost ground to a new principle, namely 'uniformitarian change'.

Galileo (1565-1642) not only substituted an earth in motion for the earth at rest and the idea of experimentation for scholasticism but developed a conception of reality which was no longer reconcilable with the traditional unity between theology, science and ethics. No less than his discoveries, the way by which he reached them and the manner in which he presented them to the public implied the rejection of what had been right and proper until then. Claiming that the earth is *not* the centre of the universe and that it revolves around the sun is one thing, but founding such a claim upon the evidence of observations – his own observations – was something else. It suggested that *seeing* is better than *believing*; that ancient usage does not necessarily bestow superior truth; that nature is not concealed by mysteries which only the initiated can comprehend, but that it can be grasped by reason – by everybody's reason. As if to underline all this he did not write in Latin as was customary but in Italian, nor did he disguise his views by scholastic arguments to reconcile them with the old authorities. Copernicus (1473-1543) had been content to do so by proclaiming *De revolutionibus orbium coelestium* (1543) a mere hypothesis. For Galileo the truth was too obvious to be disguised. The question whether his works on gravitation and motion did or did not anticipate Newton's First and Second Laws may be interesting, but it is less relevant than his demystification of nature and reality which provided those who followed with the opportunity of combining observation with logic and experimentation with mathematical analysis. Claiming that the 'Book of Nature is written in mathematical characters', he not only broke with Aristotle's logic–verbal approach, but substituted a new type of 'non-scholastic' rationalism which suited the experimental method and the temper of the incipient commercialized society. For having 'held and taught the Copernican doctrine' Galileo was sentenced to prison (21 June 1633); the sentence was later commuted to house arrest which lasted for the remaining eight years of his life.

It is fairly obvious that scientific discovery influences the direction of social and economic change or at least its rate of change. But it is equally true that social and economic perceptions permeate science. There is no need to appeal to a *Zeitgeist* to imply such a relationship. The meaning of *Zeitgeist* is that science and other social activities respond equally to some spirit of the age whose source and power are unknown.

> Yet there is nothing mystical about the way in which notions of cause and effect, choice and chance, determinacy and freedom, spread from one science to another. Equally, it is entirely within the normal picture of historical causation that general social attitudes and economic relationships between social classes should have a profound effect upon the acceptability and apparent reasonableness of scientific hypotheses. Science is, after all, a social activity... [Lewontin, 1968:V,208-9].

In the 'Age of Reason', with no longer a personal God to harness the forces of nature for mankind, man had to harness them himself and he trusted that he could do this with the help of science. *Truth* and *order* rose to a newly elevated position in the scale of social values, and science – the 'branch of study which is concerned either with a connected body of demonstrated *truth* or with observed facts *systematically classified* and more or less

colligated by being brought under general laws' (OED:1725) –
became the new source of mankind's hope. But unlike the old, the
new truth was accessible to all, and not to the initiated clergy
alone. Not only *could* it be tested in the light of everyman's
reason, but unlike revelation, it was never to be taken on trust. It
had to be examined and re-examined in order to be cleansed of
non-truth. It required *doubt* and even the expression of possibly
wrong ideas, because only the confrontation with non-truth could
confirm its trustworthiness and stimulate the search for new and
better truth. And so truth and order, together with the right to
doubt and freedom of expression, became part of the new
philosophy and life-style. The evidence for God's existence was to
be found in the recognizable order in nature, and to attain earthly
happiness, man must *discover* this order so that his social laws can
be arranged to conform with it. But to make *nature* the guide to
proper human conduct people had to believe that some things
were *naturally right* and *intrinsically good*.

There was little 'new' in this. Already Plato (427?-347? BC)
asserted that there were things which are right by nature. So did
Aristotle (384-322 BC) when he spoke of the unchangeable law
common to all men, though it is not clear whether he thought this
law was founded in nature or simply generally accepted. For
Cicero (106-43 BC) the law of nature arose equally from God's
providential government and from the rational and social character
of man. In his own words: 'There is in fact a true law, namely
right reason, which is in accordance with nature, applies to all
men, and is unchangeable and eternal' [Cicero, 51 BC:III,22]. 'Out
of all... the philosophers' discussions, surely there comes nothing
more valuable than the full realization that we are born for justice,
and that right is based not upon man's opinions, but upon Nature'
[Cicero, date unknown:I,28-9]. In the first centuries of the
Christian era the Fathers of the Church also believed in human
equality and in an absolute set of values. But they made God, and
God alone, their source. Thomas Aquinas (1225-1274)
incorporated the Aristotelian idea about the natural law in a
hierarchical system in which God's eternal law becomes the
foundation of the natural law and natural law the basis for human

law. The thought was that the latter was necessary to make natural law suitable for solving the specific problems of living in society.

In the fifteenth century, in *De concordantia Catholica* to the Council of Basle (1433), the idea of equality assumed a new form in a new context which suited the needs of the emerging middle class. It asserted a natural freedom for all members of society. One century later, in the *Vindiciae Contra Tyrannos* (1579), 'reason and wisdom' and 'an understanding mind', had already become a 'parcel of divinity'. Also the right of property had become part of man's heritage *by nature*, because 'every man loves and cherishes his own', though the argument underlying this right had not yet become utilitarian. In the seventeenth century the conception of natural rights and natural law became secularized. The revived interest in stoicism, Platonism and the new understanding of Aristotle brought with it a kind of naturalism and rationalism which could fill the gap left open by the decline in religious belief. But the new belief that the discovery of natural law was in human power was strongly supported by the remarkable progress made in mathematics and the physical sciences. This progress seemed to indicate that the world is not beyond human comprehension and could be explained by logical deduction and mathematical reasoning. Increasingly social phenomena were also regarded as natural events open to study by observation, logical analysis and deduction in which revelation or any other supernatural element had no role. In the words of Grotius (1583-1645),

> The law of nature is a dictate of right reason, which points out that an act, according as it is or is not in conformity with rational nature, has in it a quality of moral baseness or moral necessity; and that, in consequence, such an act is either forbidden or enjoined by the author of nature, God.

But this God, as Grotius pointed out, implies nothing in the way of a religious sanction. For the law of nature would enjoin exactly the same if, by hypothesis, there were no God. 'Just as even God ... cannot cause that two times two should not make four, so He cannot cause that which is intrinsically evil be not evil'. Hence, there was 'nothing arbitrary in natural law more than there is in arithmetic. The dictates of right reason are whatever human nature and the nature of things imply that they must be' [Sabine, 1961:424].

Francis Bacon (1561-1625), a contemporary of Grotius best known for contributing to philosophy the inductive method of modern experimental science, did not find it necessary to discuss how first principles were established. For him the source of philosophical ideas was *sensuous perception*, and of religious ideas *divine inspiration*. The difference between religious and philosophical first principles was only that the former stand by virtue of their divine authorization, and the latter continue to be subjected to critical inductive examination. Once first principles were accepted, it was possible in both philosophy and religion to draw logical conclusions. The world is uniform and the inductive method, namely the organization of observations according to an ordering principle around some provisional hypotheses, is valid for all sciences including ethics. Man too is constantly drawn by the all-pervading force of the whole, which is the general good, and the partial force, which is his individual good. Ethics combines the two in harmony. The key to Bacon's world is still uniformity and order, but so is the freedom to doubt and err. '*Citus emergit veritas ex errore quam ex confusione*'. (Truth is easier sorted out from error than from a confused collection of observations.) In retrospect it is the permeation of his work with the idea that careful analysis of regularities in nature can give man a degree of mastery over it and enable him to *use* nature for his own purposes, and the sense of progress – the thought that science can provide man with a new source of worldly happiness – which makes Bacon's work so very interesting and indicative of the changing mood of his time.

In the period which separated the publication of Gilbert's *De Magnete* (1600) from Newton's *Principia* (1684) the methods employed by Galileo and Descartes were refined into *the* methodology of systematic scientific endeavour. If the seventeenth century had been the century of revolutionary innovations, the eighteenth and early nineteenth century witnessed their consolidation. A brief survey of the evolution of the new ideas and of the names of scientists associated with them should demonstrate the point. The most impressive progress took place in mathematics with the further development of the differential calculus (first invented by Leibniz and Newton) by the brothers Jacob (1654-1705) and John (1667-1748) Bernoulli; and Daniel Bernoulli (1700-1782); Leonhard Euler (1707-1783), Alexis Clairaut (1713-1765); Jean D'Alembert (1717-1783); Joseph Lagrange (1736-1813); Gaspard Monge (1746-1818); Pierre Laplace (1749-1827); and Adrien Legendre (1752-1833). Most of them did not contribute to differential calculus alone. Euler founded the calculus of variations; Clairaut studied space curves and surfaces; Lagrange modernized analytical geometry; Monge advanced descriptive geometry, and Laplace turned the theory of probability into an independent branch of mathematics. Next to this they contributed to the advancement of mechanics and astronomy. On the basis of Newton's *Principia*, Euler developed the mechanics of particles. D'Alembert, Jacob Bernoulli and Lagrange developed analytical mechanics. Final proof for the existence of God was not forgotten but supplemented by Pierre Maupertius's (1698-1758) 'Law of Least Action', and other important contributions to the understanding of impact and elasticity. The former was to provide the basis for Carnot's mechanics. Lazare Carnot (1753-1823) was the first scientist to assert, in contrast to Euler and D'Alembert, the experimental character of the principles of mechanics [Dugas & Costabel, 1958:425]. Clairaut, D'Alembert, Euler, Lagrange and Laplace must also be recognized for their studies of the solar system, and for their development of the experimental parts of physics. John and Daniel Bernoulli, Euler and D'Alembert advanced the investigation of motion of fluids (hydrodynamics); Clairaut hydrostatics. Again Euler, D'Alembert, Daniel Bernoulli, Monge and Lagrange contributed to the study of vibrations, and furnished by this the theoretical foundations for the study of sound, which like the study of heat was basically experimental.

Other mathematicians who studied vibrations were Louis Carre, Brook Taylor and Jean-Baptiste Fourier. E.F. Chladni (1756-1827) demonstrated the existence of longitudinal and transversal vibrations, and measured the velocity of sound in various solids and gases. Nallet showed that sound travelled in water. The physician and chemist Joseph Black (1728-1799) developed thermo-dynamics by introducing the concept of fluid heat (the caloric) and latent heat, and distinguished between heat and temperature. Benjamin Rumford (1753-1814), an army organizer, social reformer and scientist, innovated methods of heating, lighting and cooking, and showed that heat is a form of energy and subject to the general law of the conservation of energy. In 1728 Daniel Bernoulli concluded that the pressure exerted by a gas on the walls of a container is the result of the collisions between the atoms of the gas and the walls of the container. This idea was only taken up and developed in the nineteenth century, when it became the basis for the kinetic theory of gases.

In the new branches of study, electricity and magnetism, the best known contributors were Franklin, Gray, Du Fay and Coulomb. Benjamin Franklin (1706-1790) introduced the 'one fluid' theory and the law of the conservation of charge, and in contrast to other contemporary scientists, he employed a positivist approach. Stephen Gray (1666-1736) and Charles F. Du Fay (1698-1739), both experimental scientists, discovered conductivity and induced charge; and Du Fay also discovered that there are two types of charges. Charles Augustin Coulomb (1736-1806) developed theories of magnetism (1777) and electricity (1785).

In chemistry the most important innovation was in the work of Antoine Laurent Lavoisier (1743-1794) who dismissed the idea of phlogiston. But he may no longer be regarded as a developer of earlier ideas. He is in fact the initiator of a new era in chemistry and his work needs more properly to be placed in the context of the innovations of the nineteenth century.

It is significant that in this period of scientific consolidation man's interest took a new direction. It moved away from the old matters of doctrine, from questions concerned with 'the purpose of life', and shifted toward the 'art of getting a living' [Ashton, 1955:1]; it moved away from questions relating to the nature of the state and focused on the means of increasing its opulence; it moved away from 'what was ultimately to be wished', and in the direction of 'what was immediately expedient'. The concatenation of the new direction in science, and the quest for opulence which stimulated technology, opened man's eyes to the contribution science can make to technological advancement. At the same time the advancement of technology was also supplying scientists with new and better instruments to work with. Thus, while science became subservient to the technological demands of an increasingly materialistic society, the technological achievements themselves were providing new stimuli which led to greater scientific insight. To be sure, science had not yet become a major force in the development of industry, but it was beginning to play an increasingly important role in the transformation of manufacture into industry. Many branches of technology were still unaffected by the new scientific ideas, but several of the most important ones did come under their influence. This was particularly true of the chemical industry, and through it textile manufacturing, which were increasingly permeated by innovations based upon the new theoretical ideas. This became obvious near the end of the eighteenth century when Black's idea of latent heat laid the foundation for the development of steam-powered engines. However, on the whole, the change in the foundation of technology progressed only very gradually.

From the middle of the seventeenth century more and more of the people normally concerned with economic activities were taking an active interest in science. For England a glance at the membership lists of the Royal Society in the early years of its existence, and at the *Histories of Nature, Arts or Works* sponsored by the Society, is sufficient to discover this tendency. On the Continent of Europe a similar trend can be seen from the contrast between the secrecy with which the alchemists surrounded their work and the liberality with which scientists like Descartes, Huygens and Leibniz broadcast their discoveries. Huygens (1629-1696) experimented with steam in cylinders in order to devise some mining equipment. Savery experimented with vacuum and together with the craftsman Newcomen produced an early steam-powered water pump (1712); and the combined effort of the scientist Joseph Black (1728-1799), the technician James Watt

(1736-1819), and the businessman Matthew Boulton (1728-1809), produced the famous steam engine. Black discovered a way to measure quantitatively heat-energy, and subsequently latent heat. Watt learned from him to apply scientific principles to the practical problems he was engaged with, and Boulton recognized the commercial chances this combination of scientific effort and technological ingenuity offered. In fact *businessmen* like Boulton, *craftsmen* like Watt and *scientists* like Black and Erasmus Darwin (1731-1802), Samuel Galton, James Keir, Joseph Priestly (1733-1804) and others were by this time mixing freely in the 'Lunar Society' [Singer et al. 1956:677-9].

The period in which science had been the sole province of an inquisitive elite trying to satisfy its curiosity about the nature of the world was nearing its end. The practical bourgeoisie was beginning to put science into service to meet its material purposes. The understanding of the laws governing the universe began to be harnessed to the pursuit of the material ends of an increasingly acquisitive society. Questions like 'does it work?' or 'is the theorem useful?' began to replace the question 'is it true?' Henry Cavendish (1731-1810) became better known in his time for his contributions to the development of new processes in bleaching, in ceramic, coal-tar, iron making and distillation, than for his research on inflammable air (hydrogen); and Antoine Laurent Lavoisier (1743-1794) for his contributions to the development of agriculture, gunpowder and balloons – than for his theoretical achievements [Singer et al. 1956:XXIII].

The idea that a benign God had created the world as an orderly pattern to serve some happy future purpose evoked in Locke and his followers an almost 'sentimental' trust in social harmony. The consolidation of the power of the bourgeoisie in the eighteenth century, and its establishment in the newly acquired position in the social hierarchy was accompanied by a fresh conception of harmony. The universe continued to be in motion, but it was a new kind of motion. It was motion produced by gravitational pulls between masses which attracted one another but were harmoniously held together in their particular places or orbits because they were postulated each in its right position in relation to the others. The simplicity of Newton's Law of inverse squares convinced all who wanted to be convinced that order was the very essence of the universe. In England it provided evidence of God's will; in France some thinkers were able to conceive of the orderly system even without a God to will it, namely by man ordering and classifying things which are or behave alike. However, even where no God remained to provide the absolute or eternal element in man's conception of reality this element was not entirely extinguished. It remained in Newton's assumption of absolute time and space. So, in spite of the rising utilitarianism in the eighteenth century, and the increasing tendency to substitute a utilitarian conception of morality for the search for rational standards of inherent good (implicit in the idea of natural law), the belief in an 'eternal' value system was not lost.

There is a striking similarity between Hobbes's universal egoism and Newton's gravitation. Both explain events or changes, and both provide a simple spring of action like a mechanism or clockwork to account for them. Earlier generations *described* events and when they found them to be regular, as they did with the movements of the planets, they predicted their recurrence with ingenious precision. They did not attempt to *explain* them. The question *why* never entered their minds. They knew why. It was the will of God. Not so Hobbes and Newton and others who were to follow. For them to find *explanations* was the quintessence of scientific endeavours. Hobbes's spring of action was *egoism* – each individual's striving to assure his self-preservation by attracting wealth and power to himself [Hobbes, 1651]. Newton's mechanism was *gravitation* – the mutual attraction of all bodies in the universe [Newton, 1687]. There is a wonderful symmetry here between Hobbes's and Newton's perception. Both see the universe made up of individuals, persons or particles, each of which is endowed with a kind of inherent force attracting all around it, while the system as a whole is held together by the mutual cancellation of the multitude of contrary attractions. The only difference is that Newton's mechanism dealt with inanimate matter, and Hobbes's with man in a society which still regarded egoism with disapprobation. It was therefore not unnatural for those seeking wealth and power to search for a way to reconcile their deeds with the old values and to free themselves of their society's opprobrium. The alternative they came up with was *altruism*. As the mainspring of their actions this was logically less defensible than *egoism* but more respectable. It gave to the pursuit of wealth something of the image of the benevolent creator. Consequently, as the eighteenth century turned into the nineteenth, social theory became less logical but more and more in line with the conception which suited the views and self-image of the bourgeoisie.

It may be said that the seventeenth century produced a calculus of measurement which made possible the formulation of mathematically intelligible natural laws which were believed to be of universal applicability. Nature became rational, and experimentally verified certainty took the place of arbitrariness. Reason challenged the power of faith but did not abolish it. Faith, together with the belief in the unchanging character of nature's laws, continued to provide society with a stabilizing element. Only in the eighteenth century, when men like Hume, Voltaire, Diderot and Hollbach separated ethics from religion, were the old conceptions about what constitutes proper social conduct really shaken. But even then they were shaken, not annihilated. The *grounds* for the justification of man's desired behaviour changed, not the justifications. Almost everything that had been right or wrong before continued to be so, only it was no longer right or wrong because God so willed it, but because *man* conceived it to be so. The bourgeoisie won the freedoms it required, but it did not gain the power to replace the old value system by one of its own making. 'Right gave way before claims of expediency', but expediency had not yet become the source of right [Laski, 1934:I,xii].

With Locke (1632-1704) the knowledge of good and evil was still founded in 'innate' ideas; with Shaftesbury (1671-1713) it was founded in 'instinct'. Locke rationalized his 'innate' ideas – good is what causes pleasure and evil what causes displeasure or pain – but the rewards and retributions were directly related to the *laws* in which the 'innate' ideas were formalized, namely divine and civil laws and social conventions. Shaftesbury's conception was less formalistic. For him the knowledge of good and evil remained beyond divine instruction and human experience. It was intuitive, 'natural, agreeing with nature, instinctive' [Shaftesbury, 1709:III,2]. Birds do not need a catechism to learn to fly or build their nests; they do so by instinct. Man does not need instruction to distinguish right from wrong; the distinction comes to him by instinct. Unlike Locke, whose conception of morality was legalistic, Shaftesbury can do without the scriptures and the social contract. People just *know* what is right or wrong. By studying himself (his motives) man comes to know whether his actions are morally desirable or not, and if there is a need for evidence it is found in the approbation or disapprobation of society. The thought that what people take to be their intuitions may be no more than what they were brought up to believe or disbelieve in simply escaped him. Here then was the compromise between the old foundations of morality (which being transmitted from one generation to the next by moralizing attitudes an verbal contamination continued to form the intuitions in most societies) and the foundations of the new morality, which allowed the bourgeoisie to adjust the mores to its changing needs.

The author who best reflects the new mood of the late eighteenth century, and who gave formal expression to its ethics, was Immanuel Kant (1724-1804). Kant was at one and the same time an innovator and a preserver of the old conceptions. As Friedrich Schiller (1759-1805) observed: 'there is always something about Kant... which reminds one of a monk, who has left his cloister behind him but cannot rid himself of its traces' (1795). From Rousseau Kant learned of the 'dignity of man' (which liberated him from his contemporaries' idealisation of the Enlightenment and from his own contempt for the uneducated masses); from Hume he learned the distinction between knowledge and feeling; and from Spinoza – that ideas can be independent of experience. But it was the distinction between *is* and *ought*, and his recognition that the *ought* can never be derived from the *is*, which best reflected the new mood of his time. It was the new mood of a bourgeoisie which, having won its first 'revolution', was

settling down intent upon maintaining its position. It was the mood
of people who, having attained their objective, had no more wish
for further changes; the mood of people with no more *ought* to be
desired, and no more *is* that ought to be different.

Kant was neither a pure empiricist nor a pure rationalist. Like
Helvetius and Hume he believed that knowledge begins with
experience, but like Newton he thought that not *all* knowledge
arises from experience. Reason must approach nature in order to
be taught by it. However, it must not approach it as 'a pupil who
listens to everything the teacher chooses to say but as an
appointed judge who compels the witness to answer questions
which he himself has formulated' [Kant, 1781:183]. Experience
must be complemented by an ordering of perceptions to give rise
to concepts because only by them does experience become
knowledge – 'concepts without perceptions are empty; perceptions
without concepts are blind'.

Like the mathematicians, whose influence on contemporary
thought was enormous, Kant too adopted axiom-like intuitively
given *a prioris*, but by applying *a priori* percepts of space and time
things can be understood. In other words to be *a priori* means that
these percepts are the precondition for having any sense-
experience. They are the contributions of the mind - that is of
intuition – to knowledge. By studying these *a priori* percepts, one
gains understanding of human knowledge. Similarly, by studying
morality man is unable to penetrate the things-in-themselves, the
*noumena*, but their spatial and temporal manifestations can be
understood and are the proper object of empirical study.

Morality is 'given'; one cannot know its foundations but one can
study the character of its concepts and percepts. God may be the
benevolent creator of the world, but it is also conceivable that He
is not. Either way there is no proof and, even more disturbing,
logically both propositions can be proven possible. With regard to
man one is on firmer ground. Man can be shown to have an
inclination to socialize and at the same time to be egoistic. The
conflict between these two tendencies is nature's way of promoting
human progress – of furthering man's natural capacities. Here
Kant's view comes close to contemporary English thought but the

similarity is only superficial. Hutcheson (1694-1746) believed in 'a divinely ordained harmony of egoistic and altruistic impulses in man... in which self-love always finds itself circumscribed by love for one's fellow men' [Hutcheson, 1728:193-4]; and Adam Smith (1723-1790) believed that 'man's study of his own advantage leads him to prefer that employment which is most advantageous to the society' [Smith, 1776:475]. Hutcheson and Smith obtained harmony by making social approval the object of man's egoistic impulses. 'The rich man glories in his riches, because he feels that they naturally draw upon him the attention of the world' [Smith, 1759:120-5]. 'It is the consideration of his own private profit which is the sole motive that determines the owner of any capital to employ it,' [Smith, 1776:475], but it is the study of his own advantage which leads him to the employment which is most beneficial to all, because through profits he will learn of the demands of society. 'The rich in spite of their natural selfishness and rapacity....are led by an *invisible hand* to make nearly the same distributions of the necessaries of life, which would have been made had the earth been divided into equal portions among all inhabitants' [Smith, 1759:465-6]. Moreover, the rich man 'by pursuing his own interest....frequently promotes that of the society more effectively than when he really intends to promote it' [Smith 1776:477-8].

With the English writers egoism assumes an almost moral quality; with Kant it does not! For Kant the 'good society' is one which allows men to develop their capacities, which provides the greatest individual freedom to compete. But he is wary of anarchy (the rule of the rabble) and oppression (aristocratic privileges). With him too the bourgeois state leaves little to be desired, but egoism remains the very antithesis of moral perfection. His ends of ethics remain closer to the mediaeval Christian tradition than to the justification of bourgeois expediency by his contemporary English authors. The explanation for this difference may well have been the disparity between the level of economic attainment, and of social adjustment to it, in England and the Continent. In England the bourgeois revolution reached its peak by the end of the first quarter of the nineteenth century; on the Continent this peak was only reached with the violent events of 1848.

Kant's ethical conception was dominated by a quest for self-perfection and the conscious advancement of the happiness of others. In his *Tugendlehre* (personal ethics) he lays chief stress on that attitude of character which corresponds to his general conception of the ethical. 'In his view, virtue consists in strength of soul *(fortitudo moralis)*, in the power and dignity which follows from the consciousness of possessing the law of our own action within ourselves and of being united by means of this law into one great whole' [Hoffding, 1900:II,91]. The ends of personal ethics are self-perfection and the happiness of others.

> Not our own happiness, – for we strive after this involuntarily and with such eagerness that we hold it to be other men's duty to consider it likewise. Nor the perfection of others, – for only they themselves can effect this; for perfection consists in nothing else but in making ourselves, according to our own conception of duty, our own end... [Hoffding, 1900:II,91].

Kant's conviction that *faith*, not knowledge, justifies belief in the freedom of the will, in immortality and in the existence of God, was therefore certainly closer to the mediaeval tradition of Christianity, than to his own generation's. Abandoning the Platonic and Christian search for the *inner nature* of things, he still remains assured of their existence. Although the ethical *noumena* themselves cannot be known, the ethics based upon them can be recognized. Man can act as if the maxim from which he acts becomes through his will a universal law of nature; he can treat humanity, whether in his own person or in that of another, as an end in itself – not as a means. Kant's *moral individual* is a criterion which is superior to and beyond the social order. What Kant failed to recognize was that to find such a moral standpoint, which is independent of the social order, is not only impossible but likely to render the one who adopts it a conforming servant of the social order [MacIntyre, 1967]. His basic premise does not really deviate much from the traditional. His notions of *right, good* and *the good will* are those which had been accepted before, but he gave them an 'inner' (psychological) content. 'Nothing can possibly be conceived in the world, or even out of it, which can be called good without qualification, except a *good will*' [Kant, 1785:1]. The old values had been external to man; like space and time they were *given*. With Kant they begin to lose their independent character. They begin to drift; they do not yet accommodate but become adaptable to the wishes of a changing society. Subjective intentions – good will – take the place of objective criteria – the firm dictum of Church and of tradition – and become the arbiters of ethics. The old value system was breaking away from its anchorage; it was not yet drifting, but it was no longer safely fastened in its mooring.

In summation the eighteenth century produced a compromise between a new-fangled individualism and the traditional sense of social obligation. It assumed the presence of general harmony and of a universal mechanism akin to *gravitation* which guides men willy-nilly to their proper places within the universal order. It avoids Hobbes's opprobrious egoistic mechanism as the mainspring of human action and substitutes for it the quest for happiness which can only be found within man himself and in common ends. Because there is 'a divinely ordained harmony of egoistic and altruistic impulses in man' [Smith, 1759:465], only the actions which lead to social harmony can also provide harmony in man's soul. 'The study of man's own advantage naturally, or rather necessarily, leads him to prefer that employment which is most advantageous to society' [Smith, 1776:475]. Man's actions are determined by society because to be content man requires the approval of his fellow men. The pursuit of wealth, avarice, is purged of sin because it is not the real object of man's material egoism but only the means to obtain public esteem. This *true* end puts a 'natural' limit on rapacity and transforms egoism into a mechanism beneficial to society. Riches draw upon man the attention of the world, and it is this which causes him the true happiness which he would forfeit if he allowed self-interest to overstep the socially acceptable limits and his actions become subversive of the general good. The traditional values remain intact; greed remains greed and vice remains vice, but the bourgeoisie receives a free pardon. Its particular type of greed is cleansed of sin, for it is not 'really' motivated by the evil love of gain. It is motivated by the quest for happiness which is legitimized in God's creation by the laws of nature which harmonize the private with the public good. If the poor seem less happy than the wealthy then they are deluded. Happiness is not synonymous with wealth: 'in what constitutes the real happiness of human life beggars may in no respect be inferior to those who would seem so much above them... for it consists in the esteem in which one is held by others and in health, freedom from debt and in a clear conscience' [Smith, 1759:107].

Like Newton's *gravitation*, Smith's *psychological apparatus* serves as the *mechanism* by which this universal harmony is maintained. Through profit the employer learns of the needs of society and through loss what is in surfeit supply. For producing what is in social demand the employer is rewarded by profit and for producing what society cannot use he is punished by loss. An *invisible hand*, akin to *gravitation*, maintains the world in harmony.

# 6.  Capital Accumulation and Investment

The greatest improvement in the productive powers of labour... seem to have been the effects of the division of labour... A workman not educated to this business... nor acquainted with the use of the machinery employed in it... could scarce, perhaps, with his utmost industry, make one pin in a day, and certainly could not make twenty. But in the way in which this business is now carried on... divided into a number of branches, of which the greater part are likewise peculiar trades... even poorly equipped 'manufactory' can with only ten persons make upwards of forty-eight thousand pins in a day [Smith, 1776:4].

With these words Adam Smith described the new mode of production which in scarcely two centuries was to provide mankind with amazing powers to increase productivity and transformed its entire social framework. The innovations were to make mankind the master of unprecedented powers to create wealth, but subjected it to ominous social consequences. The latter were to plague a great part of European society well into the twentieth century.

In the second half of the eighteenth century the new mode of production, ushered in by men like Arkwright (roller-spinning), Hargreave (spinning Jenny), Crompton (the mule), and Watt (steam power), caused an increasing number of people to lose control over their own means of providing their livelihood and to forego the measure of social and economic protection which customs and quasi-feudal affiliations had previously given them. The old society, in which personal nexus and common interests of people of diverse rank had offered the poor a degree of protection, was waning, while the new safeguards were slow in taking their place. In the fast growing towns traditional skills became obsolete because their masters were unable to compete with the new production technology.

There is a great deal of learned controversy among historians about the question whether the living conditions of the working classes affected by the new mode of production improved or deteriorated in the nineteenth century [Kraus, 1986; James, 1986; Dumke, 1986; Van der Veen, 1986; Lindert, 1986; Soderberg, 1986; Scholliers, 1986; Williamson, 1986; and Ransom & Sutch, 1986;]. With few exceptions, their arguments are missing an essential point, namely the *qualitative* effect of the social transformation. They ignore that the working people lost the feeling of security and social 'belonging' and that their lives became more wretched and dehumanized. Dickens (1812-1870) and Zola (1840-1902) saw and described this.

Desolation and fear of unemployment delayed workers' resistance to the new-fangled order, while the bourgeoisie was able to adjust its mercantilist attitudes to the new circumstances. The unifying element in the old hierarchical relations, which had been based on mutual obligations and duties, disappeared and a socially divisive paternalism transformed the early Christian notion of compassion into charity. In this way the old moral values were not abolished but received a new interpretation which made them applicable only where they served the public order.

There were of course objective causes for the dehumanization of labour. They were inherent in the separation of each production process into a great number of very simple operations for which little skill was required. This deprived the worker of the satisfaction that comes from seeing the fruit of his labour and turned him into something like a part of a machine. His actions became mechanical, repetitive, like the machine's, and the machine even determined his work rhythm. As Adam Smith observed,

> the man whose whole life is spent in performing a few simple operations
> ... has no occasion to exert his understanding ... He naturally loses the
> habit of such exertion, and generally becomes as stupid and ignorant as
> it is possible for a human creature to become. The torpor of his mind
> renders him, not only incapable of relishing or learning a part in any

rational conversation, but of conceiving any generous, noble or tender sentiment... [Smith, 1776:V,I].

Smith did not want this to happen. To avoid it he was prepared to abandon nature's self-regulating mechanisms in this context and to offer state-sponsored education. But what for Smith (1723-1790) was only a frightening specter became perceived reality with Malthus (1766-1834).

On the one hand the separation of tasks solved the adaptation problem. The peasants who could no longer find a living on the land, or were attracted by imaginary prospects to the towns, could almost immediately perform the work required in the new industries. On the other hand employers could easily replace 'difficult' labourers by more docile workers, a practice which was to have far-reaching consequences for class relations also in the future. In this way the luxurious life-style of the bourgeoisie taught those who were able to amass wealth the new role and power of money, and the desolation and fear which characterized the life-style of the industrial working class taught it industrial discipline. Fear of unemployment superseded pride in craftsmanship; anxiety of falling foul of one's employer replaced the traditional obligation of obedience. Employers had little cause to respect the needs of their employees, but wage workers could only disrespect the wishes of their employers in peril of their jobs and livelihood. The focus of attention shifted form the labouring *person* to the product of his labour.

As long as the productivity of labour had been low, when the labour of ten men together could perhaps provide a sufficient surplus to feed an extra person who was not himself engaged in production (such as a master, king, warrior or priest), and as long as the security and prestige of the socially superior person depended on the number of inferiors he controlled, most social and economic efforts centred around *people*. But when workers equipped with the new technology were able to produce a volume of output much greater than had been possible before, and the question of handing it over to their employers could not even arise, *people* ceased to matter and became 'labour power'. When the life and property of the rich became better protected by the state than by private armies of retainers, and the symbols of social standing could be bought for money, *people* lost their place to money as the focus of attention. Similarly, when acquisition became the object of endeavours the 'fair price' lost ground to *competition*. A society obliged to protect itself against the almost monopolistic position of Guilds and craftsmen needed a 'fair price,' but in a society in which producers were vying with each other for the sale of their goods, and profit was obtained from cost reductions by the use of new technologies, the 'fair price' lost its relevance.

Competition engendered low prices, but not all strata of society shared equally in this advantage. As the supply of labour is less elastic than the demand for goods, workers were more vulnerable than employers to market fluctuations. With little cost employers could vary the volume of their output to suit variations in demand. Workers could hardly do the same with the supply of labour. Though not always at a steady rate there was a continual accretion of people seeking employment. *Real wages* – that is wages after price variations are allowed for – did not always rise in line with productivity. Employers supplemented domestic demand by selling their produce in foreign markets, but labour had no such 'safety valve'. Consequently the distribution of the affluence the new technology provided was not equitably shared. The wealth of some entrepreneurs increased and capital accumulated, while the majority of people remained almost as poor as they had always been. The positive result of this development was that it provided the resources for investment – the *ability* to accelerate economic growth. The negative effect was the misery with which the urban working class paid for it. The fact that the incipient industry was still small enough not to depend on domestic markets, and that a good part of its produce could be sold abroad, helped to maintain the necessary incentives for investment – the *wish* to invest. It was this combination of the growing *ability* and *wish* to invest with the restricted consumption of the frightened wage workers which lay at the roots of the 'first industrial revolution'.

On the whole desolation and fear of starvation dominated the life of the steadily growing industrial working class; the spirit of acquisition, competition and rationality characterized the bourgeoisie. For centuries people had bartered commodities to satisfy the needs they could not satisfy by themselves. When money entered the transactions it was a convenient medium of exchange and occasionally a store of wealth. Some people produced victuals, others manufactured other goods; the former sold victuals to buy the other goods and the latter sold their goods to buy food. Profit was not unknown but the object of production was consumption. The new spirit of acquisition transformed money from a medium of exchange into a self-expanding value. Money became capital, and owners of capital no longer sold and bought to satisfy their normal needs but to increase their stocks of wealth. Profit became the purpose of production and the satisfaction of real wants the coincidental concomitant.

There were of course even in this period workers whose skills gave them a separate position. They organized themselves in semi-religious 'mysteries' and trade associations to protect their common interests. But the majority of workers were neither able nor dared to offer *organized* resistance to their lot. Organization was not only hindered by the hostile climate of the period in which the principle of freedom in its guise of competition was becoming the new idol of the social elite, but by the positive legislation which interpreted all attempts by workers to organize as 'ring forming', that is monopolies to the detriment of the general public. Moreover, workers were more inclined to approach the 'captains of industry' individually 'cap in hand' than to make common cause with fellow workers. They had not yet liberated themselves from the ancient habit of looking for protection and guidance from those hierarchically above them.

In the twenty-two years which separated the publication of Smith's *Wealth of Nations* from Malthus's *Essay on the Principle of Population* social relations in England underwent a profound transformation. For Malthus's generation of entrepreneurs man had become a tool to serve the needs of the economy. Misery and poverty had nothing to do with the social and economic system. For Malthus 'the most permanent cause of poverty has little or no direct relation to forms of government or the unequal division of property' because it springs from the excess of the supply of labour over its demand, that is from the poor's sexual immoderation. Consequently, 'as the rich do not in reality possess the power of finding employment and maintenance for the poor, the poor cannot, in the nature of things, possess the right to demand them' [Malthus, 1789:260]. If the lower classes could be made to realize that by making scarce 'the commodity' which they produce (children) all would be well. Malthus neatly exonerated the bourgeoisie from all compunction concerning the underprivileged and placed the responsibility for their ill plight at the poor's own doorsteps. He gave a new twist to the traditional asceticism, to the association of sex with sin, by turning it into a self-adjusting mechanism (akin to Adam Smith's 'invisible hand') by which the virtuous are rewarded and the sinful damned. For him

> the virtue of chastity is not... a forced produce of artificial society; but it has the most real and solid foundation in nature and reason; being apparently the only virtuous means of avoiding the vice and misery which result so often from the principle of population... therefore, it is in the power of each individual to avoid all the evil consequences to himself and society... by the practice of a virtue clearly directed to him by the light of nature, and expressly enjoined in revealed religion;... (because) it is the apparent object of the Creator to deter us from vice by the pains which accompany it, and to lead us to virtue by the happiness that it produces [Malthus, 1789:160-2].

Contraception was not the answer, because 'natural and moral evil seem to be the instruments employed by the Deity in admonishing us to avoid any mode of conduct which is not suited to our being' [Malthus, 1789, 83-99].

Malthus combines the traditional teachings of the Church with those of the Church of England; the ancient theology of predestination with the new protestant ethics of salvation through parsimony and work; the will of God with the law of nature; God's design with man's freedom of choice. His God is revealed on earth through 'vice and misery' but remains the old merciful God in spite of this because 'vice and misery' cease to be punishments (God's retribution for man's original sin) and become God's instrument for mankind's salvation.

> Were it not for the strong and universal effort of population to increase with greater rapidity than its supplies... I do not see what motive there would be sufficiently strong to overcome the acknowledged indolence of man, and make him proceed in the cultivation of the soil... [Malthus, 1789:446-7].

Malthus is a utilitarian moralist who believes in the improving powers of God's arrangements upon earth and in a mixture of feudal and absolutist attitudes to labour. He attacks Pitt's Poor Law of 1796, and various other charitable attempts to mitigate the distress that accompanied the transition from feudalism and mercantilism to industrial society, and pours scorn on the solutions put forward by utopians like Condorcet and Godwin.

> A writer may tell me that he thinks man will ultimately become an ostrich. I cannot properly contradict him. But before he can expect to bring any reasonable person over to his opinion, he ought to show, that the necks of mankind have been gradually elongating; that the lips have grown harder and more prominent; that the legs and feet are daily altering their shape; and that the hair is beginning to change into stubs of feathers. And till the probability of so wonderful a conversion be shewn, it is surely lost time and lost eloquence to expatiate on the happiness of man in such a state... [Malthus, 1789:10-11].

What aroused Malthus's anger was Godwin's contention that but for the irrational *institutional* restraints which society itself imposes there would be neither misery nor vice. For Malthus not the institutions, but man's 'acknowledged indolence' and weakness of character were at fault. Only each individual's pursuit of his own advantage, within the institutional framework of property, marriage, and class distinctions, can lead to greater happiness.

For Edmund Burke (1729-1797)

> some decent, regulated preeminence, some preference (not exclusive appropriation) given to birth, is neither unnatural, nor unjust, nor impolitic. It is said that twenty-four millions ought to prevail over two hundred thousand. True; if the constitution of a kingdom be a problem of arithmetic... To men who may reason calmly it is ridiculous... A

government of five hundred country attorneys and obscure curates is not good for twenty-four millions of men, though it were chosen by eight-and-forty millions... [Burke, 1790:III,296-9].

To the French Chancellor's statement that all occupations are honourable, Burke retorts that 'if he meant only that no honest employment was disgraceful, he would not have gone beyond the truth.' But asserting that 'the occupation of a hair-dresser, or of a working tallow-chandler... to say nothing of a number of other more servile employments,' are honourable went too far. 'Such description of men ought not to suffer oppression from the state; but the state suffers oppression, if such as they, either individually or collectively, are permitted to rule... Everything ought to be open, – but not indifferently to every man...' [Burke, 1790:III,296-7]. In 1790 the abrogation of legal and political privileges in France were Burke's cause of dismay, by 1793 'contempt of property' became his main concern. He feared that the events in France might serve as an example 'which could not be shut out by territorial limits' and would be emulated everywhere [Burke, 1793:IV,138].

Adam Smith (1723-1790), like John Locke (1632-1704) before him, recognized that work creates value, that the worth of a commodity is directly related to the amount of human labour bestowed upon it in its process of production. Ricardo took this observation a step further. In a letter to McCulloch he argued that the value of all goods depended upon the relative quantity of labour necessary for their production and upon the rate of profit earned for the capital which is locked up without bringing in revenue until the goods can be sold [Ricardo, 1896:12]. It is not the greater or less compensation paid for labour which affects the value of goods but the quantity of labour. The quantity of labour that includes not only 'the labour applied immediately to the commodities... but (also) the labour ... which is bestowed on the implements, tools and buildings, with which such labour is assisted' [Ricardo 1817:55-90]. But he also argued that

labour like all other things which are purchased and sold, and which may be increased or diminished in quantity, has its natural and its market price. The natural price of labour is that price which is necessary to enable labourers, one with another, to subsist and to perpetuate their race, without either increase or diminution.... The market price of labour is the price which is really paid for it.... labour is dear when it is scarce and cheap when it is plentiful... When the market price of labour exceeds its natural price... (the labourer) has it in his power to command a greater proportion of the necessaries and enjoyments of life, and therefore to rear a healthy and numerous family. When, however, by the encouragement which high wages give to the increase of population, the number of labourers is increased, wages fall to their natural price, and indeed from a reaction sometimes fall below it. When the market price of labour is below its natural price, the condition of the labourer is most wretched: The poverty deprives them of those comforts which custom renders absolute necessaries. It is only after their privations have reduced their number, or the demand for labour has increased, that the market price of labour will rise to its natural price.... [Ricardo, 1817:V,52-53].

This is a sober statement. People are a factor of production; poverty and deprivation are stripped of their human properties, labour is dehumanized; it is a commodity. Its reward depends on the laws of supply and demand, not upon the value it produces.

The constant progressive element in science and society is the widening of the likenesses man selects among the facts. Man's observations and experiences are many, perhaps infinite. By dividing them into those he believes matters and those which do not, and into what is alike or fitting into a pattern and what is not, he passes judgment on his observations and experiences, and this judgment forms the basis of his beliefs. Newton saw the likeness between the 'fall of the apple and the swirling of the moon in her orbit round the earth'; Einstein saw the unity of space and time, and the identity of energy and mass ($E = Mc^2$). Each of them saw unities, which no one had recognized before them, and produced completely new conceptions of the universe. Rousseau saw the likeness in all men and arrived at a new conception of mankind. However, unlike Newton's and Einstein's, his conception, like Galileo's, was threatening too many of the establishment's vital vested interests in his time to be readily accepted. The point is that when we discover the wider likeness, whether between space and time, bacillus and crystal, we enlarge the order in the universe; but more than this, we enlarge its unity. And it is this conception of the unity of nature living and dead for which our thought reaches that determines progress. It is this unity that presents a far deeper conception than any assumption that nature must be uniform. [Bronowski, 1951:134].

It is the shift in the judgment of things regarded alike or unlike that determines man's values in both the natural and the social sciences. When physicists discover such a new likeness their science shifts, events previously disregarded assume a new significance and the importance of events hitherto regarded significant is reassessed and value judgments are altered. When society discovers a new likeness a similar process of re-evaluation of old value judgments takes place. The ancient Greeks did not regard slaves as persons; mediaeval society did not liken itself to heathens; and (though they occasionally paid lip-service to the idea of the brotherhood of man) the bourgeoisie did not regard those unable or unwilling to adopt its life-style as people like themselves; nineteenth century Europeans never regarded Asians or Africans as equals; but Rousseau did. Where others saw the dissimilarity in colour, manners and beliefs, he noted the unity, the uniformity of human nature, and herein lies his contribution to social progress.

If Malthus reflects the link between the ancient conception of man and society with the new perception of the victorious bourgeoisie, Rousseau reflects the link of the new perception with things to come. Rousseau (1712-1778) regarded man 'the same in all ranks' and all people members of society. More than this, he believed that 'the ranks which are most numerous deserve most respect' [Rousseau, 1886:II,226]. He considered society the source and owner of all property. 'The right to property' was not an individual's right to protect what he regards his own *against* society, but a right *within* society. With him

the right which each individual has to his own estate is always subordinate to the right which the community has over all... The first man, who, having enclosed a piece of land, (and) bethought himself of saying *'this is mine'*, and (who) found people simple enough to believe him was for him the real founder of civil government and all the subsequent evil it produced. [Rousseau, 1762:182].

Man, the calculating egoist as most of his contemporaries saw him, was for Rousseau but man perverted by bad government. *True* man was sensitive and had an innate revulsion, which cannot be explained by calculating reason, against the suffering of others. The genuine sources of man's attitudes are *feelings*. Only bad government taught man to suppress his true self by allowing *reason* to govern both his thoughts and deeds. It was this perversion which permitted the poverty of some to serve the luxury of others, and is the fount of the laws and customs which give to this *unnatural* state of affairs a semblance of legitimacy and self-evidence. Rousseau did not deny the existence of egoism; *natural man* was not oblivious to self-love, but his self-love was but one among several equally weighty motivations. 'Even animals assist one another, why should man be inferior to them in sympathy and compassion?' Man uncorrupted by society has few desires and therefore little motivation to own property. Food, sleep and love are his true needs and they can all be satisfied without the subjugation of others. Only the 'artificial wants', the wants created by society, give rise to civil government and all the evils that attend it. But even bad government cannot destroy man's true self entirely. It cannot deprive him of his conscience, because his conscience is innate. Man always 'knows' the difference between right and wrong though, of course, he may not act in conformity with this knowledge. Like Locke Rousseau did not think that this inherent knowledge may also be a social product. It may not have crossed his mind that it was no more than what has been passed down from one generation to the next and became 'self-evident' by force of habit. In a sense Rousseau did little more than 'broaden the channel dug by Locke; but the latter was justifying a revolution that had happened, and Rousseau a revolution that had still to come' [Laski, 1934:xi].

There was a wide spectrum of social conceptions between those of Malthus and Burke at the one end, and Rousseau on the other, and it reflects the moral confusion of this period in which the bourgeoisie attained its coveted economic hegemony and was not yet seriously threatened by the working class. Ricardo, who was very abstract in his thought, but also a keener observer of reality than many of his contemporary writers, may serve as an example. He had a glimpse of the role of capital accumulation in providing employment, and of the changes that were beginning to take place in the material conditions of the working class. He shared with Malthus the belief that in the long run humanity was to suffer the consequences of diminishing returns from land, but unlike Malthus he did not believe that in the foreseeable future the 'subsistence wage' is constant. In his opinion a kind of *ratchet effect* relates subsistence incomes to changes in the volume of the social product.

> It is not to be understood that the natural price of labour, estimated even in food and necessaries, is absolutely fixed and constant. It varies at different times in the same country, and very materially differs in different countries. It essentially depends on the habits and customs of the people... An English labourer would consider his wages under their natural rate, and too scanty to support a family, if they enabled him to purchase no other food than potatoes, and to live in no better habitation than a mud cabin: Yet these moderate demands of nature are often deemed sufficient in countries where man's life is cheap... Many of the conveniences now enjoyed in an English cottage would have been thought luxuries at an earlier period of our history... [Ricardo, 1817:54-5].

Further,

> if the improved means of production, in consequence of the use of machinery, should increase the net produce... the landlord and the capitalist will benefit, not by an increase of rent and profit, but by the advantages resulting from the expenditure of the same rent and profit on commodities very considerably reduced in value, while the situation of the labouring classes will also be considerably improved; first, from the increased demand for menial servants; secondly from the stimulus to saving from revenue which such an abundant net produce will afford; and thirdly, from the low price of all articles of consumption on which their wages will be expanded [Ricardo, 1817:268].

These hopeful possibilities can, however, only materialize if both the 'net' and the 'gross' income of society increase simultaneously (if what modern economists would call investment in the consumer goods sector and in the producer goods sector would increase harmoniously) because 'the one fund from which landlords and capitalists derive their revenue, may increase while the other, that upon which the labouring class mainly depend, may diminish.' If this is not the case, then 'the same cause which may increase the net revenue of the country may at the same time render the population redundant, and deteriorate the condition of the labourer' [Ricardo, 1817:263-4]. Ricardo has insight; he sees things but is prevented by his paradigm from drawing what in retrospect seem obvious conclusions. Neither *labour value* suggests to him that profit is an immoral appropriation, nor does the *wages fund* destroy his belief in universal harmony.

In summary, in spite of the common postulate of all classical economists that liberty and property are the keystones of every rational economic order, and that political economy resembles a natural science in the universal applicability of its laws, important differences remained between them in approach and in their perceptions of society. Malthus continued in the mediaeval Christian tradition to seek man's destiny in moral improvement. Ricardo belonged to the new era. His work reflects the increased confidence of the propertied class which, at first only hesitantly but in the late eighteenth century with growing self-assurance, adjusted the perception of society to its economic and social position. Galileo and Descartes had shaken the immobile mediaeval perception of the universe; and the idea that there was a mechanical moving force in the universe was carried by Hobbes to the realm of social behaviour by making man the servant of his passions, while Jeremy Bentham (1748-1832) placed mankind 'under the governance of two sovereign masters, pain and pleasure.' All that mankind does, says, and thinks, is ruled by them [Bentham, 1789:IV,17]. The overriding moral principle is that one ought to aim at the greatest happiness of the greatest number. But the ontological status of this principle was doubtful. Bentham himself admitted that the principle cannot be proved, because 'it is used to prove everything else,' and 'a chain of proofs must have their commencement somewhere.' In other words, it is self-evident. Self-evidence, however, may be an appeal to one's prejudices; and therefore all he could have said is that 'a careful analysis of man's moral judgments would show that the greatest happiness principle always did underlie them, so far as they were consistent; the principle itself could then be accepted just as an aim that men did have, as a matter of fact' [Monroe, 1967:I,284]. Utilitarianism turned passions into wants and transformed acquiescence with fate into the spirit of restless activity. The explanation of observed phenomena became functional rationality – the application of reason to the choice of means for the satisfaction of wants. The recognition of realistic possibilities for material advancement stimulated the separation of ceremonial from functional elements in the pursuit of wealth and status, and permeated society with a new type of irreligious ethics. But by making the 'greatest happiness of the greatest number' the ontological premise of his utilitarianism Bentham best expressed the individualistic and hedonistic conception of the bourgeoisie, its ideal of thrift, promptness, industry, honesty-as-the-best-policy, economic expediency and the pursuit of profit. Although he himself remained in fact within an essentially traditionalist framework.

Moreover, realistic possibilities for material improvement in the eighteenth century were confined to a relatively small minority and so were the new conceptions of morality; but this minority was growing and setting the pace of social and economic change. The great majority of people, whose chances for advancement remained as remote as they had always been, had little truck with the new ideas and continued to hold on to the traditional beliefs and moral value judgments. They had no cause to put the new-fangled scepticism in the place of the consolation they could find in trust in a compassionate God. This dichotomy served entrepreneurs well. On the one hand it gave legitimization to their pursuit of wealth, and helped their efforts to fix wages and free profits. On the other it affected workers' aspirations, life-style and social standing in a manner which kept them docile in spite of the employers' increasing opulence. This combination of an active and utilitarian bourgeoisie with a compliant and submissive working class facilitated the required accumulation of capital for investment in the technologically advancing mode of production.

# 7. Birthpains of Competitive Society

From the middle of the eighteenth century onward industrialization was accelerating. The bourgeoisie was gaining power and status and a new type of people was becoming prominent. A century later it had established its revolutionary conception. But having attained its coveted social and economic position the new class was entering upon its first period of consolidation. The laws of motion became laws of dynamic stability; the study of growth became the study of equilibrium. Having obtained power the bourgeoisie had little to gain from permitting the revolution to go further.

> The static hereditary society could hardly be reconstituted, but in its place a system of dynamic stability was erected. Change and mobility were still accepted as characteristic of society but as the running-in-place rather than an overturn of the existing order... Liberal democracy... had a vested interest in maintaining the world social order but allowed individuals, on the basis of relative competitive ability, to find their own place in the social structure [Lewontin, 1968:208].

In the parts of Europe in which the middle class was gaining strength, its rise was accompanied by the growth of an urban working class. Population was increasing but the number of people engaged in farming remained almost constant, and even diminished in some regions, while the share of the population engaged in manufacturing perceptibly increased [Mitchell, 1975]. The new mode of industrial production was leading to a concentration of labour, and the concentration of labour led to a new type of relationship between employers and workers and between the

workers themselves. Very slowly workers became alienated from
employers; and their concentration in large enterprises created
new networks of communication between workers with similar
interests and grievances. What had remained of the *vertical* quasi-
feudal social links was gradually giving way to *horizontal* social
class alignments.

The dynamic force behind the rising economic power of the
bourgeoisie was competition. Entrepreneurs' constant need to
sustain or increase their market share to avoid being driven out of
business by more efficient competitors imposed upon them an
incessant search for technological innovations and improvements.
This was the progressive element which provided the constant
drive to produce better and cheaper. As Marx and Engels said in
1848, 'During its rule of scarcely one hundred years the
bourgeoisie created more massive and more colossal productive
forces than have all the preceding generations together' [Marx &
Engels, 1848:5]. The negative element, at least from the workers'
point of view, was that the new economic order prevented falling
production costs from being passed on in full to the consumers.
Competition imposed innovation and innovation required capital;
but capital could only be obtained by docking real wages to match
the falling prices, or delaying the transmission of lower costs to the
public in price reductions until it could no longer be avoided
because the competitors' technology 'caught up.' In this way the
bourgeoisie was trapped in an antagonistic conflict with the
working class. Advancing technology required more capital and
greater concentration of labour, and the concentration of labour
increased workers' ability to demand higher rewards. For several
decades it was the rapid accretion of people in the urban centres
which deferred widespread violent confrontation, but the seeds of
conflict were sprouting. Against this impending confrontation the
bourgeoisie was beginning to fortify itself when in the nineteenth
century it abandoned the revolutionary conception, which had
served it well in the struggle to wrench power from the old
regime, and turned toward the new ideology of dynamic
equilibrium.

The ideological conversion which accompanied the social and economic changes was reflected in the works of the outstanding writers and scientists of this period. Neither Darwin nor Spencer nor Hegel 'invented' the principle of competition, but they provided it with an ideological justification which could pass as scientific, that is based on the law of nature and the mechanism of causes and effects. For Herbert Spencer (1820-1903) the ideal man was 'economic man'; the man who obtains his position in society by natural selection. In the second half of the nineteenth century, he transforms Charles Darwin's (1809-1882) principle of natural selection, into *the survival of the fittest*, which becomes the ideological basis of *laissez-faire*. Friedrich Hegel's (1770-1831) dialectics provides an explanation for the *mechanism* by which society is driven – how it works. For Darwin advancement was *accidental*, the survival of variations that happen to suit their environment and therefore were perpetuated [Joad, 1953:XIV,296]. Darwin suggested a name for a mechanism, namely natural selection, to explain organic evolution; for Spencer the mechanism was purposive adaptation. He supplemented it with a selective element which gave the bourgeoisie the protection it wanted against interlopers from the lower strata of society. Unlike Darwin he considered the inheritance of acquired characteristics the major causal factor in evolution, and put the seal of legitimacy on the bourgeoisie's new status. He suggested that 'the general law of organization is that the difference of function entails differentiation and division of the parts performing them.' He chased off the last remaining elements of the old deterministic morality claiming that 'the deepest truths that can be reached are simply statements of the widest uniformities in our experiences of the relations of matter, motion, and force' [Spencer, 1862]. He rejects the theory of *special creation*, with its catastrophic or revolutionary connotations, and espoused the idea of *organic evolution* defining evolution as the 'change from a state of relatively indefinite, incoherent, homogeneity to a state of relatively definite, coherent, heterogeneity.' In the *Principles of Sociology* (1876-96) he extends this idea from biology to human society and provides a definition of evolution which implies a change from 'anarchic' social mobility to ordered heterogeneity within each class. He says, in fact, that there is nothing to be gained from recognizing the advantages or disadvantages of different systems because each system is the inevitable product of the conditions that gave birth to it. And that the conditions which gave rise to it, and not people's willed intervention, are the system's true determinants.

And yet, even at this time the individualistic and hedonistic practices of the bourgeoisie did not drive out the old conceptions of morality entirely. The bourgeoisie's pursuit of profit, its ideal of thrift, promptness, industry, economic expediency and honesty-as-the-best-policy, was founded in a more complex ethical conception than utilitarianism. It remained the product of an intellectual climate with deep roots in an idealized Christian and feudal past. Education continued to rest in the hands of those who had traditionally been responsible for it, and who wished to install in the minds of the young religious dogmas and the old beliefs. The religious sects in the Protestant countries, who wished to keep their children loyal to their persuasion, played a particularly important role in combining the rudiments of secular learning with the dogmas they wished to impress on children's minds. The Catholics were soon also adopting similar practices. The secularization of schools began much later when the state began to take over the responsibility for education. The same is true of the universities. Even in England, the 'cradle of utilitarianism', classics and religion continued to hold prime place in universities. Utilitarianism developed almost entirely outside them.

Bentham's utilitarianism had developed in a period in which traditional non-utilitarian norms of behaviour were still exerting a potent influence. It emerged in an era of wide consensus about what is and what is not socially acceptable which was anchored in the firm rules of the inherited norms of conduct. This is the reason why a society dedicated to profit-making competitive enterprise, to the efforts of the isolated individual, to equality of rights and opportunities and freedom, continued to adhere to institutions and relationships which in effect totally denied all these. The bourgeois family, and the paternalistic relationships between employers and their employees, may serve as good examples. The bourgeois family went back to a much earlier age; but it developed a new kind of patriarchal authority, privacy, and solidarity in response to the hazards and opportunities of the competitive society.

Another factor which left its mark on early nineteenth century utilitarianism was the reaction that followed the great French Revolution. Together with the restoration of clericalism (which neither the expulsion of the Bourbons (1830) nor the ascent of the bourgeoisie and awakening of the working class (1848) eradicated) an idealized image of feudalism spread, which romanticized the old hierarchical relationships in a way that made them look like a real remedy for the contemporary social ills. On the Continent it stressed the paternalistic aspects of the feudal system and presented them as a relationship in which superior members of society were obligated to accord benevolent support and protection to inferior members. Rightly or wrongly many employers began to see themselves 'as good fathers and providers to their workers, who would never of their own accord bite the hand that fed them' [Landes, 1976:662-4]. By this the conservative reaction touched upon the most painful feature of the new social and economic order, namely desolation. It presented an idealized romantic picture of the past as a yardstick by which the 'captains of industry' ought to be measured. All this does not deny the cruel new reality of the situation of most of the working class in this era, nor does it dispute the exploitative character of the economic relationship between employers and labour, but it indicates the complexity of the period's utilitarianism, and of the restraining influences which gave it its specific character. The confrontation with an idealized past not only sustained part of the social hegemony in the hands of the aristocracy, but imposed upon the bourgeoisie modes of conduct that stopped its utilitarian rationalism short of reaching its self-destructive logical conclusion. Shocked by the excesses of the French Revolution the European intellectual elite fell prey to a nostalgia for a harmonious past that never was. It longed for a sense of social security and stability but without the curtailment of established privileges.

In Britain the conservative scepticism produced men like Thomas Carlyle (1795-1881) who presented an idealized image of the lord–serf relationship as a kind of antithesis to the new social reality [Carlyle 1843]. By censuring the rich and powerful for not assuming the obligations of an idealized *pater familias* or chivalric feudal lord, Carlyle reflected the kind of standard of behaviour against which the bourgeoisie was to be measured. It caused moral discomfort and thereby restrained its more rapacious inclinations, and directed the newly acquired status of the bourgeoisie toward the traditional conception of hierarchy which could legitimize the novel social inequality. It transformed the mediaeval conception of rank, founded upon birthrights, into one based on economic success. But for this it had to accept that privilege entails responsibility – *noblesse oblige* – and that if its wealth was to be recognized as a sign of distinction it had to adhere to certain modes of conduct inherited from the past.

If the bourgeoisie wanted to claim rank it could not permit itself to be seen flouting the obligations society associated with it, at least not overtly. Consequently a new code of conduct evolved which like mediaeval society did not recognize the money value of labour services, but accepted as natural the enrichment of some people by the appropriation of part of the fruits of the labour of others. In this way the bourgeoisie had no need to deny its exploitative character; it could simply ignore it. Even Ricardo, who did more than any other writer before him to demonstrate that value is the product of labour, did not draw from this the ultimate moral conclusion. He neither claimed that wealth grew out of paying workers less than the full value of their work, nor that it came from charging customers more than the 'true' worth of their purchases. Such a conclusion was simply too alien to be reached in a society still witnessing the death-throes of the feudal order. In fact most people even in the industrially more advanced countries were still unaffected by the new modes of production and by the social transformation associated with them. For most people the class relationship that displaced the mediaeval estates was just an aberration. The 'captains of industry' were judged by the same standards that had been applied to the traditional 'superiors'. The good army captain had always been expected to care for his troops, and the good lord for his tenants; now the good industrialist was expected to do the same for his workers. If he did not, he was unworthy of his rank and status. The true character of the newly evolving economic order simply escaped even most of its critics in the early nineteenth century. They censured the new social relationships from the point of view of an earlier society whose social arrangements and economic reality was either waning or no longer in existence. It was these critics, and the egalitarians and utopists (and not the critics who were to raise their voices in the later part of the nineteenth century) against whom the bourgeoisie had to defend itself. Against them classical economics invoked the law of nature and the whole body of Newtonian science to show that it was neither the inequitable distribution of property nor pure rapacity which were the causes of the new kind of misery. They did not take the utilitarian stand to claim that it was not the business of the rich to care for the poor, but simply insisted that 'the rich do not in reality possess the power of finding employment and maintenance for the poor' [Malthus, 1789:260]. They remained well within the traditional conception of social responsibility, and in the end it was this that provided the degree of stability without which early nineteenth century society might have fallen into the kind of insecurity and anarchy which marked the last days of the Roman Empire.

The salient point with regard to this period's conceptual paradigm is that it was not the conservatives alone who maintained the principle tenets of traditional ethics but also the utilitarians and radicals. Godwin, who believed in an altruistic human nature, and Bentham, who believed that man cannot be trusted to act for the 'general good' unless guided towards it, both clung to the principle of 'the greatest happiness of the greatest number.' For both the happiness of society meant the sum total of the happiness of its individual members. Both took it as the fundamental criterion for good; alone with Godwin the notion of good remained traditional, that is absolute and definitive, while with Bentham it was not. All men seek happiness and avoid pain, hence happiness is good and pain evil. With him good and evil are introspective and measurable, which makes morality a calculus of pleasure and pain – less unconditional than it had been and more mutable. Both Godwin and Bentham were progressive in the sense that they extended *humanity* beyond the limits of the mercantilist conception that had divided mankind into people who 'matter' and people who do not. But unlike Godwin, Bentham opened the door for future redefinitions of social values by expediency. By denying the presuppositions behind the rights and obligations of natural and positive law he rejected in principle (though perhaps not in practice) the very basis of the entire traditional value system. It was through this door that a new bourgeois conception of morality crept in and within half a century vacated Bentham's happiness-founded moral calculus of its progressive elements. By attaching weights to different kinds of pleasure the bourgeoisie quickly reinstated in its favour the old class separation by giving the pleasures of the rich more, and the pleasures of the poor less, weight in the sum of society's total fund of happiness. By the end of the century the process was complete, and happiness ceased to be a criterion of morality. For J. Bentham (1748-1832) 'pushpin' had still rated 'as good as poetry', for J.S. Mill (1806-1873) it did not; and for H. Spencer (1820-1903) 'to play billiards' was altogether 'the sign of an ill-spent youth'. The restraining notions had become socially less relevant than they had been fifty years before. Determinist morality with its clear dicta about right and wrong was approaching its end. 'Man' had become 'economic man'. There was no more use for an established church, for organized colonialization, for poor relief or any other social legislation. In fact there was no use for anything which interferes with 'natural selection'. Even education was superfluous; it does not protect society against crime and cannot protect its private property, because 'the moral sense develops independently of education and ignorance has no connection with evildoing' [Spencer, 1850].

The period's 'pregnancy' of all things with their contrary is well reflected in Hegel's dialectics. The German term *Aufheben* may illustrate the point: it can mean *raising*, as in *etwas vom Boden aufheben*; it can mean *cancel*, as in *den Befehl aufheben*; and it can mean *retain*, as in *die Theaterkarte bis Morgen aufheben*. Here in one word is the entire 'law of motion'; the whole mechanism of change from *thesis*, to *antithesis* and *synthesis*. Georg Wilhelm Friedrich Hegel (1770-1831), like Schiller and Schlegel, reacted against Kant's ascetic dualism which separated the *is* from the *ought*. He sought the unity behind diversity – the absolute in which all contradictions are resolved into unity and matter and mind are one. His dialectics not only reflected the complexity and transient nature of the social relations in his time but indicated the mechanism of change which moved them from one unity through the disclosure of opposites to another unity. Half a century later Friedrich Engels (1820-1895) would elaborate the same idea:

> Let us take a grain of barley. Billions of such grains of barley are milled, boiled and brewed and then consumed. But if such a grain of barley meets with conditions which are normal for it, if it falls on suitable soil, then under the influence of heat and moisture it undergoes a specific change, it germinates. The grain as such ceases to exist, it is negated, and in its place appears the plant which has arisen from it, the negation of the grain. But what is the normal life-process of this plant? It grows, flowers, is fertilized and finally once more produces grains of barley, and as soon as these have ripened the stalk dies, is in turn negated. As a result of this negation of the negation we have once again the original grain of barley, but not as a single unit, but ten, twenty – or thirty-fold [Engels, 1885:186-7].

For Hegel the struggle between opposites was the natural mode of existence, and life's aim *achievement* and not happiness. 'Nothing great in the world has ever been accomplished without passion... Periods of happiness are the blank pages in the history of mankind they are periods of harmony and stagnation unworthy of man's genius.' Worthy of man's genius are the periods in which, driven by the *Zeitgeist*, one genius after another becomes in a dialectical progression the midwife of revolutionary progress. Each situation bears the imprint of its past and the seeds of its future. The key to ethics is man's desire to attain the ends designated by society. But as these ends are changing with the passage of time, and differ from one society to another, there can be no *absolute* morality. Consequently only fools can try to reform existing institutions on the basis of *their* reason, because existing institutions are the embodiment of 'historical reason' which is a much sounder basis.

Yet the majority of people, the peasants and the urban poor, were hardly affected by all this. They continued to keep faith with the old beliefs. The new rationalism had little to offer for the solution of their problems, and scepticism provided no solace for people whose fate was either determined by the vagaries of weather or the wishes of their powerful 'betters'. However, this does not mean that all workers remained entirely unaffected by the material changes which were taking place. The relative labour shortage in the first half of the eighteenth century enabled some sections of the labour force to press for, and obtain from time to time, higher wages. Consequently even mercantilists could no longer maintain that 'workers' wants are strictly limited,' and their predilection for low wages simply became impracticable in many instances. As a result of this domestic demand expanded and was gradually becoming an increasingly important source of profit. Also the progress of technology required a new type of better educated labour which also made it impracticable to continue to regard all workers as 'non-people' [Brenner, 1966:16-17]. There were of course attempts to mitigate the effects of the skilled-labour shortages by attracting skilled immigrants from other countries and by training 'the poor' but on the whole this did not solve the problem. At least from time to time skilled labour had to be well remunerated. In this way already in the eighteenth century the rise of the middle class was matched by a growing number of better educated and less submissive urban workers. As yet their resistance to exploitation was confined to individual demands for better wages and personal redress for grievances, but the seeds of the new class conflict were already sown.

In conclusion the hundred years which separated the middle of the eighteenth from the middle of the nineteenth century witnessed a great number of contrary developments. Wealth accumulated and created the material basis for economic growth, but the fruits of growth were inequitably distributed. Technological innovations increased productivity, but the person employed to operate it was subjected to work routines which restricted his ability 'to exert his understanding,' [Smith 1776:303] and deprived him of work satisfaction. The aristocracy's feudal prerogatives were abolished, but new privileges reserved for the bourgeoisie were taking their place. Mysticism was banished from science and rationalism spread to most spheres of thought and activity, but it created utilitarian attitudes which introduced relativism into the tenets of morality. What was materially expedient was becoming morally commendable. Competition introduced a powerful compulsive mechanism for innovation and economic growth, but made almost all human activities and achievement subordinate to and dependent upon economic success. The new mode of production produced an increasingly affluent bourgeoisie, but it also created a new stratum of underprivileged workers, namely the urban working class. Altogether, it was a period in which 'machinery, gifted with the wonderful power of shortening and fructifying human labour (was) starving and overworking it,' and 'new-fangled sources of wealth turned by some strange weird spell into sources of want,' and in which 'the victories of art (were) bought by loss of character, and at the same place that mankind master(ed) nature, man became enslaved to other men or to his own infamy' [Marx & Engels 1958:I,359]. In one sense the bearers of progress, the 'captains of industry,' were providing mankind with the technology capable of freeing it from material want; in another they became mankind's worst detractors.

Reactionaries who were searching the past for inspiration became the protagonists of social progress. Innovators, radicals and revolutionaries revived old doctrines, and their conservative and reactionary opponents became the inventors of new ones [MacIntyre, 1967:227-9]. The bourgeoisie, which under the banner of the Rights of Man and the slogan of 'Liberty, Equality and Fraternity' set out to destroy the old iniquity, was setting up a new socially divisive order which was less humane and even harsher in its consequences for the poor than the order it replaced. Aristocrats, clerics and other admirers of the old world inspired and promoted new progressive and humane ideas. Men like Claude Henri de Rouvroy Saint–Simon (1760-1825), who believed in Christian ethics and feudal economic arrangements, and Jean Charles Leonard Sismondi (1773-1842), a romantic conservative in the Christian spirit, and Charles Fourier (1772-1837), and Robert Owen (1771-1858) who put their trust in social utopias, and cooperatives and non-profit stores, became the bearers of progressive visions.

As yet all these contrary developments were only tendencies, but the conflict inherent in the contradictory characteristics of the new social and economic order were becoming visible. In the late nineteenth and early twentieth century they were to determine the face of capitalism.

# 8.   'All Things pregnant with their Contrary'

In the second half of the nineteenth century the bourgeoisie consolidated its position and strove to fortify it against the working class. Its economic philosophy was *acquisition, competition* and *rationality*. The purpose of all endeavours was acquisition, the means competition, and its methods were strictly rational. The new spirit of *acquisition* eclipsed the restriction inherent in the mere need of earning a livelihood and replaced it by desires which have no upper limits. *Competition* claimed the assertion of individuals' natural capabilities and freedom from traditional and conventional restrictions; the *methods* implied the use of precise cost–benefit calculations, a predilection for long-range planning, the development of indirect methods of production, and the strict adaptation of means to ends. Together the aims, means and method established the supremacy of business interests over all other values and gave rise to an almost purely utilitarian valuation of people, objects and events. In fact, the spirit of acquisition not only seized upon all economic phenomena but reached over into the entire sphere of human activities and relations [Sombart, 1953:III,195-208].

Accumulation of capital, advances in cost-reducing technology, and the spreading of trade, *defined* progress. Human beings became 'labour power,' and nature a 'factor of production'. Quantification, ably introduced by Lavoisier into chemistry in the second half of the eighteenth century, became in the nineteenth century an essential tool of social stratification. As the discovery of mechanisms was regarded the quintessence of science, the regulative effect of price and profit fluctuations became the scientific basis of economic theory.

Acquisition took prime place among all other human drives, and systematic rational behaviour became virtue. Compassion became derisive sentimentality, and individuality (except in the pursuit of economic aims) eccentricity. As a result of this all individual activities were guided by the principle of highest rationality, but the system as a whole remained conspicuously irrational. Its overall coordination was left with a self-regulating mechanism founded upon a metaphysical trust in a particular kind of natural order which was supposed to lead man by an 'invisible hand through the study of his own advantage' willy-nilly to employ his resources in the way most beneficial to all.

It was this coexistence of well nigh perfect rationality with trust in a metaphysically ordained natural order from which the numerous strains and stresses of the capitalist system originated. The assertion of natural rights in the pursuit of profit (only marginally restricted by usage and laws to forestall criminal dealings) enabled the bourgeoisie to study dispassionately all the material aspects of nature, but prevented the application of rationality to the analysis of man's social arrangements. There simply was no motive force equivalent to the quest for profit to stimulate individuals in suitable social positions to study the structure of society as a whole and to question the assertion of social and economic harmony. The poor were ill equipped to do so, and preferred to seek their salvation as individuals within the framework of the system; and the better off had little to gain from it. The exceptions, men like Marx, were therefore singularly unsuccessful in their time with their efforts to transform their theoretical insight into revolutionary practice. They simply could not make those most in need of change conscious of the irrationality of the entire social order.

The idea which was spreading in the natural sciences, namely that by better understanding nature man can 'recreate' it to serve his purpose, found little echo in the social sciences. For ages man had known to make steel by combining suitable iron ores with coal and controlling its carbon content. He did this by the difficult and unreliable process of stopping the blast in the furnace at precisely the correct moment. In the late nineteenth century, the systematic approach to nature and the formulation of theories about the composition of substances and how they affect each other, taught man to synthesize and form hitherto unknown compounds. It taught him to make high quality steel, and many other things, with certainty and confidence. He no longer guessed or learned from hard and costly experience when to stop the blast in the furnace to obtain the quality of steel he wanted, but could simply burn out all the carbon and add the required measure later. No similar ideas were making many converts in the realm of the social sciences. Some thinkers understood that the social system is a human artifact, that its 'laws of motion' have no universal applicability, but their views were still too far removed from people's everyday experience to make converts. After all, the transformation of a social system does not require one person to be conscious of alternatives but millions must be organized and prepared to accept the deprivation associated with a struggle for change. In the nineteenth century the few who were conscious of the alternatives and capable of organizing the underprivileged were those most likely also to find personal salvation within the ruling system. There simply was no mechanism akin to competition to motivate an *individual* to challenge the social order. Only when the practical possibilities for changing the system became apparent, and the chances of improving one's life within the system seemed hopeless, thoughts about more rational alternatives began to spread. But for this the time was not yet ripe. Throughout the first half of the nineteenth century the organizational efforts of labour were little more than collective attempts by individuals to redress the immediate evils they experienced personally, and to mitigate the system's worst excesses. They were spontaneous outbursts of discontent not yet designed to replace the system by another, and they were lacking a practicable positive perception of an alternative society.

During the second half of the nineteenth and early twentieth century the number of people employed for wages in manufacture, construction and other non-agricultural services was very rapidly

increasing. On average they increased annually in the United
Kingdom by approximately 150,000, and in Belgium by 47,000
[Mitchell, 1975]. But although wage workers were acquiring most
characteristics of a separate social class their class consciousness
developed only very slowly. In part this can be explained by the
fact that the middle class was more open to entrants from 'below'
than the aristocracy had been, but there were also deeper causes.
Class consciousness requires either common descent or a
recognizable similarity of occupation, wealth, education, life-style
and stock of ideas which enable individuals to meet one another
on equal terms [Ginsberg, 1934:III,536-8]. Both Marx and Weber
described only the *objective* class reality and not the constructive
element, namely the claim to power. Neither described the
*subjective* self-classification that serves as a foundation for
constructive class consciousness. In the definition of class Marx
emphasized the economic factors and Weber the separation of
class from status, and reserved the former term for the economic
and the latter for the quality of perceived social interaction – that
is for the positive or negative estimation of persons or positions.
Objective class consciousness only takes notice of similarity of
conditions and relates them to the vicissitudes of fate; subjective
class consciousness relates them to the social system. The point is
that the existence of a large group of people in a common
economic position need not lead to a *conscious common* effort.
People in the same situation may exhibit similar attitudes and
behaviour without having a sense of class consciousness. In 71 BC
many Roman slaves revolted. Led by Spartacus they dominated for
a time a great part of southern Italy. They were a group of people
in a common economic position who exhibited similar attitudes
and behaviour. All the same, they can hardly be defined as a class,
because they did not develop a class consciousness. They neither
strived to abolish slavery as an institution, nor to confront Roman
society with an alternative social structure. In fact they accepted
the existing order except for their own place as individuals within
it. This was also the reason for their undoing. It explains why the
Roman establishment was saved from the menace of a much wider
uprising all over the empire. In other words, consciousness is

heavily weighted by the cultural environment and by the ideas common to a society. It is not solely determined by purely economic relations. Antagonism toward higher strata may develop spontaneously but class consciousness among the lower strata will only arise when the collective opportunity to eliminate their inferiority is demonstrated, and when this inferiority is recognized as a product of an existing order. None of this had reached maturity before the middle of the nineteenth century.

Even late in the nineteenth century the conflicting interests of employers and workers were seen within the context of the market system. There were buyers and sellers of labour trying individually to obtain the best bargain for themselves. When workers found it useful and practicable to combine in their trade or in their work-place in order to improve their bargaining position, they tried to do so. Before the 'anti-ring' law forbade the practice, London coal-bargers did this very successfully. It did not require much social perception; but class consciousness does. Throughout most of the nineteenth century the working class had neither an intellectual leadership nor objectively the prospect of greatly improving most people's living standard by a more equitable income distribution. The level of technological efficiency was simply not yet sufficiently advanced. Class consciousness was developing but only in the wake of the growing discrepancy between affluence and poverty, following the rise of labour unions which were struggling to improve workers' conditions *within* the ruling social and economic system. From within the system labour's progress was also facilitated by internal contradictions within the bourgeoisie. For this the struggle between landlords and industrialists (reflected in the wrangle between Tories and Liberals about the Corn Laws) can serve as an example. It weakened the bourgeoisie's political hegemony and afforded labour opportunities to act in unison, and to display class characteristics. To serve its particular advantage one or the other sections of the bourgeoisie found it expedient from time to time to extend more political rights to workers. Sometimes this took the form of a rearrangement of electoral constituencies; at other times of reducing the minimum franchise qualifications, and other times again, of abolishing restraints on labour unions [Brenner, 1969:161-70].

While *class consciousness* was in its infancy, the division between 'us,' the poor, and 'them,' the rich was rapidly dividing industrial societies into what Disraeli (1804-1881) called 'the two nations.' This division reflected class coherence, common experience and life-style, but not 'class consciousness'. It acknowledged the obvious manifestations of the ill-effects of the economic order but not its causes. As a result of this it identified class with life-style, with the culture of poverty in one class and of affluence and power in the other. There is little mention of exploitation in the proletarian *belles-lettres* and folk-songs of this period, and much about the sufferings the poor had to endure. Workers regarded all who did not share their life-style, the culture of poverty, as 'them' and the middle class used the term 'proletarian' as a pejorative. This not only deprived the working class of the ability to recognize the objective causes of its distress, which were inherent in the economic system, but also of the ability to gain the support of the lower strata of the middle class and the intelligentsia who objectively were its natural allies in a struggle to ameliorate or change the reigning economic order. Neither the middle class nor the intelligentsia had good reasons to maintain a system based on economic inequity and exploitation, but there was little attraction in exchanging their reasonably comfortable life for a life-style whose sole *raison d'être* was poverty. Therefore, by allowing the consequences of poverty to become the hallmark of its class, the proletariat enabled the bourgeoisie to maintain its social hegemony by simply presenting the image of poverty as the sole alternative. For almost a century the legacy of this identification of poverty with membership of the working class remained so strong that even the attempts by the end of the century to stress the true societal importance of labour – for example by extolling the 'dignity of labour,' were ineffective in alleviating the fears of the middle class of being reduced to proletarians. But these were not the only reasons for labour's inability to dislodge the bourgeoisie from power.

In the early days of the bourgeoisie's ascent, in the era of merchant capitalism, manufacture thrived on expanding foreign markets. In this period the backbone of resistance was the journeymen. But journeymen had it within their prospects to become employers. They were therefore on the whole less motivated to reject the entire social and economic order than to find solutions to immediate problems. Often they did this by setting up cooperatives to eliminate middle-men and sometimes, when they were desperate, by resorting to a kind of Proudhonian anarchism. Later, when merchant capitalism became technological capitalism, labour separated into two camps: one increasingly inclined to abandon capitalism altogether, and another prepared to bargain with it on its own terms. In the 1880s these strategies divide the labour movement into a variety of streams ranging from communists and syndicalists, to Guild socialists and industrial unionists. Some were seeking the solutions politically and the others in craft unions. All were driven by the desire to protect or improve workers, living standards, but the *revolutionary* stream took its inspiration from Marx's theory of dialectical and historical materialism, and the *neoclassical* (unionist) stream from the logic of the capitalist system itself. The latter simply regarded unions as rational constructs, like business firms, to maximize members' share in the fruits of production. *Revolutionary* unionism contained a class perception of society which implied an ethical dimension, namely a distinction between exploited and exploiters. *Neoclassical* unionism, which became more common in North America than in Europe, was less 'ideological,' and did not embrace an alternative perception of society and made no claim to labour's moral ascendancy *vis-à-vis* the bourgeoisie. The *revolutionary* part of the labour movement adopted Marx's ideological premise as its guide to action. It regarded Marx's dialectics as the general law of development by which prediction becomes possible through the analysis of the past and the understanding of the present. *Neoclassical* unions had a pragmatic approach. They confined their efforts to improving their members' living conditions by struggling for higher wages and better workconditions without invoking any particular ideological premise or moral stand.

Marx himself never escaped the values he inherited from his Jewish–Christian background. He had no other values by which to judge the bourgeoisie except those to which it was still paying at least lip-service itself. But the use of moral vocabulary always presupposes a shared form of social order. Appeal to moral principles against some existing state of affairs is always an appeal within the limits of that form of society; to appeal against it one must find a vocabulary which does not presuppose its existence. Such a vocabulary one finds in the form of expression of wants and needs which are unsatisfiable within the existing society and require a new social order. Marx appealed to the wants and needs of the working class against the social order of the bourgeois society. But he never raises two questions which are crucial for his own doctrine. The first concerns the role of morality within the working-class movement, 'we remain uncertain as to how Marx conceives it possible that a society prey to the errors of moral individualism may come to recognize and transcend them.'

> Marx's second great omission concerns the morality of socialist and communist society. He does indeed speak in at least one passage as though communism will be an embodiment of the Kantian kingdom of ends. But he is at best allusive on this topic... [MacIntyre, 1967:214].

By converting Ricardo's *economic* labour value theory into an *ethical* issue involving a property right, Marx claimed for labour moral hegemony. Ricardo had shown that value was the product of labour and, allowing for scarcity, of labour alone. But if labour was the basis of value then profit must be theft. It could only arise from paying the worker something less than the value he produced. This was the source of Marx's moral indignation. Invoking, as it were, the bourgeoisie's own conception of property rights, and applying them to work, Marx supplied the labour movement with the ammunition for fighting the bourgeoisie upon its own ethical premises. Before long the bourgeoisie will parry this assault by abandoning the labour value theory in favour of *utility* as source of value. But the new theory could only soothe the consciences of the rich; it could not stop workers from recognizing what feudal and early capitalist society had consistently ignored, namely the money value of labour services.

In his examination of Eugen Duhring's ideas and their rejection, Friedrich Engels (1820-1895) wrote a particularly lucid description of the mechanism by which profit transformed into theft.

> Let us assume, that the means of subsistence represent six hours of labour time daily. Our incipient capitalist, who buys labour-power for carrying on his business, i.e. hires a labourer, consequently pays this labourer the full value of his day's labour-power if he pays him a sum of money which also represents six hours of labour. And as soon as the labourer has worked six hours in the employment of the incipient capitalist, he has fully reimbursed the latter for his outlay, for the value of the day's labour-power which he had paid. But so far the money would not have been converted into capital, it would not have produced any surplus-value. And for this reason the buyer of labour-power has quite a different notion of the nature of the transaction he has carried out. The fact that only six hours' labour is necessary to keep the labourer alive for twenty-four hours, does not in any way prevent him from working twelve hours out of twenty-four. The value of the labour-power, and the value which that labour-power creates in the labour-process, are two different magnitudes... On our assumption, therefore, the labourer each day *costs* the owner of money the value of the product of six hours' labour, but he *hands over* to him each day the *value* of the product of twelve hours' labour. The difference in favour of the owner of the money is – six hours of unpaid surplus-labour, a surplus-product for which he does not pay and in which six hours' labour is embodied. The trick has been performed. Surplus-value has been produced; money has been converted into capital – a profit has been realised [Engels, 1885:282-3].

The bourgeoisie reacted by abandoning the labour theory of value in favour of a less morally incriminating one. It adopted *utility* as source of value and placed greater emphasis on scarcity. The idea of *utility* as source of value was hardly new. Dating back to Aristotle (384-322 BC) it was revived by Ferdinande Galiani (1728-1787), Etienne Bonnot de Condillac (1714-1780), Jean Baptiste Say (1767-1832) and James Maitland the Earl of Lauderdale (1759-1839). It had suffered from its inability to explain why some of the most useful and necessary things like water were free or cheap while useless things like diamonds were costly. Galiani solved this problem by making *value* the *ratio of utility to scarcity*. He abandoned the search for an *objective* measure of value and gave it a *subjective* or relative definition. He made *value* dependent on the utility derived from a good by whoever wanted it, the intensity of his desire, and its scarcity. In the words of Condillac 'a more keenly felt want gives to things a greater value... a thing does not have value because of its cost... but it costs because it has value' [Condillac, 1776:74]. In the nineteenth century Fleeming Jenkins would formulate the same ideas more directly to oppose the labour theory of value.

> The fact is, that labour once spent has no influence on the future value of any article: it is gone and lost forever... But though labour is never the cause of value, it is in a large proportion of cases the determining circumstance, and in the following way: Value depends solely on the final degree of utility. How can we vary this degree of utility? By having more or less of the commodity to consume. And how shall we get more or less of it? By spending more or less labour in obtaining a supply... Cost of production determines supply; Supply determines final degree of utility; Final degree of utility determines value [Jenkins, 1870:12].

Here then was a theory capable of delivering the bourgeoisie from moral depredation.

In fact the bourgeoisie's departure from the classical labour theory of value was not simply an expedient to elude the moral implications of this proposition but part of a wider change in late nineteenth century perception. Locked in the grip of competition the bourgeoisie became accustomed to seek practical solutions to immediate problems. If the age of Enlightenment was dominated by the search for answers to the question *why*, for the *noumena* of events, the new age was governed by the search for answers to the question *how*, for the *phenomena*. The rise of the bourgeoisie put man in the centre of the universe and made his senses the final judge of reality. Only what his senses or the mind could perceive became *real* knowledge. Hence, as value cannot but price can be directly perceived, price alone became a worthy object of analysis.

In the late eighteenth century Antoine Laurent Lavoisier (1743-1794) introduced quantification and turned 'the scales into the most important physical instrument of all.' It gave to the old word *atom* a new meaning. At about the same time electric energy was also converted into a measurable quantity, namely the ampère. In chemistry such units of measurement as volt, gauss and farad (all named after their inventors) were spreading.

> From Priestly to Dalton, more and more elementary bodies came to be defined by their characteristic atomic weights... (and) because all the new units seemed to fit into a coherent framework, some scientists gained the impression that physics had discovered the very mainspring of the universe – *that man had at last discovered God.* However, most scientists preferred to restrict their observations to the taking of readings, leaving metaphysical speculation to the philosophers. In Kant's day it had still been possible for men with open minds to take an over-all view of human knowledge but in the nineteenth century... no scientist worth his salt could continue to prize speculation above experiment... the age of positivism had dawned [Moraze, 1961:III,2].

Henceforth, and until Einstein was able once again to show the inadequacy of our senses for grasping the full meaning of reality, true knowledge was thought to be founded exclusively on sense experience and all inquiry into ultimate origins was abandoned. To be sure, even Henri Poincaré (1854-1912) had already run up against some of the problems that nineteenth century positivism imposed upon science, but it was not before Einstein that the system was eventually shaken. But when Albert Einstein (1879-1955) showed that 'the unity of the beholder must give pride of place to the unity of the external reality he beholds,' that 'time and space are interrelated in ways which transcend common experience,' the bourgeoisie was already losing its economic and social hegemony.

It is not that phenomenalism and nineteenth century positivism were not extremely successful in solving many practical problems on man's road to the conquest of his natural environment, but that by their very character they avoided the questions which could have thrown doubt on the logic of the prevailing social arrangements. The nineteenth century posed as questions worthy of answers those questions which the middle class needed to be answered to serve industry. By the time they consolidated their economic primacy, they had already created conditions which made labour resistance practicably unavoidable and they called on science to serve their narrow requirements. This does not imply that science, and in particular applied science which until close to the last quarter of the nineteenth century was governed by extreme empirical elements, was unimportant. But the technological achievements of this period were mainly the product of the accumulated experience of craftsmen, the enterprise of managers, and the skill of individual designers [Singer et al., 1956:V,vi]. The point is that until the end of the century, only that science which had direct technological applicability was supported by the bourgeoisie. And when international competition no longer permitted the bourgeoisie to ignore the more profound scientific discoveries, few scientists were involved in the designing of factories and products.

In conclusion it may be said that by the middle of the nineteenth century a system of production, involving social relationships, in which the primary object is the gain of profit through exchange, was well established in Western civilization. But its bearers had not yet liberated themselves from all the moral values they inherited from earlier ages. They made rationality the determining factor in their economic and technological decisions, but retained religion and mysticism in almost all other spheres of their existence. They continued to pray and to live in fear of divine retribution, but they no longer expected their prayers to have the same results as their own determined efforts. They grasped the political and economic hegemony out of the hands of the landed aristocracy but continued to hanker after land and titles. They embraced utilitarian ideas but did not take the universities out of church control. They made rational scepticism the new 'master of society' but left the majority of people to be guided by churches and evangelical sects.

# 9.  Labour between Reform and Revolution

The purpose of all labour movements and trade unions was to protect and improve workers' living conditions. The revolutionary unions aspired to achieve this by changing the entire social and economic system; the non-revolutionary 'neoclassical' unions by obtaining advantages for their members within the prevailing social and economic order. But even within the revolutionary movement there were large differences. At the one end of the spectrum were the *radicals*, and the *anarcho-syndicalists*, who did not believe in a peaceful or gradual transformation of the system [Perlman, 1968]. At the other end were *reformists*, who were revolutionary in their aims (the abolition of capitalism) but evolutionary or piecemeal in their method.

Marx believed that the development of human society is ruled by necessity and that necessity is independent of people's consciousness. He thought that recognition of necessity, and the formulations of policies in conformity with it, are the essence of progressive labour leadership. In his view the laws of necessity do not operate automatically. The laws determine the general trend, which is the product of objective situations, but the actual course of events and their timing depends on the pull of contradictory forces. In this way socialism is bound to replace capitalism – a historical necessity – but the manner in which it will occur and the actual date of the downfall depend upon a variety of circumstances. The forces which provide these circumstances are the product of ideas, or the ideas themselves. Scientific socialism, in his opinion, is the reflection of the conflict between the old capitalist productive relations and new productive forces and the

127

superstructures which arise from each. The *recognition* of the new reality eventually causes the transition. The idea, that is the recognition of the new economic and social reality, becomes an integral part of a cause which can unite people and lead them to conscious practical action. In this sense an idea when taken up by the masses becomes a material force [Marx & Engels, 1958:362-3]. In any given situation the correctness of labour policy depends upon its leaders' correct appreciation of the situation in its widest historical context. But facts seldom speak with a single voice; and the question how one can ever be *sure* to have the proper appreciation of the consequences of one's actions became the source of far reaching differences of opinion in the labour movement. The orthodox converts to social–economic determinism believed that scientific Marxism – the method of historical and dialectical materialism – provided a unique answer. But at least three other streams in the revolutionary union movement, with alternative assessments of historical situations, came up with different interpretations of reality, and therefore with other prescriptions to guide their policies and actions.

The left wing of the social democrats, the communists, denied the practicability of a gradual or reformist approach. In the light of what they called scientific socialism they regarded an intensification of class contradictions and a violent confrontation with the bourgeoisie historically inevitable. Selecting from the works of Marx what suited this interpretation of 'historical necessity,' and ignoring what dit not, they argued that the increasing rate of capitalist exploitation, and the accumulation of capital that attends it, must inevitably result in a decline in the profitability of capital and in investment, and therefore to workers' sagging living standards. Ignorant of, or ignoring, the fact that workers' living conditions were on the whole improving in the industrial countries, they continued to maintain this scenario well into the twentieth century. According to this scenario the recurrent, and continually more intensive economic crises inherent in the capitalist mode of production eventually leaves the labouring masses no other choice but to revolt. Aware of this threat, the bourgeoisie surrounds itself with persons who can be 'bought' to protect it. It allows some intellectuals and the professional elite a greater share in the fruits of production and takes control of the army and police to suppress the discontent. It engages the nation in colonial exploits, or plunges the world into a war [Lenin, 1917a]. Consequently, labour's struggle must be political rather than economic. The role of unions is to prepare the working class for the eventual confrontation; their economic role – the haggling with employers about wages and work conditions – is necessary but subordinate. Once the main objective, the overthrow of the system, is achieved, and socialism replaces capitalism, the role of unions is revised. With the passing of the means of production into the hands of the people, or the government acting on behalf of the people, the struggle for higher living standards ceases to be a matter of class contradictions and becomes 'the struggle of man against nature,' and against managerial or bureaucratic arrogance. The unions become the guardians of efficiency and of the rights of individuals.

The foremost representatives of this line of reasoning were the Bolsheviks, led by Vladimir Ilyich Lenin (1870-1924). The Bolsheviks contended that the working class need neither wait until the proletariat has gained class consciousness before it seizes power, nor that it should necessarily do so by parliamentary majority. It could attain its ends by armed insurrection led by a well organized centrally directed revolutionary elite. All factions of the social democratic movement could agreed that in Russia, where autocratic rule and the remaining feudal structures still dominated all social, political and economic life, 'all obstructions on the road to capitalism must be eliminated.' The peasantry and the urban petty bourgeoisie, as well as sections of the capitalist class itself, must be united in a combined struggle against autocracy and mediaevalism. Where they separated was regarding the role of the industrial working class. Lenin believed that the industrial proletariat was already sufficiently advanced in Russia to take the lead in this struggle. He regarded its leading role as not only desirable but necessary, because he feared that as soon as the bourgeoisie had attained its ends it would abandon the revolution and oppose it. Moreover, as the industrial proletariat constituted only a small minority in the predominantly agrarian population of Russia, Lenin was worried that without an alliance with the peasantry the chances for survival of a socialist government once it was established would be small. He was therefore prepared to make considerable concessions to peasant individualism in order to obtain the peasantry's support.

To prepare for the seizure of power Lenin favoured the establishment of a small, disciplined party. In his opinion spontaneous proletarian insurrection would deteriorate into purposeless riots and personal acts of violence, which leads nowhere. The opponents preferred to appeal to the masses and to cooperate with the 'bourgeoisie' who they believed were destined to be the driving force in the *first* stage of the revolution. These differences first came to light during the debates in the Russian Social Democratic Party's congresses of 1903. Julius Cederbaum, *Martov* (1873-1923), and Pavel Borissovich Axelrod (1850-1928), were in favour of a decentralized mass movement, and Lenin favoured a small group of professional revolutionaries. At this time Lev Davidovich Bronstein, *Trotsky* (1879-1940) supported Martov; and the leading Marxist social philosopher in this period, Georgi Valentinovich, *Plekhanov* (1857-1918), sided with Lenin.

During the general strike of 1905, Lenin's faction, which henceforth called itself the *Bolsheviks* (the majority) wanted to turn the unrest into armed revolt. It was then that Lenin coined the slogan the 'democratic dictatorship of the proletariat and peasantry'. The other faction, the *Mensheviks* (the minority), now supported by *Plekhanov,* did not believe that Russia was already ripe for socialism and favoured political reforms and cooperation with the moderate socialist following of Alexander Feodorovich Kerensky (1881-1970). *Trotsky* and his following argued for a third option, namely to extend the strike in order to obtain a labour government, but opposed Lenin's readiness to make concessions to 'peasant individualism.' While these divisions were specifically related to the Russian situation they were to leave a deep mark on the future development of the entire movement, as will be shown in a later chapter.

A completely different ideology on the radical left of the labour movement was anarcho-syndicalism. Anarcho-syndicalists did not believe in the determinism of 'historical necessity'. In their opinion the capitalist system is held together by a universal pursuit of gain which permeates society to the last individual. Providing each individual with an illusion of security of life and property the system leads him to approve of arrangements like the bourgeoisie's legal system which enables him to enjoy what earnings or property he has but leaves him unmoved by the fact that if he is a worker it prevents him from receiving the full value of his labour. In this way the worker is led by immediate notions of self-interest to approve of one type of 'theft' in order to be protected from another. Unconsciously the system turns him into its protector and denies him the security he is actually striving for. Competitive pursuit of gain becomes a necessity for survival, and the wish to survive gives rise to the pursuit of gain – a vicious circle with an inescapable internal logic which makes the system unassailable from within. Thus because of its internal consistency capitalism may last for a long time. It can be destroyed only from outside – by acts unexplainable in terms of bourgeois reason.

There is an illuminating parallel between anarcho-syndicalist ideology and contemporary developments in conventionalist science. Nineteenth century conventional science held that as science advances the power of empirical evidence recedes. If Newton's mechanics can be 'saved' from experimental refutations by the introduction of auxiliary hypotheses capable of reconciling the anomalies with the general theories, then this is done (Henri Poincaré 1854-1912). As long as every experiment is itself at least partially dependent upon the acceptance of the general theory, no experiment can ever be sufficiently 'crucial' to make scientists abandon it. To assert the uniformity of thermic expansion a scientist uses a thermometer, but the assumption of uniform thermic expansion is already built into the thermometer. Similarly the use of microscopes presupposes the acceptance of part of optics. This makes science a complex system theory – a system of interrelated hypotheses, experimental equipment, and methodological procedures. It means that when a hypothesis is tested and refuted there is no way of deciding whether it is the hypothesis that is false or any one of the many other factors, including the observation when it involves the reading of an instrument. According to Edouard Le Roy (1870-1954) and other extreme conventionalists, the scientist who believes in the law governing free fall who observes a body falling in a manner not expected by this law, must not attempt to modify the law but deny the very possibility of a free fall (that is reject the theory as a whole). Anarcho-syndicalism did precisely this. It rejected capitalism's 'laws of motion' as a whole. This was of course plainly in conflict with the more moderate labour movement's conceptions which were closer to the belief of Pierre Maurics Marie Duhem (1861-1916) who held that no physical theory ever crumbles under the weight of refutations, but may well crumble under the weight of continual repairs.

The roots of anarchism reach far back into the classical and romantic heritage. Anarchism arose out of the proposition that man is essentially good but corrupted by the institutions of authority. Spontaneously he is individualistic and creative and tends toward voluntary cooperation and fulfilment, but the unnatural structures of the state and its institution of private property force him into situations which impair his creative individualism and his sense of social responsibility. Hence, take out private property, and the state, which serves no other purpose than the protection of such property, becomes superfluous. Without private property mankind is liberated from Hobbes's war of all against all and spontaneously finds its *natural* forms of social cooperation. In short, anarchism bestowed upon man the qualities Christianity had attributed to the Deity which man was encouraged to emulate. Man's *original sin* was the institution of private property and of the state to protect it.

These then were the values which stirred the hearts and minds of men from so varied a background as Proudhon (1809-1865), Kropotkin (1842-1921), Czolgosz (1873-1901) and later of the Andalusian peasants who fought Franco. What they all had in common was confidence in man's inherent goodness, an exaltation of individualism, and a disgust for the institutions of authority that corrupt man and subvert society's natural harmony. Where they differed was in the suggested methods for overthrowing the system. William Godwin (1756-1836), who may be counted among the forefathers of anarchist ideology, was apparently convinced of the powers of education to bring about a voluntary piecemeal transformation. Pierre Joseph Proudhon (1809-1865), who coined the phrase 'property is theft' abhorred violence, but admitted that it may be unavoidable. And so did Peter Kropotkin (1842-1921) and Mikhail Bakunin (1814-1876), the so-called prophet of anarchism, collectivism and atheism. In contrast, Georges Sorel (1847-1922) fathered the anarcho-syndicalist dream of bringing capitalism to its knees by a general strike. He recommended organized (union) action led by revolutionary elites. For him democracy was but 'the triumph of mediocrity'. It goes without saying that this recommendation was hardly consistent with the original conceptions of anarchism; and indeed his writings later found considerable echo in the Fascist movements. Finally there were also anarchists like Leon Czolgosz who not only advocated violence but practised it; and 'Big Bill' Haywood who was among the founders of the Industrial Workers of the World (I.W.W.), and who was thrown out of the socialist party for preaching violence.

In spite of the internal differences anarcho-syndicalism must still be regarded as the purest form of union opposition to the growing omnipotence of the capitalist state. While the majority of socialists were tempted to fight capitalism by the bourgeoisie's own institutions, that is politically in parliament, and by piecemeal reforms; and while the non-revolutionary unions were ready to come to terms with the capitalist state for a greater share in its wealth and power, anarcho-syndicalism wanted no dealings either with it or with any of its institutions.

An essential difference separating anarchists from socialists was their attitude toward the state. Socialists regarded the state as a necessary evil, which at least in the early post-revolutionary period had to be retained. Anarchists denied this necessity. The state was the source of all evil and had to be abolished forthwith. In the socialist scenario the proletariat seizes the state power and transforms the means of production into state property. Taking possession of the means of production in the name of society is the state's 'last independent act as a state.' After this, in one sphere after another, 'the interference of the state power in social relations becomes superfluous and then ceases of itself. The government of persons is replaced by the administration of things and the direction of the processes of production. The state is not "abolished", it withers away' [Engels, 1885:306-7]. This was not the anarchists' idea. Against the background of their philosophical tradition, ranging from Zeno of Citium to the Levelers, they were convinced that the state 'has a life of its own' which is intrinsically evil irrespective of the purpose it serves.

With all this anarcho-syndicalism was never really representative of true anarchism. This was not only due to tactical differences but because of the inherently individualistic elements in the pure anarchist conception. For example, French anarcho-syndicalism, which became quite formidable in the last decade of the nineteenth century, combined Proudhonist emancipationalism and distaste for state authority with the Marxian conception of antagonistic class contradictions. It found in Sorel's belief in the role of the militant elite, and in Bakunin's predilection for violence, a powerful basis for opposing all parliamentary or other political activity. It urged 'direct action,' and above all the *general strike*.

Italian syndicalism, which was greatly influenced by Sorel's ideas, cooperated with the socialists, and for some time even shared in government. It did this under the banner of 'realism,' which meant the need to adjust the strategy to suit political reality. Spanish syndicalism was the most impressive and long-lasting. It upheld its claim to spontaneity, retained its hostility to the state and to its bureaucratic institutions, and continued to oppose the Church. Paradoxically, however, its most heroic period came when it joined forces with other movements in the leftist government during the Spanish civil war.

In all these countries the increasing tendency to give to *means* precedence over *aims* deprived anarcho-syndicalism of anarchism's most progressive element, namely its liberating individualism. The more tactical considerations made it necessary to form organizational frameworks, the more did the intellectual speculations of the pure anarchists lose ground. In the end anarcho-syndicalism became entirely divested of its anarchist tenets. This process reached its summit with Edouard Berth's anti-intellectualism, ('deeds rather than thought') anti-semitism, and eventually monarchism. Nevertheless, on the eve of World War I, unionists were convinced of the imminence of the social revolution. They denounced socialist intellectuals for their party politics but, unlike Sorel and Berth, did not make a cult of anti-intellectualism and anti-rationalism. They urged direct action but not violence. For the intellectuals the *general strike* was the great social myth but for the union's rank and file it was a real tactic for pragmatic purposes.

Of the other countries where anarcho-syndicalism gained some influence the Netherlands and the United States deserve to be mentioned. Under the influence of Christian Cornelissen (1864-1942), and in a different manner under the influence of F. Domela Nieuwenhuis, Dutch anarcho-syndicalism was mainly theoretical, while American anarcho-syndicalism was influenced by men of action like the leaders of the I.W.W. (Industrial Workers of the World). The latter's aggressive rhetoric and lack of discipline, and their opposition to the war, eventually provided the American bourgeoisie with the opportunity to suppress the movement. Having carried anti-authoritarianism and worker exclusivism to fatal extremes, its decline was precipitated in the 1920s by its hopelessly impractical organizational structure, its internal dissension, and the competing new appeal to revolutionaries of communism.

The reformist wing of the socialist movement was convinced that persistent pressure on employers to raise labour's share in the fruits of production and to increase workers' influence on the running of enterprises would eventually lead to a peaceful socialization of industry. Some even proposed to use union funds to create union industries in order to eliminate capitalism by its own means, that is by competition. The champion of this idea, Eduard Bernstein (1850-1932), believed that the establishment of union enterprises would influence the level of remuneration

everywhere because wages in the union sector would raise
workers' incomes in the private sectors and eventually the union's
sector would force private enterprise altogether out of business.
Managers of union enterprises, being less dependent than private
management on profit maximization, would be free to devise long-
term economic policies toward this end. Instead of investing in the
sectors and regions where profits are highest, as private enterprise
management must do in order to meet shareholders' expectations,
union managers would pursue investment policies which in the
long run can serve the cause of labour [Bernstein, 1898]. Unlike
in private industry, workers in union enterprises were expected to
support their managers; to moderate wage claims in periods of
recessions or when prices had to be lowered to eliminate private
enterprises.

On the moderate right of the union movement were the
socialist–pragmatists, men as Hayes and Berger (and later Sam
Gompers of the pre-1924 American Federation of Labour). To the
left of them were the German social democrats and communists
like Rosa Luxemburg (1870-1919) who were for revolution but
against armed rebellion; for the elimination of capitalism but only
with the democratic support of a conscious working class – with
'the complete spiritual transformation of the masses' [Luxemburg,
1918]. Opposing Lenin, she wrote in her *Treatise on the Russian
Revolution*,

> Without general elections, without unrestricted freedom of press and
> assembly, without a free struggle of opinions, life dies out in every public
> institution, becomes a mere semblance of life, in which only the
> bureaucracy remains the active element. Public life gradually falls asleep,
> a few dozen party leaders of inexhaustible energy and boundless
> experience direct and rule. Among them, in reality, only a dozen
> outstanding heads do the leading and an elite of the working class is
> invited from time to time to meetings where they are to applaud the
> speeches of the leaders, and to approve proposed resolutions
> unanimously – at bottom then, a clique affair – a dictatorship to be
> sure, not however of the proletariat but only of a handful of politicians...
> Such conditions must inevitably cause a brutalization of public life;
> attempted assassinations, shooting of hostages, etc. [Luxemburg, 1922:71].

The non-revolutionary neoclassical unions, which work with and within the capitalist system, were and continue to be primarily concerned with the immediate wants of their members, with wages and working conditions. They do not relate to any particular vision of a future society but operate like any business organization trying to maximize its members' dividends. Their leadership is less concerned with ideology than with wages and the level of employment. But even these relatively limited concerns have increasingly forced them to adopt ideologically and politically significant standpoints. Often they cannot avoid exerting their power as pressure groups to prevent or support some piece of state legislation which concerns their freedom of action. Perhaps more significantly, they find it increasingly necessary to be represented on management boards or other employers' decision-making bodies to gain the required information for realistic assessments of their chances to succeed with wage claims, and to protect their members' jobs. Recurrent periods of mass unemployment and inflation have led some of even the least revolutionary unions to adopt political positions which are in fact revolutionary in content, though not by design. Their attitude is pragmatic but this pragmatism leads to modifications in the capitalist system. The theoreticians of the non-revolutionary unions are concerned with organizational problems, with the selection of suitable instruments for the attainment of objectives, and with the relationship between wages, prices and employment in general, but only seldom with the ideological and ethical principles of the capitalist system. The most powerful unions are also concerned with the macro-economic relationships between wages, technological improvements or innovations, and with various price-elasticities. They find this necessary to protect their members' interests but willy-nilly it involves them in controversies which have much wider ideological and ethical implications. In spite of all claims to the contrary in sections of the bourgeois press, union leaders are usually well aware of the limits to their wage claims. This has little to do with ideologically prescribed desires to keep the system alive (which are sometimes attributed to them by the extreme left) but is the result of their pragmatic approach to the need to maintain their members' working places and not have wage increases cancelled by inflation. In addition, they often press for social legislation to improve working conditions, social security, and pensions, which are issues which have become no less important than wage improvements as time has gone by. Finally they are concerned with taxation and subsidies because these too have a bearing on union members' living standards. As a result unions, whether neoclassical or revolutionary, have taken an ever increasing share in the running of the bourgeois states and reduced its excesses. They have, however, not touched the core of the system – the profit hunger that permeates all aspects of capitalist society. Marx had recognized and feared this possibility. In the controversy about Gladstone's speeches of 13th February 1843 and 17th April 1863, he wrote:

> *Wenn die Arbeiterklasse 'arm' geblieben ist, nur 'weniger arm' im Verhaltnis, worin sie eine 'berauschende Vermehrung von Reichtum und Macht für die besitzende Klasse produzierte, so ist sie relativ gleich arm geblieben. Wenn die aussersten Grade der Armut sich nicht vermindert haben, haben sie sich vermehrt mit den aussersten Graden des Reichtums...* [Marx, 1972:42-6].

For Marx the issue with capitalism was as much a moral as a practical issue and for this reason he would hardly have been appeased by the truly impressive economic achievements of the trade unions in the rich countries, and he would have been appalled by the 'achievements' of 'socialism' in the East.

In conclusion, the era of bourgeois consolidation in the nineteenth century provided both the *ability* and the *wish* which are necessary for economic progress. It established a legal system by which property rights were protected, for and against, the state, and thereby created conditions favourable for the accumulation of funds; and it provided a powerful mechanism, namely competition, to stimulate investment. In one class it based personal social and economic advancement upon competitive ability, and in another class it left individuals with almost no other alternative but to seek employment for wages. In this working class, people have no choice but to increase their efficient work and a high degree of work discipline in order to to stave off the threat of unemployment, hunger, poverty and destitution.

Thus the fear of destitution and the 'love of gain' provided capitalism with both dynamism and labour discipline. The desire for power, for social acclaim, even to serve the public good, were retained, but by virtue of an inner logic they all became subordinate to profit-making, because they could no longer be attained without economic success. But among those excluded from reaping the fruits of the ensuing economic progress the seeds of opposition were already germinating. On the basis of the system's own logic it took the form of labour unions; on the basis of the hope for a better society it took the form of anarcho-syndicalism and revolutionary socialism.

The second half of the nineteenth century was the watershed which separated the era in which the bourgeoisie had been struggling to wrench power from the feudal establishment, and the new era in which it began to feel besieged by the emergent working class. The spirit of acquisition, competition and individualistic economic rationality ingressed all spheres of life, but, at first hesitantly and individually, workers began to demand redress for the hardship the new social order imposed on them. In the second half of the nineteenth century their individual resistance was gradually developing into collective action. As yet their opposition vacillated between reaching out for political power or employing economic means, but the stage for the struggle for the emancipation of the working class was set.

# 10.  Improvement of Living Conditions

In England the beginnings of organized labour opposition were punctuated by sporadic outbursts of violence. Such were the Luddite riots of 1811 and of 1816. They were hardly conscious attempts to change the ruling social and economic order, but explosions of rage and fear of unemployment occasioned by the introduction of machines. Efforts to challenge the bourgeoisie's hegemony came only in the wake of the *Reform Bill* (1832) and the *People's Charter* (1838). However, these were abruptly terminated in 1848 with the suppression of the Chartist riots. During the prolonged prosperity, and skilled-labour shortage, which followed the middle of the century, the skilled workers' unions were able to reorganize and obtain a great many economic advantages for their members. The new model unionism was less militant and restricted itself to industrial action. The depression which began in the late 1880s disclosed the weakness of this new-style unionism. It proved powerful in times of labour shortage, but weak in periods of widespread unemployment. Within a decade its importance was overshadowed by the rise of unskilled workers' unions in docks, mines and gas-works. Unlike the skilled workers' unions of the 1860s and 1870s, whose leaders had tacitly accepted the bourgeois system, the unskilled workers' unions were led by socialists. In spite of this, until close to the end of the century, the unions never became socialist. The leaders simply did not succeed in enlisting rank and file support for political objectives, nor even to disassociate the rank and file from the Liberal Party or the Lib-Lab alliance. When the British working class finally established its own political representation in the early years of the twentieth century, namely the parliamentary Labour Party, the party was dominated by the unions; and it was not until 1918 that it adopted socialism as part of its official programme [Webb and Webb, 1920:113-20; Cole, 1925-27:53-78; Brenner, 1969:18].

It may therefore be said that until the end of World War I, the British labour movement was hardly revolutionary. It adopted a kind of 'Guild socialism', promoting workers' control over industry at shop floor level, or a reformist, *Fabian*, approach steering a middle course between French-style syndicalism (which rejected party politics and economic bargaining and favoured the abolition of capitalism by a *general strike*) and German-style union activities (which were dominated by the Social Democratic Party). During the post-war economic stagnation of the 1920s, the labour movement suffered a setback. Its membership diminished, the general strike (called by the TUC in 1926) failed, and the passing of the *Trades Disputes and Trade Union Act* (which declared strikes in sympathy etc. illegal) marked the end of this phase in British unionism. Henceforth the centre of gravity passed from the unions to the Labour Party. But the party did not fare much better. The minority government it formed in January 1924 was defeated in November. In 1929 Labour was once more in a position to form a government, but it was unable or perhaps unwilling to pursue socialist policies. Its most memorable achievement was the extension of franchise to women over the age of 21 years. With the 'cotton lock-out' and two millions unemployed, and the financial crisis, Labour was defeated in 1931 and replaced by the national government.

Except for a short spurt of action following the events of 1848, there was little union activity in Germany until the 1860s. In 1863 Ferdinand Lassalle (1825-1864) organized the first German political workers' party. His aim was to achieve universal suffrage and through it workers' control over the state. Recognizing the state's power to levy taxes, extend credit and give subsidies, he wanted to use it to promote workers' producer cooperatives. What he was aiming at was a state-supported system of workers' cooperatives. His belief in the *iron law of wages* (namely that when wages rise above subsistence level the population will also increase and force wages down again) led him to doubt the adequacy of unionism for solving labour's problems. He therefore favoured the elimination of the wage system without the abolition of private ownership. This split the German labour movement. Unable to accept Lassalle's approach, Marx formulated his objections as follows:

> If I abolish wage-labour, then naturally I abolish its laws also, whether they are of iron or sponge. But Lassalle's attack on wage-labour turns almost solely on this so-called law. In order therefore, to prove that Lassalle's sect has conquered, the wage system must be abolished together with the iron law of wages and not without it. It is well known that nothing of the iron law of wages belongs to Lassalle except the word iron borrowed from Goethe's great eternal iron laws. The word iron is a label by which the true believers recognise one another. But if I take the law with Lassalle's stamp on it and consequently in his sense then I must also take it with his basis for it. And what is that? ... it is the Malthusian theory of population.... But if this theory is correct, then again I cannot abolish the law even if I abolish wage labour a hundred times over, because the law then governs not only the system of wage labour but every social system. Basing themselves directly on this, the economists have proved for fifty years and more that socialism cannot abolish poverty, which has its basis in nature, but can only generalise it, distribute it simultaneously over the whole surface of society [Marx, 1938:ii].

Lassalle and his followers retained the main tenets of German idealistic philosophy, and Marx and his followers 'materialized dialectics' into class struggle. Lassalle set his hopes upon the state as an instrument to assist workers to organize themselves into producers' cooperatives, and to promote this aim, he established the Universal German Working Men's Association (1863). Marx sought a more radical solution. After forming in London the International Working Men's Association (1864), the *First International*, to unite workers of the world for the aims he had elaborated in the *Communist Manifesto*, Marx sent Wilhelm Liebknecht (1826-1900) to Germany to organize his labour movement, which was later led by August Bebel (1840-1913). In 1875, Lassalle's and Marx's movements united and formed the

German Social Democratic Party. During the short period of its early existence (before it was prohibited) the new united party was dominated by Lassalle's wing of the labour movement. In October 1876 the *Reichstag* passed legislation which prohibited meetings, publications and collections of money for socialist or similar parties which, in the words of the law, were aiming 'to overthrow the existing order of state or society'. With this the German labour movement was driven underground. When it re-emerged into legality in 1890 it had become Marxist.

It was during this time that Germany rose to take third place (following hard upon Britain and the USA) among the industrial powers. The number of people whose livelihood depended on industry increased in Germany to more than sixteen millions, and the number of people living in towns with more than 20,000 inhabitants grew to over eight millions. To take the wind out of the sails of the socialists, whose underground influence was increasing in pace with the growing industrial labour force, Bismarck introduced several measures to ameliorate the condition of the working class. The most important of these measures were *Sickness Insurance* (1883), *Accident Insurance* (1884) and *Old-Age and Invalidity Insurance* (1889).

In 1890 the bill extending the anti-socialist legislation was, after two readings, suddenly forgotten. The new Emperor (William II, who had succeeded to the throne in 1888) favoured a policy of social legislation to dissuade workers from supporting socialism. July 1890 saw the establishment of industrial courts to solve labour disputes; the restriction of employment of women and children; and the declaration of Sunday as an obligatory day of rest. In June 1891 factory inspection was improved, and workers were given the right to form committees to negotiate employment conditions. In March 1892 a Department of Labour was established to deal with labour problems in general. In 1899, socialists and liberals pressured Hohenlohe to pass a law permitting a federation of societies. In 1900, under Bulow, the social insurance legislation was extended, and so was sickness insurance in 1903. In 1908 the conservative government (formed in 1907 to combat centre and socialist policies) restricted factory work for women and children, and in 1910 an insurance code was passed which consolidated all previously made arrangements and extended their provisions. In spite of these efforts to improve the conditions of the working class 'from above', socialism continued to spread.

After the repeal of the anti-socialist legislation in 1890, the socialists returned to the *Reichstag* with 35 deputies. In the following year their congress in Erfurt adopted a Marxist programme. From 1890 to 1906 the Social Democratic Party shared power with the unions. But its failure in the elections of 1906 greatly strengthened the (revisionist) non-Marxist wing.

In the 1912 elections the socialists polled more than four million votes and became the largest party in the *Reichstag*. But by this time it had become moderate, favouring gradual parliamentary reform over revolution. Though it continued to be influenced by radicals, especially by Karl Kautsky (1854-1938) and Rosa Luxemburg (1870-1919), it followed the moderate course of the rapidly growing trade unions. This tendency for moderation was reinforced after the socialists' election setback in 1907. The party became reformist, and ready to cooperate with the progressives in the *Reichstag*. By this, though not in theory but in practice, it conceded hegemony to the bourgeoisie. In 1914 the trade unions and the Social Democratic Party approved in the *Reichstag* credits 'to defend the *Fatherland* against autocratic Russia'. Nationalism had gained the upper hand and routed the forces of internationalism. As a 'prize' unions were given representation on many government boards during the war. Thereafter they gained power and prestige and official recognition in the Republican Constitution. The socialist leader, Scheidemann, who in November 1918 proclaimed the German Republic and the Republican Constitution, confirmed the trade unions' official status, and forbade discrimination against union members, making 'yellow unions' (company unions) illegal. The working day was reduced to eight hours, and a number of joint conciliation boards were set up to solve labour disputes.

In conclusion German social democracy obtained considerable economic advantages for the working class. It achieved this without challenging the core tenets of the capitalist system. But challenging the system was precisely what the revolutionary political wing of the labour movement had in mind. The *Spartacus* revolt (1919), against the social democratic government was a reflection of this conflict. It was the confrontation between those who accepted the bourgeois system and tried to reform it, and those who believed that the system was in the long run inherently incapable of sustaining the economic achievements which the reformists could obtain. Logic was probably on the side of *Spartacus* in 1919, but concrete achievements, and the traditionalism which goes for 'common sense', were on the side of the reformist government. In the end the crushing defeat of the *Spartacists* put the final seal on the split in the German labour movement.

Until 1932 the German Social Democratic Party remained the largest party in that country, and the German Communist Party the most powerful communist party outside the Soviet Union. But both sections of the German labour movement had grown so far apart that they were unwilling to cooperate even in the face of the Fascist threat. Since 1929, Hitler's *national socialists* were putting the achievements of the unions and the social democrats in jeopardy. In the presidential elections of March 1932, Hindenburg secured 18,651,497 votes and Hitler (supported by the middle class, disappointed workers, industrialists and landlords) secured 11,300,000 votes. The communist Thalmann obtained 4,983,341 votes. In 1920 the trade unions had still been sufficiently strong to defeat a reactionary monarchist *coup d'état* by a general strike. Twelve years later, in 1932, a large part of the German working class was no longer able even to recognize Hitler and his policies for what they were. The defeat of the *Spartacists* had rid German social democracy of its revolutionary wing and left the party in the hands of moderates who continued to accept the bourgeois world and without wanting it its inherent economic instability of alternating periods of prosperity and depression. Having no alternative perception of society capable of replacing the bourgeoisie's, the social democratic leadership was therefore almost 'programmed' to disappoint its followers. The achievements it gained in prosperity were partly lost in the depressions. Therefore, by not attacking the roots of economic instability but only tackling its symptoms, social democracy lost face with the working class. Not challenging the socio-cultural hegemony of the bourgeoisie it left the door wide open to left and right demagoguery. In other words, the split in the labour movement deprived Germany of a constructive alternative perception of society capable of appealing to both workers and progressive members of the middle class. In the absence of such an alternative the depression raised the old fears of destitution and revived the middle class's fear of being reduced in social status. Worst of all, the absence of attainable solutions within the bourgeois system produced a climate conducive to escape to irrationalism. This climate, which always tends to spread when the gap between the desired and the attainable becomes too wide to be bridged by rational endeavours, took the form of rabid nationalism in Germany. The heritage of nineteenth century nationalism, and the hurt pride of having lost the 1914-18 war, combined with the frustrated expectations for economic security and advancement, and gave to the two words *national* and *socialism* just the right ring to convey the illusion of an answer. The lack of a rational solution within the bourgeois system, and the inability of the extreme left at this time to advance a credible alternative to the bourgeois state, left the doors wide open for a mythical leader and father figure, who thinks and decides for all, to deliver each individual from the impossible task of finding solutions for himself.

In France trade unionism was restricted by law until 1884. From 1884 until 1895 its development was impeded by its intricate relationship with no less than five rival socialist parties. From 1895 to 1902 it was mainly under the influence of the syndicalists. The *Confédération Générale du Travail* (CGT), which was organized at the beginning of this period, reflected the French workers' frustration with both the political and the trade union activities of the labour movement. The political engagement had achieved little by way of transforming the system 'of production for profit' into 'production for use', and the trade unions' demands for collective bargaining 'unmasked' them (in the eyes of the radicals) as partners, or at least as prepared to 'trade', with capitalism. In 1902 the *Confédération Générale du Travail* amalgamated with the *Fédération des Bourses du Travail* and unionism was separated for almost a decade from party politics. This period, in which labour made fairly good progress in the improvement of workers' living standards, was terminated by the approaching war which also put an end to the era of political withdrawal. Like German social democracy, the French labour movement supported its country's war effort, and was 'rewarded' by some union leaders being given seats in the French Cabinet.

After the 1914-18 war, in 1920, the failure of the general strike, and in 1921, the court order to dissolve the *CGT*, led the union to abandon its syndicalist tendencies. The syndicalists' dream, of labour taking over the economic enterprises and replacing the profit-minded managements by workers' cooperatives intent upon the satisfaction of men's *real* needs, had anyhow been waning. So, at least for a time, the *CGT* became a union like most other unions, resorting to political militancy and to industrial action as the occasion demanded. Next to the *CGT* there were also other unions pressing for improvements in France: the *Confédération Générale du Travail Unitaire*, the communist trade union and a number of Catholic unions. But the lack of political engagement by most of the French unions did not imply an absence of working-class political activity. The contrary is true; there was no other country in which the working class was equally class conscious or militantly socialist working class. Unlike in other countries, French working-class consciousness was not only the product of economic grievances but had deep roots in the political history of nineteenth century France. In particular the bloody events, which in May 1871 terminated the Paris Commune uprising, left a legacy the French working class was never to forget. Together with the separation of party politics from union membership, this legacy spared French labour some of the difficulties which were causing a great deal of confusion in the other industrializing countries. When long-term policies clashed with immediate needs; when considerations of a general nature could not be harmonized with immediate union requirements; when overall policies of workers' parties were in conflict with specific union demands in particular enterprises or parts of industry; the differences were less likely to weaken labour's general position in France than in most other countries. This does not mean that as a rule the unions were not massively supported by the labour parties, or that on the whole the union members did not vote for the political left, but it does mean that both the unions and the parties maintained great freedom of action in their separate spheres. The parties could concentrate on the political promotion of their aims and the unions on industrial action.

The fact that industrialization started earlier in France than in Germany, but progressed at a slower pace, may account for some of the differences in the character of the two countries' labour movements. The existence of a much greater cooperative business sector added in France a 'class' of partly self-employed working men whose interests and concerns did not always concur with those of the rest of the working class. In spite of periods of cooperation (for example in 1936 when the communists supported the *popular front* government of radical socialists and socialists) this division made the definition of labour's stand on many issues difficult and deepened the estrangement between socialists and communists. The socialists' moderation in the struggle against the bourgeois state alienated many of the more revolutionary inclined workers but the communists' identification with the Soviet Union's foreign policies (even with the Russian–German non-aggression pact of the summer of 1939) prevented them from finding their place in the ranks of the communists. While the socialist revolution in Russia scared the Western bourgeoisie to the point of making economic, social and political concessions to their working classes, the excesses of this *first socialist state* removed it so far from the Western cultural heritage and value system that it also frightened a great part of the Western working class, and even more so the progressive middle class.

The French communists adhered by Leninist principles. Their leader Maurice Thorez (1900-1964), with all the credit he deserves for his party's struggle against Nazi Germany (after the invasion of the Soviet Union), never became more than a dogmatic follower of the Soviet system and its policy. That nonetheless the

French Communist Party survived as a powerful political factor can only be explained by the earlier mentioned historical events which left the French working class much more suspicious of the bourgeoisie than any other Western working classes, and by the sub-culture or 'family spirit' which surrounded French communism.

One of the most painful 'by-products' of industrialization everywhere was the breakdown of the sense of security which was part of rural family life, of Guild association, and even of the feudal system. Until late in the nineteenth century, capitalism offered little to compensate for this loss – but the French Communist Party did. Unlike most other communist parties the French communists were organized by working place and not by regions. This created a feeling of solidarity among workers and led to the provision of a wide range of social services by the party for its members from Kindergartens to medical care. Therefore, to be in conflict with the party implied more than politics. It meant to risk expulsion from 'the great family', loss of solidarity at work, and the forfeit of the social services which the party offered. As a consequence class consciousness was often reduced to little more than animosity toward the bourgeoisie and opposition to exploitation. In fact, it led to a 'depoliticization' of the party cadres and the substitution of party discipline for consciousness, and party loyalty for independent thought. In the end policy decisions became the province of the party leadership alone which workers accepted in spite of the frequent Moscow-inspired political 'somersaults'.

The non-communist left, namely the socialists and the radical socialists' were more like electoral associations than disciplined party organizations. The socialists remained a 'class party' as it had been before the communists broke away from it in 1921. Its aims continued to be the socialization of 'the means of production and exchange', and the abolition of the bourgeois state by democratic means. Like labour's parliamentary representation in Britain, French socialist representatives in the *Chamber* were more ready to compromise with the bourgeoisie than their party organs, not to mention their party rank and file. The radical socialists were non-Marxist. Their support came from a wide array of progressives and from the liberal middle class.

In the United States of America labour's greater share in the fruits of production was mainly obtained by what is called 'neoclassical' efforts. Since the middle of the nineteenth century American trade unions were on the whole non-political. They resembled capitalist business enterprises adhering to the principle of profit maximization, which in their case meant the maximization of their members' immediate economic advantages. In this sense they were not only ideologically not committed to the abolition of the capitalist system but part of it. They were prepared to employ political pressure when it served their purpose, but *within* the system and on its own terms. They achieve this by promising to politicians aspiring to office the union's block vote, in exchange for post-election labour legislation. Members did not expect their unions to solve long-term national or world-wide social and political problems, but to wrench from employers the best possible wage rates and working conditions. That in the long run this *ad hoc* 'here and now' achievement would add up to a general transformation of the capitalist system was sometimes recognized but not considered part of union policy. The fact that the government of the United States became increasingly burdened with responsibilities which did not lie strictly within the competence of a *capitalist* state had little to do with 'union ideology'. The directional interference in the country's economy, and the provision of social services by the state on the scale Franklin Delano Roosevelt (1882-1945) introduced them, and the growth of the state – owned and state – controlled industrial sector since World War II, were not the direct result of union pressure, though some unions and indirectly all unions did play a role in it. This was so because in the absence of a strong socialist movement to promote labour solidarity it was the unions who taught American workers to act in unison to protect and improve their living standard. In the strongly individualistic society, composed of people from different cultures and countries of origin and with one wave of new immigrants after another joining the melting-pot this was of very great importance. Moreover, in spite of their lack of ideological commitment, the unions willy-nilly undermined the capitalist system. In the first place they raised labour's working conditions, and struck at the roots of 'the universal applicability of the *price* or *market mechanism*' by enforcing the principle of *collective bargaining*. In the second place, by using the votes of their mass membership in national and local government elections to influence the results, they wrought from the state a great number of social and economic concessions, culminating in the *New Deal* which in effect transformed old-style capitalism into something like a regulated capitalism which acknowledged the state's responsibility to provide work and a degree of social security for all its citizens.

The new-style capitalism, and the growing state ownership and control of essential means of production, did not mean of course the abolition of free enterprise; American capitalism continued to be governed by bourgeois principles, and production continued to be dominated by the urge to maximize profits rather than to satisfy 'real' wants, but American capitalism lost some of the worst ills attending this urge, namely the cold fear of starvation of those who have nothing else to sell but their labour. It would be an exaggeration to claim that European-style opposition to the system was altogether absent in America (the songs of Joe Hill, Aunt Molly Jackson and Sara Ogan Gunning bear witness to this) but it never gained the kind of influence it had in Western Europe.

The difference between American and European labour opposition to inequity and poverty was the product of the diversity of the historical circumstances which gave rise to it. In America the availability of 'free land' until well into in the nineteenth century made the struggle for reasonable minimum wages less pressing than in Europe. The availability of land prevented wages from falling for long much below what a household could earn by farming. Consequently American workers became accustomed to a minimum living standard which set the level at which 'voluntary unemployment' started at considerably higher earnings than were acceptable in Europe; and because of social obduracy this difference persisted even after its initial cause had disappeared.

The relatively high American wages were both a cause and a consequence. On the one hand they forced employers to search for and introduce labour-saving technologies, that is to raise per capita output; and on the other, it provided employers with a market for their produce which grew more or less in line with the increasing labour productivity.

Another reason for the difference between American and European unionism was that the successive waves of immigration made American labour very difficult to organize. The newcomers to the American labour market did not only raise language and communication problems, but often also introduced racial and national antagonisms, which impeded the development of the kind of cohesion without which no organized action can be undertaken. In addition, each new wave of immigrants provided employers with the opportunity to replace organized workers by new hands who had not yet become adjusted to their new surroundings. As American wages were well above those earned by the new immigrants in their countries of origin, initially most of them seldom felt the need to organize. For all these reasons American unionism never got really off the ground before World War I, and between the wars its membership and influence even declined. But by this time the gap left open by the unions was filled by *political* pressures for progressive labour legislation, and during the spells of economic prosperity and labour shortage by individual deals between workers and employers [Underwood Faulkner, 1963:603-82; Brenner, 1969:171-6,204-16].

Between the beginning and the middle of the twentieth century, the gross national product of the United States increased approximately fourfold and disposable personal income increased more than fourfold. At the same time average weekly hours of work declined from about 58 to 39. It must therefore be concluded that in the first half of the twentieth century, technological progress accompanied by competition improved the conditions of American labour in spite of the absence of a socialist opposition and of a class conscious union movement. The means by which American and European labour obtained higher living standards may have differed but the results were similar.

# 11.   Fascism and the 'Proletarian Counterculture'

The 'Crash of 1929' put an end to what for many people had, in spite of war and severe economic reversals, been an era of optimism and rising living standards. The depression of the 1930s was of hitherto unknown severity. For many young persons in Europe and America promising careers were blocked off. For older people it meant layoffs which often turned into permanent unemployment. For those who were able to retain their jobs it frequently engendered wage cuts, fear of unemployment and frustration. Engineers wasted their talents serving as petrol-pump assistants; doctors had to contend with unpaid bills and patients with unattended medical needs. For the unemployed, the alternatives to starvation were scarce and rarely sufficient to maintain their human dignity. Many had to rely on 'soup lines' and resort to begging – 'buddy can you spare a dime'. For the poorest the depression meant starvation. Numerous parents saw their children go hungry, without adequate medical care, and without the kind of environment that would allow them to develop into secure, healthy, dignified individuals. In short, 'the depression meant an intensification of all social evils: crime, juvenile delinquency, broken homes, the growth of racial and religious hatred, lapses into violence, and a growing audience for demagogues...' [Hamberg, 1961:47-9].

The most loathsome fruit this situation bore sprouted in Germany, namely the rise of Hitler. In a vain effort to stop him and his party from coming into power, social democrats and trade unions joined forces in 1932 with the Catholic and with the liberal parties of the bourgeoisie to elect the royalist, protestant and conservative, Hindenburg as President of the Republic. Together they polled 18,651,497 votes. Hitler received 11,339,446, and the communists, who put up their own candidate, got 4,983,341 votes.

The problem was that neither the bourgeoisie nor the left had a credible alternative, immediately practicable policy, for the termination of the crisis. The bourgeoisie had led the country into it and had little new to say; and communist and socialist propaganda had mainly been calculated to expose the evils of capitalism, which needed little stressing at this time. Worst of all, they had too little to offer. Germany's industrialization had not attained the level of efficiency required to provide an appreciable rise in the living standard for all citizens. What attracted a not inconsiderable part of the German intelligentsia to communism at this time was less the presence of a realistic solution to the crisis than a gut aversion to Nazi irrational populism, and the dream of social and economic equity. Paradoxically therefore, it was precisely the liberal bourgeois heritage, its individualism, and the lingering influence of the Old Testament's demand for justice and the New Testament's trust in the deliverance of mankind, which, stripped of its religious connotation, found an echo in Marxist aspirations. It was this legacy of nineteenth century intellectual liberalism, together with the reaction against vulgar utilitarian materialism (the revulsion against the repugnant conduct of the *nouveau riche* 'Babbitts,') and the discontent with the oppressive authoritarian education and life style, which drove a good part of the German intelligentsia toward communism. It was this that forged a bond between the socialist proletariat and the German intellectual elite and produced slogans as 'the dignity of labour' (*Arbeit Adelt*), and gave rise to the vast proletarian literature. In the radical camp this climate of opinion was best represented by authors like Stefan Heym, Heinrich Mann, Bertolt Brecht, Fritz von Unruh, Anna Seghers, Johannes R. Becher, who matched writers like Thomas Mann, Hermann Hesse, Feuchtwanger, Zweig, Werfel, Holthusen and later Borchert, in the liberal bourgeois camp. Together they made German culture sane and seemingly unassailable.

Earlier in the discussion the term *progress* was related to the unifying elements in man's perception of the universe. Economic progress was related to man's ability to overcome the reticence of nature and its control for his material advantage. From this point of view national socialism was certainly reactionary. It stressed the dividing characteristics of men – colour, race and status; and it regarded nature uncontrollable by human rationality. In comparison the bourgeoisie was progressive. It recognized class and race differences but did not endow them with rigidity and false attributes; and it maintained confidence in man's rational ability to understand nature and wield it to his purposes. Socialists believed not only in the equality of man but also in mankind's propensity to control nature and provide plenty for everyone. In this respect what separated the bourgeoisie from socialists was the conception of equality. For socialists equality was unconditional. The bourgeoisie's conception was conditional, namely a belief in the potential, not the actual, equality of all. Provided people are diligent and parsimonious, and live according to the rules, then, irrespective of background, race and colour, they have an equal *chance* to share in what society can offer. The socialists regarded the *ought* as the *is*, they claimed that all men are equal, which was visibly not the case. The bourgeoisie only claimed an equality of chances which offered *hope*. The socialists could claim that inequality was an aberration, the product of capitalism, but they could not prove that the abolition of the ruling system would actually lead to equality and affluence. Unable to produce such evidence they gave the impression that all they had to offer was a redistribution of the available – a little more for the poor, less for the not so poor, and much less for the rich. Before the depression this could appeal to the destitute and to the moralists among the intellectuals, but not to the great mass of people with something, even if it was very little, to lose.

Marx had asserted that the level of productive technology – the economic infrastructure of society – determines its cultural, social and legal relationships:

*Eine Gesellschaftsordnung geht nie unter, bevor alle Produktivkräfte entwickelt sind für die sie weit genug ist, und neue höhere*

*Produktionsverhältnisse treten nie an die Stelle, bevor die materiellen Existenzbedingungen derselben im Schoss der alten Gesellschaft ausgebrütet worden sind.*

Germany's social democrats and communists were unable to give to the working class the insight – the class consciousness – that would have been required to effect the 'leap' from capitalism to socialism, because with all the technological advancement that had taken place before the middle of the twentieth century, capitalism had not yet reached maturity – had not attained a level of productivity capable of meeting simultaneously the required resources for more investment and the spreading demand for higher living standards. Marx had regarded the baking of the 'cake' as the historical task of capitalism; the task he foresaw for socialism was its eventual equitable distribution. But capitalism, in spite of appearances, had *not* completed its historical task in pre-World War II Germany. Not until the late 1960s did science and technology in the economically most advanced countries reach the level of efficiency which gave mankind the power to satisfy the material needs of *all* people at a standard of consumption which even the better remunerated would consider adequate. The choice of 'less more' for the rich and more for the poor had not arrived yet. More for one group was still implying less for the other.

The majority of the votes received by communist and social democratic parties between the end of the nineteenth century and the Fascists' rise to power were therefore above all votes of protest. They reflected labour's, and part of the liberal bourgeoisie's, exasperation with poverty and exploitation. They were votes of protest which could switch to any other opposition, and in the Great Depression indeed switched to national socialism.

Unlike the liberal bourgeoisie and the left, Hitler's national socialists – the Nazis – did not have to contend with reality. Instead of a solution they proffered *escapism*. In the place of rationality they offered the mystic of national honour, a desire to avenge the lost war of 1914-1918 and its aftermath; in the place of individualism they proffered unconditional loyalty to their leader. They did not promise to the bewildered German people rational hope for economic welfare, which would be difficult to meet, but a new value system. They offered a myth, popularized by ancient prejudices against socialists, intellectuals, Jews, pacifists, liberals and communists, and propagated a conception of society insensitive to individual deprivation, which perceived the individual meaningless outside the nation. They did not promise to eliminate poverty and destitution but made them acceptable – they aimed, in their own words, 'to take the sting of shame out of poverty.' Their propaganda reduced the complexity of human existence to the most simplistic demagogic propositions: '*cows* may rightly be concerned with food, but men ought to aspire to higher things – Socialists demean mankind making it "think" with their stomachs, but Germans should seek their spiritual salvation by devotion to duty, to their national state, and to its leader.'

In this way national socialism was able to offer something to almost everybody. To the middle class it held up the illusion of deliverance from its fear of being reduced in status, and it gave the opportunity to get rid of Jewish competitors in business and in the professions; to the working class, it provided an escape from confrontation with its depressing economic reality, and a feeling of sharing in the nation's 'great mission'; to the unemployed and destitute, it gave bread and uniforms in the ranks of the Storm Troops, which in their own esteem gave them 'social status'; to the industrialists, the mass support they needed to fend off the dread of social revolutions and the hope for greater work discipline and 'devotion to duty' from their labour force together with a market for military hardware; to the aristocracy (some of whom actually despised Hitler and his pseudo–philosophies but who were ready to support him all the same) it gave the illusion of regaining respect for blue blood and rank.

In one respect Hitler was successful. His parliamentary predecessors had failed to provide employment and he did. The means by which he solved the unemployment problem was simple. He forced labour to accept low wages and skimmed off the savings to finance new employment in armament industries and public works such as the construction of the famous motorways. This hardly increased the workers' welfare but it spread poverty more evenly.

Bertolt Brecht captured this in his *Deutsche Marginalien* (1938).

*Die Arbeiter schreien nach Brot.*
*Die Kaufleute schreien nach Märkten*
*Die Hände, die im Schosse lagen, rühren sich wieder:*
*Sie drehen Granaten.*

The final bill for this 'success' was of course only presented a decade later.

One thing which national socialism had in common with true socialism was that neither could conquer without destroying first the bourgeoisie's social and cultural hegemony. But while genuine socialist movements attacked the bourgeois values on the basis of their own rational and materialistic point of view, giving prime place to welfare and the satisfaction of real wants, national socialism's onslaught on the bourgeoisie was directed against its liberal individualism. Without a meaningful philosophy of its own, and fed only on people's disillusionment with the bourgeoisie's economic system, the Nazi leadership passed off for ideology a formula which could mean anything to anybody. Claiming an affinity for its 'ideology' with the German irrationalist philosophical tradition of the nineteenth century, namely to Schopenhauer and Nietzsche, it not only provided its hotchpotch of ideas with a semblance of respectability but latched on to the sombre pessimistic mood of the depression.

Nineteenth century irrationalism assumed that *life controls reason* – not reason life. This did undoubtedly strike a cord with thousands of people who had planned their future in the 1920s and found their dreams shattered in the 1930s. More than that, nineteenth century irrationalism maintained that a natural (herd) instinct, inherent in race or blood, guides nations to their destinies, and that the pursuit of individual happiness runs contrary to man's true urge for heroism which comes from devotion to duty and from sacrifice. It maintained that *instinct*, not reason, is the great mover of society because life is too deep and complex to be grasped by the common human mind. It may be grasped by intuition – though *not* by divine intuition but by the instinct of the genius. In other words, it proposed that neither the bourgeoisie's weighing of costs and benefits, nor the scientists' patient weighing of facts, nor even divine insight, but the instinctive *will* to act is the true source of genius. It was a philosophy capable of lifting the burden of responsibility for their fate from the millions of people who saw no way out of their predicament; a doctrine that dangled 'action' – 'the deed' – before the eyes of the unemployed; promised status to all who had none; rejected the tenets of the bourgeoisie that had failed them – its utilitarian individualistic rationalism, and offered instead a romanticized revival of a feudal past, as if it were a real alternative to the life of endless hopeless struggle against forces most people could not understand.

To be sure, Schopenhauer (1788-1860) really did consider life an 'endless striving to no purpose' – a struggle of a blind force 'will', and an 'incessant mutual confrontation of conflicting wills never to be satisfied and therefore condemning mankind to eternal suffering'. But he neither despised the bourgeois efforts for improvements, nor its scientists' vain hope to comprehend reality and to press the world into their 'rational laws' of human logic. But Schopenhauer felt compassion for this eternally suffering mankind and thought that in the face of this 'destiny-of-sorrow' all men were equal. Nazism had no use for this. It could not serve its purpose but some of Nietzsche's ideas could. Nietzsche (1844-1900) truly despised the bourgeoisie's much-vaunted culture (*Unzeitgemässe Betrachtungen*) and described a counterculture more suited for the Nazi purpose: a culture founded on the predominance of a 'Superman' – a genius as opposed to common man – who rejects almost all the accepted moral values, including compassion, in a universe moving in a succession of identical cycles (*Also sprach Zarathustra*).

Nietzsche's last great work, 'Will and Power,' *Der Wille zur Macht* (1886), remained unfinished. He suffered a mental breakdown from which he never recovered. In this work the 'natural aristocrat,' the man 'made' by the will to power – the superman – is like Machiavelli's Prince, 'Beyond Good and Evil,' (1886) and destined to destroy decadent democracy. But here too the Nazis needed to ignore that Nietzsche hardly assigned this role to them. He had neither been a nationalist, nor ever showed an excessive admiration for Germany. In fact his 'new vast international aristocracy' was better fitting Jews than Germans. Though he favoured restricting further immigration of Jews into Germany, his writings were never really anti-semitic; he admired the Old and disliked the New Testament. What the Nazis were able to take from him was the spectre of a new paradigm. But what real prospects did it hold for the solution of the German people's pressing problems? It could transform their fear into a lust for power – into an eternal need to subjugate all others to avoid being subjugated themselves. For Hitler this meant a fresh *'Weltanschauung'* which transformed the state from 'a product of economic necessity or of the political urge for power' into the means for the racial division of mankind into more and less valuable individuals and societies. The belief in the equality of nations, according to him, engenders a belief in the equality of persons, which goes against nature's 'aristocratic' foundations, that is against nature's gradation of races and creatures according to their worth. At the top of the scale of individuals stands, of course, the Führer himself; and at the top of the racial pyramid the Germans. Together, the Führer and the German people are called by 'history' to solve the great problems of the world: *'Wir alle ahnen, dass in ferner Zukunft Probleme an den Menschen herantreten können, zu deren Bewältigung nur eine höchste Rasse als Herrenvolk, gestützt auf die Mittel und Möglichkeiten eines ganzen Erdballs, berufen sein wird'.*

As things turned out, the first such great problem that faced the world, and required a global effort to be solved, was Hitler and his dazzled 'Herrenvolk' themselves. Whether Hitler's *'Völkische Weltanschauung'* really contained alternatives to bourgeois utilitarian materialism is doubtful. The Nazis' desire for legitimacy – their appeal to the philosophical tradition of Schopenhauer and Nietzsche – shows their lack of spiritual independence, and how little the proponents of a 'new order' were able and willing to free themselves from their petty bourgeois world. What can be more petty bourgeois respectability than that farce in the besieged bunker in Berlin when Hitler ceremonially marries Eva Braun before they commit suicide? What can be more banal than the fact (and the record of his trial in Jerusalem leaves no doubt about it) that Eichmann, who was responsible for the technical execution of the greatest crime in modern history, was more upset that another bureaucrat of no higher rank than himself was assigned to be his superior than by the heinous crime he was ordered to commit.

Escapism, fear, bureaucratic competition, and cravings for petty bourgeois 'respectability,' and not Schopenhauer or Nietzsche, were the true sources of the 'new order' and the 'great Arian mission'. There was little 'new' in racism or religious persecution. But the magnitude of the millionfold murder and of the other atrocities committed by the Nazi regime were unmatched by earlier generations, and they were perpetrated at a time when liberal and humane values had seemed to be striking firm roots. What Nazism really broke with was the Jewish–Christian heritage and the era of Enlightenment's bourgeois individualistic and rationalistic legacy. But even this it was unable to achieve. With all its efforts to 'dehumanize' Jews and the other 'inferior' peoples, Nazi propaganda never dared to tell the German people the entire truth about their deeds. Even after a decade of massive indoctrination and disorientation of society they feared that most people would rather abhor than approve their loathsome practices. The puzzle how in spite of this the Nazi leadership was able to recruit the men and women who actually operated the extermination campaigns is not difficult to solve. In all countries misfits and psychopaths who are capable of anything can be found. Under normal circumstances they have to follow their urges privately without official sanction. When found out they are committed to prisons or lunatic asylums. The fear of this has a restraining influence, but once their urges are legitimized and given the approval of the state, many who would otherwise have suppressed them feel released from inhibitions. Their crimes, which the regime tried to keep secret, do not provide evidence of what Kuhn may call a shift in the cultural paradigm, but it does show the potential of people with great political power to create an atmosphere in which normal people, even without fear of retribution (though in this specific case fear also played an important role) will condone, or ignore, things that are alien to the values they have learned to respect since childhood. Fortunately the Third Reich did not last long enough to produce a generation which was both in early youth and adulthood subjected to its influences. Had this been the case, it would not be unthinkable that the irrationalism, which to begin with was no more than the reaction to the loss of hope to achieve the material advancement and security people had expected from capitalism and its magnificent scientific and technological successes, might have in time led society back to the barren mysticism of the Middle Ages and the inhumanity of the last days of the Roman Republic.

Altogether, then, the rise of national socialism must be regarded as the result of the successful exploitation of the failure of the bourgeoisie to satisfy the material expectations by a group of political opportunists. Having no real solution for the problems which the bourgeoisie had been unable to solve, national socialism offered a surrogate which evaded the real issues. In spite of the short spurt of nationalistic enthusiasm that accompanied the movement in its victorious years of war, as soon as Germany recovered from the Great Depression and its immediate aftermath, German society reverted to utilitarian materialism. No other country, not even the United States of America, has in the post-war period been more dedicated to the pursuit of wealth, and its citizens more devoted to 'money-making,' than West Germany. Dr Adenauer's *Wirtschaftswunder* provides unequivocal evidence for the perseverance of the bourgeoisie's acquisitive spirit, and his efforts to make restitution to the Jews for the survival of the old values.

While Nazism 'solved' the German unemployment problem by preparing for war and diverting workers' attention from their material reality; and while socialism had no convincing immediate solace to offer to the victims of the depression, a new type of capitalism was beginning to take shape in the United States. This modified capitalism also allocated to the state the task of sponsoring employment, but unlike Nazism it genuinely regarded the revival of the faltering economy as its prime objective and considered neither war, nor the subjecting of labour to politically inspired wage restraint, either practicable or even desirable.

Like their European counterparts many American intellectuals were gradually becoming disenchanted with the dark side of capitalism. In the early part of the twentieth century, American literature was still dominated by the search for eternal values – by the theme of *time and eternity* – but gradually an increasing number of writers became interested in the American here and now. The precursors of this change were men like Walt Whitman, Mark Twain, Henry James, O. Henry, and Jack London. But with Theodore Dreiser (1871-1945) and Upton Sinclair (1878-1968) the description of the 'here and now' became social critique. Dreiser's *Sister Carrie*, the story of a working girl who forms two liaisons as steps to social advancement, was still withheld from circulation (1900) on the grounds of 'immorality'; but Upton Sinclair's *The Jungle*, which he wrote under the impression of an investigation of the Chicago stockyards (1901), became a best-seller and led to some reforms in the Chicago meat-packing industry. Other authors who abandoned 'time and eternity' in favour of a critical description of society without joining the revolutionary stream followed. The foremost among them were Sinclair Lewis (1885-1951) and Ernest Hemingway (1898-1961). In his book *Babbitt* Sinclair Lewis depicted the emptiness and conformism of middle-class life in the United States and its shallow meaningless idealism. Ernest Hemingway portrayed the pleasure-seeking disillusioned generation of post-World War I Americans, and reflected the violence of American life. Significantly, his best known work, *For Whom the Bell Tolls* (1940), was set in Spain among the people who fought Fascism.

In the 1920s American literature gained social consciousness. In spite of what in retrospect seems to have been a decade of economic prosperity, it was for intellectuals a time of disillusionment. The works of Eugene O'Neill (1888-1953) were in the tradition of 'time and eternity' – the relationship of man and God. So were the works of Thomas Wolfe (1900-1938); but William Faulkner (1897-1962) also analysed the perversions of American bourgeois society. In the depression which followed 1929 authors like John Steinbeck, John Dos Passos, James T. Farrell and later the writers of the American proletarian literature circle (men like Erskine Caldwell, Albert Maltz and Richard Wright) produced a wide array of socially critical literature.

The economic crisis shattered the illusion that American society was classless. Frustration, unemployment, poverty and hunger brought writers face to face with class distinction.

> Poverty opened their eyes, but tradition still tied their tongues. As members of society they were forced to acknowledge the reality of class struggle; but as members of the ancient and honorable caste of scribes, many continued to be burdened with antiquated shibboleths about art and society, art and propaganda, art and class [Freeman, 1935; introd].

Like their European brethren a decade earlier, they were able to rouse the conscience of the liberal section of the bourgeoisie but unable to stir the working class to action.

In the 1932 elections the American socialists polled close to a million votes. Their influence went far beyond their numbers, but it was hardly enough to rock the system. It may have contributed to the acceleration of the changes the ruling American establishment was ready to concede but it was not their driving force. American society was more pragmatic than European society and it was less bogged down by traditions and class mythology. While in England John Maynard Keynes tried in vain to convince the government of the folly of the traditional solutions to the unemployment problem, in the United States the greater part of the political establishment was practical. It acknowledged that the old approach did not work and that it was no longer sustainable in the face of an increasingly irate electorate and drew its conclusions. With the 1932 elections approaching, both major parties contesting for the presidency put forward ideas which did at least give the impression to the voters that they would solve their most immediate problems. It would hardly have been a reasonable election platform to offer to the many voters who were experiencing unemployment, wage cuts, and falling living standards, to continue with the old remedies of allowing things to get even worse until, who knows when, the self-regulating mechanism of prices would restore prosperity. Thus, even if only for the purpose of vote-catching, it was unavoidable for politicians in the USA to come up with new ideas about how they would solve the economic problems. Therefore, it was neither socialist agitation nor unionized labour, nor even theoretically convincing arguments, which accomplished the American 'leap' to the new type of regulated capitalism. Democracy, capitalism's own creation in the course of its struggle for ascendancy, made the repudiation of the old economic credos almost unavoidable. Before long the centre of gravity in economics shifted from the business sphere – from micro-economics and the problems connected with the optimal allocation of resources – to the social sphere of macro-economics in search of full employment.

The American president who first identified with this new trend was Franklin Delano Roosevelt (1882-1945). To be sure, even Herbert Hoover, Roosevelt's predecessor, had already made allowances for the new mood, trying tax reductions and state support for agriculture; he appealed to private enterprise to keep up production and called on state governments and municipalities to advance some construction programmes, but it was all to no avail. Yet these efforts prepared the way for the change from the capitalism of *confrontation* to a capitalism of *consensus*. Eventually, it was Roosevelt's slogan 'A New Deal' which caught the imagination of the masses. It signalled the coming of the new approach by which government ceased to be a mere guardian of law and order, a government impartially watching over the nations' economic activities, and turned it into one responsible for people's welfare. For several decades the ballot paper became a powerful instrument in the hands of the American working class for the improvement of its living standard.

The New Deal was ushered in by a host of social and economic legislation. To relieve farmers the *Agricultural Adjustment Act* (1933) re-established parity for farm products by the removal of agricultural surpluses through crop curtailment which was financed by licensing and taxing the processors of farm produce. It was followed by the *Farm Mortgage Refinancing Act* and the *Farm Mortgage Foreclosure Act* (1934) which helped farmers with refinancing their farm debts and to redeem farm properties owned by them before the foreclosure. At the same time the *Frazier-Lemke Farm Bankruptcy Act* and the *Crop Loan Act* made agreements between distressed farmers and creditors possible and granted the former time to remain in possession of their land, permitting the administration to extend loans to farmers for crop production and harvesting.

To relieve home owners the New Deal *Home Owners' Refinancing Act* and the *Home owners' Loan Act* facilitated the refinancing of mortgages and financing of house repairs. To relieve the unemployed and destitute, the New Deal *Federal Emergency Relief Act* (1933) made $500,000,000 available for emergency relief; and the *Civil Works Emergency Relief Act* (1934) and *Emergency Relief Appropriation Act* (1935) made first $950,000,000, and then $4,000,000,000 available to increase employment by the continuation and creation of new, useful work projects. Next to all these a *Social Security Act* (1935) introduced payments to support the aged, needy and disabled, and provided funds for the relief of short-term unemployed. Finally there was also a new *Wealth Tax Act* designed to limit the unfair 'concentration of wealth and economic power.'

How to pay for all this? No problem – by *deficit financing*. As the Depression causes idle funds to accumulate, interest rates are low. The state can borrow cheaply. As those who have the money to lend belong to the higher income brackets some of the interest paid by the state is recovered by the additional tax revenue on it. If the borrowed money is spent on creating new employment, social expenditure to sustain the unemployed is saved, and new income is earned from taxing the newly employed. Next to this their additional spending power also creates new taxable incomes from those who supply the goods and services to meet the new expenditure. Eventually, the economy moves again toward prosperity, the state's revenue increases, and before long interest rates rise once more. When this happens, the initial lenders to the state will gladly redeem their lending certificates and the state's finances will regain an equilibrium.

Roosevelt was re-elected president of the United States on 3 November 1936, with 524 electoral votes against the republican candidate, Landon, who obtained a mere 7 votes. In the following years there were many more social relief acts, and many court decisions declaring them unconstitutional, but step-by-step resistance to the new approach faded. Labour unions continued to press for further improvements. From time to time there was labour unrest, notably the widespread troubles in 1937 which resulted from employers' efforts to prevent the C.I.O. (American Federation of Labour – Congress of Industrial Organizations) from organizing the workers in the automobile and steel industries. The (sit-down) strike which spread from General Motors to the Chrysler Corporation and from there to the Republic Steel Corporation, Youngstown Sheet Steel and Tube Company, Inland Steel, Bethlehem Steel and other large corporations, divided public opinion and even caused bloodshed, but in the end led to the unionisation of the industries and the acceptance of the principle of collective bargaining. The era of 'regulated capitalism' and 'Keynesian economics' had begun.

# 12.  Keynes and Regulated Capitalism

Classical capitalism looked upon labour as a factor of production. Labour is hired when required and dismissed when no longer needed. The consequences of unemployment are sad but unavoidable. Moreover, mass unemployment can never last very long because it is little more than the result of temporary maladjustments in the system which are automatically corrected. As an economy goes into a recession, wages and prices fall and consequently the value of purchasing power of money increases. People who hold money find that they can buy more than they previously could, the demand for goods and services increases and leads to a rise in output and back to full employment.

On the macro level, as Jean-Baptiste Say had shown, supply always creates its own demand. First money needs to be expended on machines, materials and wages, and only later a product materializes which can be sold. Thus the incomes generated in the processes of production provide an aggregate purchasing power which is precisely equal to all costs (including profits) incurred by the creation of the output. Given this identity of the aggregate expenditure incurred in the processes of production with the aggregate purchasing power generated by it, demand can only diminish if some price or prices exceed earnings. But then, competition will adjust prices. The shortfall in demand will drag down profits and investment, which will be followed by a diminution in wages and in the cost of other factors of production, including the price of loanable funds, which is the rate of interest, until full employment equilibrium is restored.

In other words, as no money can be received without somebody handing it over, all income must equal all expenditure; and everything earned – the *national income* – can only either be consumed or not consumed – which means saved. Money spent on everything produced – the *national product* – is equal to everything earned – the *national income*. But the *national product* is also everything produced for consumption and investment; hence, as the mechanism of prices ensures that all that is produced for consumption is consumed, it must follow that *savings* are also always equal to *investment*.

The prices of some factors of production, particularly wages, may be 'sticky' and delay the readjustment, but in the end all must turn out the way it should. In conclusion: the economic system tends towards an equilibrium in which supply is equal to demand at a full employment level of national income.

In other words, conventional wisdom held that the way to recovery from the recession was to wait. Stocks will gradually deplete; nominal wages, interest rates and other costs will fall to their 'natural' level; and eventually depleted stocks, low production costs, and the rising real income resulting from the lower prices will encourage new investment. Then employment will revive and with it demand will also increase, and before long the economy will once more approach the full employment equilibrium. In short, low wages and low interest rates, the 'normal' concomitants of unemployment, will by themselves restore prosperity. Ergo, the best course of action for a government is to do nothing at all except, perhaps, to try to prevent trade unions from keeping wages up, to reduce its own expenditure in order to keep the rate of interest down, and to make investment as attractive as possible by tax concessions and similar measures.

In reality unemployment in Britain reached 10 per cent in 1921 and never fell below this level until the eve of World War II. The Great Depression only made unemployment more severe but the problem had already plagued the country much earlier. However, the economics establishment was unperturbed and held fast to the credo: if the facts do not fit the theory, too bad for the facts! In the USA public works programmes, financed by state borrowing, were considered pragmatically. They became the essence of Roosevelt's policy for the restoration of prosperity. In Britain they became the subject of academic controversy, but did not gain government support until the end of World War II. In 1929 (through the Liberal Party manifesto of Lloyd George) John Maynard Keynes (1883-1946) proposed a public works programme to take 500 000 men off the dole queues. But the Treasury held the view that: 'Whatever might be the political or social advantages, very little additional employment can, in fact, and as a general rule, be created by State borrowing and State expenditure' [Smith, 1987:8]. The Treasury's point of view prevailed.

Seven years later Keynes launched his general assault on the established economic dogma. In his *General Theory*, first published in 1936, he argued that in no sophisticated economic system, in which money is used as a medium of exchange, would wages, prices and interest rates fall far enough and fast enough to restore full employment once a major fall in investment or increase in saving had occurred.

> Ignorance, inertia, bear speculation, human nature itself, would prevent the kind of instantaneous adjustment of wages, prices and interest rates that classical theory assumed; and this inevitable, fatal, delay in adjustment would permit the *Multiplier* to come into play, amplifying the original fall in consumption or investment, and driving the economy into a cumulative decline [Stewart, 1972:138-145].

The concept of the *multiplier* was first introduced into economic theory by R.F. Kahn in an article entitled 'The Relation of Home Investment to Unemployment,' in the June 1931 issue of the *Economic Journal*. The concept set out to show how the general level of the national income will react to changes in investment. It is based on the assumption that the main component of national income, namely consumption, rises or falls as incomes rise or fall. An initial increase in investment causes incomes in the investment goods producing sector of the economy to rise. The recipients of these incomes increase their purchases of consumer goods. The producers from whom they make these purchases therefore also receive increased incomes and in turn they too increase their consumption. In this way the process is spread over a wider and wider range of producers and consumers. But given that most recipients of additional income will tend to save a part of it, there comes a point at which the spread of the additional income will eventually cease. This will be when the original increase in investment has 'leaked' back into savings. For example, if the initial new investment is $100 and each subsequent group of recipients spends 90 per cent of its new income and saves 10 per cent, the total flow of incomes would cease when the initial stock of new income, namely $100, has 'leaked' back into savings. By this time the total flow of incomes would have increased by $100 multiplied by ten, that is by $1000 which is the sum of 100 + 90 + 81.9 + 73.71 + 66.34 + and so on, until the initial stock of $100 leaked back into savings and too little of the 'new' money is left in the flow to make an appreciable difference.

What is true for an increase in investment is of course also true for a reduction. An initial reduction in investment sets in motion a cumulative fall in the level of incomes. Given a similar propensity to divide income between consumption and saving, a cutback of $100 investment would cause the flow of incomes to diminish by $1000. This means that the shortfall in consumers' demand would be much greater than the increase in savings and consequently the fall in interest rates will hardly suffice to raise potential investors' confidence to encourage them to borrow and invest.

The point is that *savers* are not necessarily the same persons as the potential *investors*, and as investment is made in the *expectation* of profit, it is neither the level of wages nor the rate of interest alone which determines investment. It is the expected effective demand for goods which encourages investment and the borrowing to fund it. But *expectations* do not 'fall out of the blue.' On the whole (there are exceptions) they rest upon experience. Investors know the value of the technological coefficient which relates their output to the available equipment. For example, they know that in their branch of production machines costing $1000 are necessary to produce an annual output of 50 units of their product, each worth $10, and this gives them a good idea how much they need to invest to meet a certain volume of demand. It follows that the rate of addition to their investment is closely related to their expected rate of increase in demand. Therefore, if a depression has been lasting for too long, no realistic rate of interest can be low enough to encourage potential investors to borrow for expansion, while a rise in effective demand for goods *is* likely to encourage it.

*Ex post*, the classical or neoclassical economists are of course right. Given the mechanism by which prices adjust supply and demand, the realized or actual level of demand is always tending toward equilibrium, but *ex ante*, the intended level of activity need not coincide with it. Furthermore, a speculative motive for holding *money* makes the classical economists' inherent tendency of the economic system to tend towards full employment equilibrium a possibility but hardly a necessity. According to Keynes, full employment equilibrium is a special rather than a general case. He called his book the *General Theory of Employment, Interest and Money*, 'placing the emphasis on the prefix *general*', because the postulates of the classical theory are applicable to a special case only and not to the general case, the situation which it assumes being a limiting point of the possible positions of equilibrium. Moreover, the characteristics of the special case assumed by the classical theory happen not to be those of economic society in which we actually live, with the result that its teaching is misleading and disastrous if we attempt to apply it to the facts of experience [Keynes:1936:3].

Strong words and clear language, but it hardly prevented his adversaries from insisting that it is his rather than their theory which reflects a special case, namely the particular case of downward inflexibility of wages. They argued that if wages and prices were flexible downwards, then the real balances effect, namely the increase in demand for commodities for consumption as a result of individuals' portfolio adjustments following a change in real money balances, would lead to the restoration of full employment without government intervention. But they were ready to concede that in practice, wages and prices are seldom flexible downward, and that even in recession there is great resistance to a fall in wages or prices. But this was *not* Keynes's argument. He did not say that classical theory is correct so long as wages and prices are flexible; and that since in practice they are not, classical theory is wrong. What he said was that the real balances effect, or Pigou effect, would simply not be of much importance by comparison with all other changes that occur when the economy turns into recession.

In the *General Theory* Keynes discussed the ways in which changes in the prices of goods or financial assets affect the volume of expenditure on consumption or investment. He devoted a good deal of attention not only to the manner in which an individual's consumption could be influenced by changes in his wealth resulting from changes in the price of any government securities he possessed; but also to why a rise in purchasing power due to falling costs and prices can be no more than a minor offset to the contradictory effect of falling incomes, consumption and investment, particularly when account is taken of the multiplier. Unlike the socialists, he had no quarrel with the essential tenet of the capitalist system, namely with the profit motive, but he believed that profit was just as much dependent on high revenues as on low costs. If it was true that the level of the *national income* determined both investment and consumption, then the way to recovery was to raise the *national income*. If then the level of *national income* is determined by the rate of investment and its multiplier, and capitalists can only be expected to invest when they have reason to believe that their investment will yield a profit, i.e. when they believe that there will be a sufficiently large demand for their prospective output, it is plain that only an 'independent actor' – one who is *not* necessarily dependent on the expectation of profit – can offer solace to the situation. Such an 'independent actor' is the state. Therefore the state must not be passive but play an active role in the revival. It must invest (naturally where such investment will not produce a good which will compete with those offered by the private sector) and hope that by way of the multiplier incomes and private expenditure will rise sufficiently to revive the profit expectations of the regular investors. When this happens increased purchasing power will revive profits, and revived profits will stimulate production. Production will raise the demand for labour, and consequently the demand for goods and services.

With this Keynes not only sinned against the sacred principle of *laissez-faire*, but deprived the bourgeoisie of two of its most cherished idols, namely the ideology of low wages and low interest rates, and 'Victorian morality.' He not only denied that wage claims were the core cause of depressions, but proposed to put tax-payers' money into workers' pockets by providing employment with borrowed funds when state revenue is low. To restore employment he expected the Treasury not only to spend current surpluses and reserves, but borrow on account of future incomes. All that was held prime virtue – thrift, thou shalt not spend more than you can afford, and the unrestricted freedom of the market mechanism – was to go by the board. Economics was to be converted from 'the study of wealth' (Adam Smith) and 'the practical science of production and distribution of wealth' (John Stuart Mill), in which in spite of the declared or hidden ideology, man seemed almost to have been created to serve the economy rather than the economy to serve the needs of man, into a discipline in which the welfare of most citizens became the true focus of attention. The state was to be converted from the mere guardian of law and order into an active custodian of all citizens' welfare.

Later there was to be a great deal of clever controversy about the validity of one or the other of Keynes's theorems, but it was this fundamental change in attitude which formed the essence of the *Keynesian revolution*. It provided the study of economics with a new moral content, and finally destroyed the lingering mercantilist conception which divided society into those who are encouraged by the 'love of gain' to perform great deeds and are 'naturally' able to enjoy the better things in life, and the others who can only be stirred into activity by the fear of starvation and enjoy only the much simpler pleasures.

By acknowledging the dependence of profit-seeking investment on consumers' demand, Keynes in effect deprived the bourgeoisie of its self-appointed patronizing social hegemony and restored economics to the social sciences. From a study which had become primarily concerned with techniques for obtaining the optimum allocation of resources in the micro-economic interest of those who control them, he turned economics into a macro-economic science concerned with the welfare of the entire nation. He presented an alternative between the traditional bourgeois hegemony and the Marxist total rejection of a profit-driven economic system; and provided a theory which reflected the technological level of attainment and industrial organization of his time and suited the changing political developments.

Keynes was not alone. There were others who independently arrived at similar conclusions, for example M. Kalecki (1899-1970), J.G.K. Wicksell (1851-1926), and in his own way even L. Walras (1834-1910), but none, including Keynes, were able before the war to sway government policy anywhere in Western Europe. The point is that democratic institutions, at least in Britain, which were well established in Keynes's time, were not sufficient to ensure democracy. Oligarchic 'eternal vigilance' is not enough; there must be widespread and informed public participation to make democracy play its social and economic emancipating role. It is not necessarily 'class consciousness' which is required, but a widespread public awareness of alternatives to the established modes of thought, and absence of inordinate cultural obduracy. In America there was much less social and cultural obduracy than in Europe, and Roosevelt's election campaigns provided his New Deal with the required publicity to make the public aware of the alternative it offered. In Britain social and cultural obduracy was strong, and those in power felt neither the need nor the wish to give publicity to alternatives which in the end would howsoever force them to make concessions. In Germany, Italy and Spain, the bourgeoisie tried to employ Fascism as its remedy against labour's mounting opposition. It almost also destroyed the bourgeoisie itself. 'It is heartbreaking,' wrote Thomas Mann in 1938,

> to see the weakness of the older cultural group in the face of this barbarism; its bewildered, confused retreat. Dazed and abashed, with an embarrassed smile, it abandons one position after another, seeming to

concede that in very truth it no longer understands the world. It stoops
to the foe's mental and moral level, adopts his idiotic terminology,
adjusts itself to its pathetic categories, his stupid, spiteful and capricious
propaganda – and does not even see what it is doing. Perhaps it is
already lost.

The bourgeoisie had attained its position of almost unbridled
power in the second half of the nineteenth century. The Great
Depression forced it to acknowledge its inability to hold on to it.
The war shook Europeans out of their customary way of life and
tore many far away from their habitual surroundings. This put an
end to the pre-war political inertia. The war was fought under the
banner of democracy, and it alerted many to the possibilities
inherent in this system for shaping a new social and economic
order. As the war went on it was becoming increasingly apparent
that once it was over, far-reaching concessions to the working class
would be unavoidable. This was already reflected in the *United
Nations Charter*. Its signatories declared their objectives in the
social and economic sphere to be

> the promotion of a) higher standards of living, full employment, and
> conditions of economic and social progress and development; b) solution
> of international economic, social, health, and related problems, and
> international cultural and educational co-operation; and c) universal
> respect for, and observance of, human rights and fundamental freedoms
> for all without distinction as to race, sex, language, or religion [*UN
> Charter* Ch.IX, Art.55].

These objectives had been agreed upon by Roosevelt and
Churchill during the darkest period of the war several years before
the *Charter* received its formal recognition. In the place of 'the
pursuit of happiness' or 'wealth', came 'freedom from fear, and
freedom from want', in place of 'survival of the fittest' and 'market
forces', came the quest for 'fair labour standards and social
security' [*Atlantic Charter* 14 Aug.1941].

During the war the reformers on the left were gaining prestige,
and even the communists obtained well earned esteem for their
part in defeating Fascist barbarism. In July 1945 Labour won the
general elections in Britain and set in motion an ambitious

socialization programme with the ultimate objective of making the country a socialist state. Parliament repealed the *Trade Dispute Act* of 1927 which had restricted the trade unions' freedom of action. It consolidated national insurance legislation and introduced free national health services (1946). Transport (1948), gas and electricity (1949), and iron and steel (1951) were nationalized. In France in the October 1945 elections for the Constituent Assembly (with women voting for the first time in this country) there was a strong shift to the left. The communists obtained 152 seats, the socialists 151, and the *Mouvement Républicain Populaire* only 138. In 1946 the elections to the Constituent Assembly in Italy showed a similar trend. The Christian democrats still topped the list of the Assembly members (207), but the socialists and communists (115 and 104 respectively) together received a greater number of votes. In 1946 in Germany the first local elections (in the Western occupation zones) returned the Christian democrats as the largest party, but the combined list of social democrats and communists (S.E.D.) received a clear majority. In 1949 the Federal Republic of Germany adopted a new *Basic Law* which did not essentially differ much from the *Weimar Constitution*, and East Germany came increasingly under communist rule. In Belgium the Catholic Christian socialists received the largest number of votes in 1946 and 1949. In the Netherlands the Catholic People's Party, closely followed by socialist Labour, won the 1946 elections. In 1948 the government lost some votes. In the new coalition Dr Beel was replaced as Prime Minister by the Labour leader Drees. In Denmark Vilhelm Buhl, a social democrat, formed in 1945 the first post-war Cabinet. In three subsequent elections (1945, 1947, 1950) the socialists emerged as the strongest party. In Norway, Eivar Gerhardsen, the leader of the Labour Party, formed the first post-war coalition government. Labour received a majority of the votes in the elections of 1945, and increased its majority in 1949. In Sweden Per A. Hansson replaced the coalition government, which had ruled the country till July 1945, by a social democratic cabinet. Again in 1948 the electorate gave the greatest number of votes to the social democrats. Industrialized Western Europe had taken a step to the left, but the old conflict between labour and capital was temporarily pushed into the background while both left and centre shared in the efforts for Europe's reconstruction. For a time the working class had won moral hegemony and took the lead in the reshaping of post-war Europe. The discordant sounds from the extreme left were as yet little more than a rumble, the far away sound of the rising storm of the future struggle for political hegemony between the USA and the USSR. The working class had ceased to be the servant and became a partner in the economic process.

Once the principle of full employment was established as a political objective the objections to Keynes's call for state intervention in the economic system were simply no longer sustainable. But there was more to the Keynesian revolution than its practicability. It was part of a much wider revolution, which was transforming man's entire conception of the universe and his place in it.

For centuries man's dominion over nature had spontaneously increased. By trial and error he had learned to solve concrete problems. Wanting in strength he learned to employ wind and water and domesticated animals to do his work. Finding the generosity of nature inadequate to feed a growing population he learned farming. Chancing upon suitable iron ores and coal he learned to control the low but vital carbon content required to obtain steel by the unreliable method of halting the blast in the furnace at precisely the necessary moment. All these improvements were not the result of new fundamental insights but the product of isolated innovations which were directly related to some work at hand. The dramatic change which since the last quarter of the nineteenth century transformed technology was that spontaneity yielded to the organized effort of modern science. It was the result of the establishment of a body of systematic principles, *theories*, which were not limited by man's direct practical requirements. The theories gave man a model of nature, a reflection of order and regularity, which, until undone by contrary observations, could form the basis for the formulation of fundamental laws of wide applicability. Man could formulate a law of gravity which enabled him to construct a rocket capable of overcoming the attraction of the earth; he could formulate a kinetic theory which gave him an understanding of matter which made possible splitting the atom to gain control over incomparably more potent and less spatially restricted sources of energy than wind, water and animal power. Genetical, biological and biochemical theories gave him an understanding of life which enabled him to interfere with natural growth mechanisms in order to obtain predictable results and to reap not only more but better and greater varieties of crops than ever before. Theories about the composition of substances and of their effects upon each other, chemistry, taught man to synthesize and form materials more suitable for his purposes than those nature had provided. He could obtain high-quality steel without resorting to the old uncertain method, simply by burning out all carbon from iron and restoring precisely the amount required. In short, by forming a picture of a mechanism which could be responsible for the observed phenomena (though he could never be sure if it is the only picture which can explain the observations) man obtained powers to dominate rather than be dominated by the natural environment, even to 'recreate' nature to suit his will. This is the context in which the Keynesian revolution must be seen.

Before Keynes economics, like the other sciences, had developed in the shadow of a search for a single mechanism. Newton's gravitation was Smith's 'invisible hand'. For Newton *time* and *space* were *absolute* and alike to all observers. His science was a sequence of before and after, of causes and effects. This was no longer true for Einstein. For him reality lost this sequence. Time and space were related and part of a single reality in which the structure of space was inseparable from the matter embedded in it and time depended on its measuring clocks. Max Planck demonstrated that at least for very small events a strict universal sequence of causes and effects does not apply. Heisenberg added a proof that at least in the fundamental sub-atomic world there can *never* be absolute certainty and that any description of nature must contain a degree of uncertainty; and van Neumann showed that even the limited objective of stating the results of alternative choices of action can only provide *probable* and not definite answers. One knows that half a lump of plutonium will have undergone radio active decay in 25.000 years, but not which half. Nor can one say of any grain whether it will decay or survive [Bronowski, 1951:80-9]. Followers of Einstein, Planck, Heisenberg and von Neumann abandoned the search for a *universal* mechanism of cause and effect and put in its place a more limited purpose, namely the description of the world in an orderly scheme capable of helping man to predict the probable outcome of a choice of actions.

For the classicists the capitalist economic system was 'given.' Man could do little more than to adjust to it. Smith believed in the economic system's eternal striving toward equilibrium. For Newton reality was a continuum held in balance by gravity; for Smith the economy was a continuum held together by the movement of prices. Both Newton and Smith believed in a separation of a fact from its observer. Their approach left man at the mercy of forces outside himself. For Marx it was a social artifact which by an inner logic, and by growth of consciousness, transforms itself into another system. Keynes's approach made man part of these forces. For him the system was a positive fact, but one which can be moulded to suit man's requirements. Apples fall down, not up, but the study of the rate of acceleration of their fall allows man to devise a rocket which enables him to reach the moon by exceeding this rate. Setting a man on the moon does not invalidate the law of gravity but indicates that gravity need not prevent mankind from reaching for the stars. Keynes's proposed intervention in the economic system did not deny the validity of its laws, but indicated that they can be employed to serve humanity. He confined economics to the limited purpose of describing the world in a manner which should enable man to look ahead – to forecast how the system would react to several courses of action between which he is free to choose.

Both approaches in science described nature for the purpose of explaining it, and for taking the explanation as a guide for human action. But modern science is at once more modest and more ambitious. It gave up the pretention to have found laws for all eternity, but it describes nature to imitate or 'reproduce' it. The order the new scientific approach imposes on nature is dictated by convenience – by the wish to predict and control. Experience remained the basis of scientific laws. But the realization that experience can never yield absolute certainty was strengthened. The old realization that all we know is that a course of action taken several times in the past yielded similar results; or that a given course of action (for example Mendel's experiment) has yielded a result which can be defined in a precise value indicating the probability of, or the odds for, its recurrence was supplemented by the realization that by interfering in these predictions probabilities may change in a irreversible way, thus creating new causal laws.

In the Middle Ages, when man had little chance of influencing his fate by his own effort, he believed in predestination. With the rise of the bourgeoisie, when man, at least some men, discovered a world and a society in motion, people believed in a mechanism of sequences – of causes and effects. But when man learned to synthesize, to mimic the work of nature, he substituted his own will for the will of God, and he recognized that all living is action, and human living thoughtful action. However, the characteristic of human action is that it is a choice at each step between what are conceived to be several alternative courses.

Heisenberg in his later years emphasized the role played by the intuition of those trying to interpret phenomena in the forming of new scientific concepts. He did not think that the philosophical background influences the scientist's answers but that it does determine his *questions*. 'The results of scientific work can be quite different if you either try to find out the plan according to which nature is constructed, or you just want to observe, to describe and to predict the phenomena. But the final understanding can depend on this decision' [Heisenberg, 1975]. Mediaeval man was interested in theology, his philosophy was neo-Platonic. Much later arose the interest in the empirical side of natural science. In the era of scholasticism, Aristotle became the undisputed authority. But in the Renaissance Plato's ideas were rediscovered and the search for the underlying plan for all natural phenomena began again. After Copernicus and Galileo the Platonic tendency to look for a plan underlying the natural phenomena was gradually once more supplemented by pragmatism,

> the wish to make use of the scientific knowledge for practical purpose, or quite generally for the benefit of mankind. So the practical applications of science played an ever increasing role in the historical development. The steam engine was invented before the laws of heat were understood, and electrical engineering was earlier than Maxwell's equations. The practical applications offered in fact a solid basis for a thorough knowledge of the phenomena, and therefore they helped eventually in looking for the mathematical forms adapted to the observations and for the concepts which led to a real understanding. In so far the two tendencies did not get into conflict. But the weights were changed. Science became important because it was *useful*; not because it enabled us to read God's second book, Nature [Heisenberg, 1975].

The nineteenth century did not really understand heat and electricity; the new 'non-Newtonian' concepts were not easily received.

> The final change was brought about by the theory of relativity... Again it had turned out that behind the infinite variety of phenomena there was a unifying principle of form, in this case a simple mathematical group, just as Pythagoras and Plato had hoped in the old times ...
>
> The convincing power of the new theory rested entirely on its fundamental simplicity. Like the heliocentric system of Aristarchus and Copernicus the theory of special relativity connected many complicated phenomena in a surprisingly simple way. Many physicists could co-operate in testing the predictions and in analysing various observations on the basis of the new ideas; the success confirmed their validity [Heisenberg, 1975].

But the real conceptual change was only produced by quantum theory.

What was the philosophical background of all this? In the literature it has frequently been suggested that positivism played an essential role in the invention of relativity and quantum mechanics. The heuristic value of Mach's positivism cannot be doubted, but it was hardly generally accepted and did not constitute the common philosophical background. Very few understood the price which has to be paid for actually taking it as the basis for physics. According to Heisenberg 'the true basis for the quantum theory remains the conviction that behind the infinite variety of phenomena there is a simple unifying principle of form' a principle that cannot be invented, only discovered [Heisenberg, 1975].

One reason for the long lasting reign of the modern vision of Democritean materialism, which Heisenberg failed to see or mention, is that it so admirably reflected the character and ideological needs of the bourgeoisie. What better description can there be of utilitarian individualism than that of tiny particles in constant motion held together by a Newtonian system of some kind of self-centred gravitation? Only the gradually growing recognition that self-interest alone cannot assure the future of society provided the mental climate for the abandonment of the long scientifically disproved nineteenth century creeds. Only when it became evident to all that organized collective action of bodies such as governments, unions, or action groups, is necessary to counter the new collective hazards which simply cannot be met by an individually powered mechanism of self-interest (long-term mass unemployment, and later water and air pollution and nuclear disasters, may serve as good examples), did the new approach in science really vanquish. People originate or adopt theories which reflect their life experience; when their conception of their everyday reality is changing their theories adapt. When society began to understand that in its totality it may not be best served by the freedom of each individual to pursue his narrowly defined self-interest, scientists too recognized a field theory, one which once again suggested that behind the infinite variety of phenomena there is a very simple unifying principle of form, though it differed from the Platonic and mediaeval principle because it no longer accepted the 'real' existence of indestructible particles. Similarly it was only when the Great Depression drove home the fact that free enterprise is not the only possible system within which all economic and social laws have to be sought, that the economics profession became ready to accept the Keynesian theory.

Man is aware that the present is not like the future, but he also knows that it is not entirely unlike it. He understands that the present provides a set of signals which hold a meaning for the future, and he hopes that as more and more signals reach him with the passage of time he can interpret these signals in an ongoing process of correction. But it is an activity which must involve the whole society, not a single observer or actor – it is a process of collective adaptation. This process is not guided by expediency but by truth, which in this context means what man can act upon with confidence. In this sense the search for *truth* may be taken as a constant social value.

If all conscious action is forward looking and implies choice, and choice depends on the degree of confidence one has in the expected outcome of one's chosen course of action, then confidence remains the closest thing to (unobtainable) certainty, and the search for truth must be a need which is independent of place and time. It becomes an eternal social value – something 'good' in itself. The foregoing excursion into the history of science reveals two tendencies in our search for an understanding of the world. One stresses the unity of nature and the other its diversity; one emphasizes the abstract thought which goes beyond the notions obtained by the senses, and the other the results of reality as they present themselves and materialize to our senses. Marx illustrated this difference in the social sphere by contrasting the abstract with the concrete relations in the realm of capitalist production. On a concrete level the relationship between a capitalist employer and his employee may be excellent, they may be friends and belong to the same sports club, but on the abstract level, which Marx calls the objective level, the relationship remains of exploiter and exploited. The concrete relationship reflects a transient and particular situation, the abstract a lasting and collective affinity. The one is akin to atoms in a stream of gas that move each in its own direction, or to persons pursuing their individual aims in the current of history; the other is more similar to the stream which determines the direction and the limits within which each atom can move, or the degree of freedom an individual is allowed within the current of time.

In the nineteenth century a Democritean approach had the upper hand in the natural sciences. It coincided with a fragmented social reality – each individual finding his place according to his competitive ability. Gradually more social needs came to light which were not met by individuals' pursuit of their immediate interests. Step by step society was increasingly becoming aware that the welfare of all required the provision of some services which are not automatically met by the mechanism which was supposedly harmonizing private 'vices' with the 'public good'. One by one provisions were made to correct the system where individualistic self-interest failed. These 'corrections' ranged from education and health, which Adam Smith had already recognized, to state intervention in order to promote growth, stability and equity, which Keynes was eventually to insist upon. But only when the necessary corrections became so numerous and overwhelming that they were penetrating almost all spheres of life, did man begin to question the underlying truth of his earlier conceptions. It was then that society began to ask whether it was really valid or useful to assume that an 'invisible hand' leads individuals' pursuit of their own interests willy-nilly to the attainment of the greatest possible good for most people.

# 13.  The Age of Prosperity

To say that in order to serve its citizens the state must *regulate* the economy is one thing; to say *how* and *when* it must do so is another. If it is true that investment by way of the *multiplier* determines the level of national income and savings, and that the resultant rise or fall in income influences the rate of investment, then the stability of economic growth with full employment hinges upon a stable rise in consumers' demand. This implies that the share of the national income which goes to consumption must constantly be kept precisely sufficient to induce savers to turn their savings into productive investment. The state must regulate the volume of consumers' demand by the instruments at its disposal: it must stimulate spending when there is a tendency to unemployment and restrain spending when there is a tendency toward inflation. The instruments the government is able to employ for this purpose can be fiscal and monetary. It can influence the volume of private expenditure by varying the level of taxes and subsidies and relaxing or tightening consumer credit controls, and by raising or reducing the volume of social security disbursements. Similarly, by taxation and subsidies the government can influence the propensity to invest, and it can directly increase or decrease investment by extending or diminishing its own current and capital expenditure. Sometimes these measures may cause government revenue deficits and other times surpluses, but in the long run this does not really matter. In addition, or alternatively, the state may use its control over the money supply to influence investment and consumption. It may cause money to be tight or readily available and thereby raise or reduce interest rates, or

186

produce a change in the demand for commodities as a result of changes in the value of money holdings when they are measured in terms of the quantity of goods and services they command. In any given situation the choice of instruments to effectuate this 'fine tuning' will depend on their efficacy, and on the aims or priorities the government has set itself. All this seems fairly straightforward as long as power factors and economic growth are left out of the picture, and questions about the timing and the measure of state intervention are ignored.

In the late 1940s and in the 1950s the problem of maintaining the balance between investment and consumption to ensure full employment was mainly discussed in the shadow of the Hansen–Samuelson model. In his article in *Review of Economic Statistics* [Samuelson, 1939:75-8] Samuelson suggested that the level of income depends upon the level of investment (the multiplier); and that the level of aggregate net investment depends on the expected change in output which is indicated to prospective investors by the previous rate of change in income (the acceleration principle). The idea behind this is that entrepreneurs are believed to wish to maintain a fixed ratio of capital stock to meet the expected demand for their output. The directors of firms know how much capital they require to produce a certain volume of their produce. They expect that the trend in demand they experienced in the previous year will continue, and their investment decisions are determined by this. But through the multiplier their investment decisions become 'self-fulfilling prophecies.' All the government needs to do is to see to it that income in each period is a constant multiple of income in the previous period.[1]

The first conclusion from the interaction of the multiplier and the acceleration principle is therefore that it need neither lead to any stable equilibrium for income, nor to cyclical fluctuations. 'Instead, it leads to a cumulative movement, which could be either upward or downward, away from a notional point of unstable equilibrium' [Matthews, 1959:16]. But there are 'time-lags' which subject the cumulative movement to a regulating mechanism which works with some delay and may therefore require a degree of intervention to prevent a change of direction. Beside this there are also the 'buffers' (such as full capacity employment at one end and depreciation replacement at the other) which limit the cumulative process in the upward or downward direction.

This suggests that as long as a government 'fine tunes' the rate of growth in demand in line with the rate of growth of the labour force and the rise in productivity, the economy will grow at a fairly stable pace. But for this the trend of labour force accretion and of technological progress would have to be known. Without this information the government can hardly determine the desired rate of demand or investment which is consistent with stability and full employment; nor can it determine when or how strongly it must intervene. Premature intervention would stifle the growth of welfare, tardy intervention would precipitate inflation.

The first who addressed themselves to these dynamic problems of what may be called the Keynesian approach were R.F. Harrod [1939:14-33] and E.D.Domar [1946:137-47; 1947:34-55]. They examined whether steady-state growth with full employment was possible and probable, and if so, whether the warranted rate of growth could be stable. By differentiating between a *natural* and a *warranted* rate of growth, they showed that when the labour force is increasing and technology is progressing, and savings are a constant proportion of real income, the warranted rate of growth would be the ratio of savings to the capital–output ratio. But in reality neither the propensity to save, nor the supply of labour, and least of all technological progress can be made to follow a knife-edge path.

For the long run all this implies that stable economic growth at full employment requires prices to fall exactly in line with cost-reducing innovation, so that both savings and consumption grow in proportions which precisely match demand to supply. Putting it differently, long-term growth requires that the ratio of the increase in consumption to the increase in saving will be equal to the ratio of increasing output to investment.

In his *Studies in the Theory of Business Cycles 1933-1939* (1966) M. Kalecki shows that if national income is divided into profits received by capitalists and wages received by workers; or into investment and consumption by both capitalists and workers (and workers are assumed to spend their entire earnings on consumption), then the income of capitalists (profit) is equal to the value of the goods purchased by capitalists for consumption and investment. This means 'that the capitalists can increase the share of national income they receive as profits simply by increasing the amount they spend on investment, with the higher level of investment leading, of course, to an increase in aggregate output based on the multiplier;' and that 'even if the capitalists consume their profits in "high living" rather than investing, they do not suffer a reduction in their profit income' [Kregel, 1979:52]. In other words, capitalists' income is maintained independently of how they spend it.

This conclusion, that capitalists' consumption increases rather than diminishes their profits, may seem a contradiction because we are used to think that the more we consume the less we save. This is true, but only for a single capitalist, and not for capitalists as a class.

> If some capitalists spend money, either on investment or consumer goods, their money passes to other capitalists in the form of profits. Investment or consumption of some capitalists creates profits for others. Capitalists as a class gain exactly as much as they invest or consume, and if – in a closed system – they cease to construct and consume they could not make any money at all. Thus capitalists, as a whole, determine their own profits by the extent of their investment and personal consumption. In a way they are 'masters of their fate'; but how they 'master' it is determined by objective factors,... Capitalists' consumption is a function of gross accumulation. The gross accumulation which is equal to the production of investment goods is determined by investment orders which in turn were undertaken in a past period on the basis of the profitability in that period, i.e. on the basis of gross accumulation and the volume of capital equipment in that period [Kalecki, 1971:12-13].

It is probably less confusing to avoid the sociological distinction between capitalists and workers and employ the economic distinction between *income from property* and *income from work*, because workers and capitalists can receive part of their income as a remuneration for work and part as rent, interest or dividends. To some extent capitalists can therefore be regarded as workers and workers as 'capitalists.' What matters is that capital accumulates and becomes a self-expanding source of property and consumption does not. For example, let it be assumed that there are only two kinds of produce, *investment goods* and *consumer goods*, and only one capitalist producing both. Suppose further that one-third of the labour force is engaged in the production of investment goods and two-thirds in the production of consumer goods. Together all workers earn a national income. However, the volume of the produced consumer goods is only equivalent to the output of the two-thirds of the labour force engaged in its production, but the entire labour force must purchase the consumer goods it needs. It follows that the entire national income is spent on the produce of only two-thirds of the labour force, and by hypothesis, it returns is its totality to the one capitalist. In other words, while the produce of the remaining third of the labour force (the real capital) remains his property from the start; in the end he is left with investment goods valued at the output of one-third of the labour force (less the depreciation of old equipment) plus the income earned by all workers which they spent to obtain his consumer goods. In this way investment in real capital adds to wealth but at the same time reduces the volume of goods available for consumption. The more the capitalist invests in real capital formation the more his wealth grows, but the smaller becomes the output for which consumers must vie to satisfy their needs. The greater the share of investment in real capital, the higher will be the prices of consumer goods, and the less workers will be able to consume. In conclusion, the capitalist's income from the sale of consumer goods remains the same whether he does or does not increase his own consumption.

There is, however, a mitigating factor in this process because investment in real capital tends to raise productivity. The reduced labour force engaged in the sector producing-consumer goods, and the greater employment in the capital-producing sector, is usually made good, and is often over-compensated, by the increasing output generated by the higher productivity engendered by the new capital formation. Consequently, productivity is the key to stable economic growth; and therefore growth with full employment requires a judicious distribution of the fruits of productivity between the share going to consumption and the share consigned to further capital accumulation. If too large a share of the fruits of increasing productivity is going to consumers it will cause inflation; if too large a share is going to savers, it will cause a shortfall in consumers' effective demand, to idle production capacity and less investment, and even with favourable interest rates, to unemployment. In other words, *regulated capitalism* requires a distribution of the national income between consumption and investment so that taking account of population accretion and technological advancement, demand neither exceeds output nor rises insufficiently to induce savers to turn their savings into investment. This means that *regulated capitalism* requires that the warranted rate of growth of national income, the rate of growth which can maintain equality of planned saving with planned investment through time, is known. But without knowing the long-term trend of growth it is not possible to determine *when* and in what *measure* the state must intervene. A premature intervention would cause growth to be less than optimal; late intervention would subject the economic system to inflation or recession. Alas, the long-term trend is elusive and beset by distortions of perspective [Reijnders, 1990:120-48]. What can be done by the state, and was done in the post-war era of Keynesian economics, is to watch key indicators such as employment and prices and react once prices show a tendency to rise or unemployment to increase. This cannot eliminate the economic fluctuations but can, and for a time did, substantially reduce them.

Already Marx had recognized that *competition* is the progressive element in capitalism. In his own words, competition compelled the bourgeoisie to create 'more massive and more colossal productive forces than have all the preceding generations together' [Marx, 1848:5]. His emphasis was mainly on one type of competition, namely between employers for their market shares. But since the time he wrote these words, this type of competition has gradually been eroding through the growth of monopolies, monopsonies and oligopolies, while another type of competition was slowly filling the gap. This was, and continues to be, the competition between capitalists and organized labour. Since Marx's days labour's ability to organize to protect and raise workers' purchasing power has increased. The combination of both types of competition, the persisting *competition between the capitalists themselves*, which continues to force many of them to pass on in lower prices the gains from cost-reducing innovation, and the 'new' type of *competition between capital and labour*, which forces employers to share with labour, through wage improvements, the gains from innovation when monopolistic practices prevent prices from falling in line with cost reductions, made the growth process more complex but did not change the nature of its driving force. Whether driven by the one type of competition or by the other the growth mechanism remains intact because it makes little difference if it is the fear of being forced out of business by more efficient producers or if mounting wage claims oblige capitalists to innovate in order to maintain the necessary profit for financing the application of new technologies. The one kind of competition as much as the other imposes upon entrepreneurs the inexorable need to make technological and organizational improvements.

In theory this dual mechanism of competition also assures that actual economic growth cannot for long be far removed from the warranted rate of growth. Labour can hardly obtain a larger share of the fruits of production than capitalists can pay without going into liquidation; and capitalists will not invest unless consumers' share suffices to clear markets at prices which allow a reasonable margin of profit. In other words neither excessive wages nor excessive profits can last for very long; the former will be corrected by inflation and loss in business confidence and the latter by a shortfall in effective demand, followed by falling prices and diminished profits. It may therefore be said that while the system is inherently unstable it fluctuates around a rising trend which though not optimal is still close to society's technological growth capacity. When demand and supply fall out of line and a recession causes prices to fall, the real value of monetary wealth increases. The holders of such wealth are tempted to reduce their increasing real money balances by spending the excess money. This in turn raises aggregate demand and restores the economy to full employment. The price of economic growth inspired by competition is therefore instability. The free market system is self-correcting but at the cost of recurrent bouts of unemployment and business failures. The equitable distribution of its growing wealth is also 'automatic'. Competition between employers forces them to reduce the prices of their produce more or less in line with the rate of productivity improvements; and when monopolistic influences obstruct this process, then labour's ability to raise wages corrects this anomaly.

Sometimes in the past this distributive mechanism was bypassed through exports making good the deficiencies in domestic demand. During the era of colonial expansion British industry amassed capital by selling abroad while wages in England remained too low to clear the domestic market [Brenner, 1969:196-212]. Similarly, in the 1930s, Japanese corporations were growing by exporting goods they could hardly hope to sell domestically as wages lagged behind the rising productivity [Brenner, 1969:229-37]. But in the absence of extensive export markets, even neoclassical economists do not deny that although theoretically the *wealth effect* seems powerful enough to restore effective demand, and in its wake investment and prosperity, its empirical validity is weak.

All this implies that long-run economic progress can only be assured by an effective combination of both types of 'competition'. There must be *competition between entrepreneurs* to force them to adjust prices downward when rising productivity engenders cost reductions so that effective demand suffices to sustain employment in line with economic growth; and there must be *competition between capital and labour* so that when price competition between entrepreneurs flags, and cost reductions are not sufficiently passed on to raise demand in line with productivity, trade unions restore the balance by making larger wage claims. But when neither price competition nor wage-hikes re-establish the necessary distribution between savings and consumption, the state alone can fill the gap by skimming off excessive savings by taxation and restoring the purchasing power to consumers by regulated spending. This, however, needs to be done judiciously and without detracting too much from the 'self-correcting' powers of the *wealth effect*, because changes in the amounts of money based on private debt held in the private sector (inside money) and bank holdings based on bank holdings of the public sector debt (outside money) have different *wealth effects* which influence the money stock. The point is that a fall in the real value of inside money due to higher prices leaves the net value of wealth in the private sector unchanged, but a change in the value of outside money diminishes the private sector's net real wealth while the balancing change in the public sector's real wealth remains unaffected.

Since the early phases of the industrial revolution, improved farming techniques decreased employment in agriculture and reduced food prices. The lower food prices left consumers with more money to spend on industrial goods and increased employment in industry. In turn, rising labour productivity in industry decreased the need for labour in this sector of the economy but reduced the prices of industrial products which left people with more money to spend on services and thereby created new employment for the redundant industrial labour force. In this way, by passing on the advantages of greater productivity to consumers by lower prices or higher wages, capitalism ensured its phenomenal success.

In 1800 primary goods production (mainly agriculture) contributed more than 75 per cent to the national product of the United States. In 1920 its share had fallen to about 20 per cent, and in 1960 to less than 5 per cent. But during the same period the share of the secondary sector (mainly industry) increased from about 10 per cent in 1800, to 30 per cent in 1920, and fell back to only 20 per cent in 1960. The tertiary sector (trade, utilities, schools etc.) contributed about 15 per cent to the national product of the United States in 1800, just under 50 per cent in 1920, but its contribution rose to about 75 per cent in 1960. The share of the working population engaged in the service sector in the United States was 55 per cent in 1948 and 67 per cent in 1974. In France it was 20 per cent in 1950 and 44 per cent in 1970; and in West Germany 28 per cent in 1950 and 42 per cent in 1968 [Dettling, 1977:66].

To be sure, the road to capitalism's success was bumpy, the 'two-pronged mechanism' of competition hardly ever ran smoothly and every time it staggered it caused widespread human misery, economic reversal or stagnation. But for a quarter of a century government intervention – the post-war 'Keynesian compromise' – successfully reduced the 'staggering' and markedly diminished its disgraceful social consequences.

In fact the Keynesian compromise between free enterprise and regulation did much more than this. Within two decades it transformed state intervention from a tool for reducing mass unemployment into a purposefully employed instrument to promote the public's welfare. From a kind of 'fire brigade' coming to the system's aid when it required to be saved, government intervention became a device for attaining well defined social objectives. A new perception of *democracy* and the increasing *complexity of industrial society* were the driving forces behind this transformation.

Post-war democracy had a much broader grass-roots base than pre-war parliamentary government. In most industrialized countries it made people conscious of the power of the ballot paper in the struggle for higher living standards and greater social security. More than this, it acknowledged that social and economic objectives are legitimate concerns of the state.

The increasing interdependent complexity of industrial production created more and more collective needs which went beyond what private enterprise could meet. The new technology required an infrastructure which private enterprise, powered by the mechanism of competition, could not provide. It necessitated highly developed transport, communication and education systems, and a measure of coordination and foresight which broke the direct links with individual firms' cost–benefit accounting. Adam Smith, not to mention John Stuart Mill, had been aware of the limitations of the market mechanism in matters like education and national defence, but they could hardly have imagined how many more allocation problems were still in store for industrial society which can neither be settled individually nor determined by the market.

Thus, while the economics profession was squabbling about whether the Keynesian theory was *general* or only a *special case* (such as when wages are insufficiently flexible in a downward direction), or trying to integrate Keynes into the old paradigm (for example, by means of the IS–LM model and similar constructions, where IS is the curve of the schedule detailing interest rates and levels of national income and the LM curve the contribution of investment rates and levels of national income which ensure equalization in the money market), the general public gave its own meaning to Keynesian economics. If government can intervene to revive employment in depressions it should also be able to intervene to attain other objectives. In the eyes of the general public Keynesian economics had not only shattered the trust in the self-correcting powers of the market system but the belief in the inevitability of the system's consequences. Earlier generations had acquiesced in the thought that 'the rich do not in reality possess the power of finding employment and maintenance for the poor,' and therefore that the poor 'cannot possess the right to demand them' [Malthus, 1789:260]. Rightly or wrongly the post-war generation had a different idea. It was convinced that within limits the state *can* mould the system to its wants. Next to full employment new claims were made for public health care, general and free education, pensions for the aged, free or heavily subsidized milk and orange juice for infants and so on, which together became in some countries the foundations of a new type of state-regulated economic system, namely the 'welfare state'.

With the new mood came the politicians who espoused the new demands. Whether out of ideological and humanitarian convictions, or simply to ensure their election or re-election, they actually realized many of the popular demands. But this implied a redistribution of the national income by increasingly progressive and heavier taxation. Consequently within three decades the share of government in national expenditure and employment surpassed the share of private enterprise. The rich did not like it, but as long as most people consciously used their ballot papers to further their own interests, opposition was subdued. In the 1970s, when public consciousness eroded and meaningful democracy was loosing its vitality, the rich grasped their opportunity for the 'return match'. Armed with the Laffer-curve, supply-side theories, and monetarism, they contested the Keynesian compromise with a vengeance.

Under any economic system the limits of what can be realized are strictly circumscribed by the country's level of productivity. Available resources and the current levels of technology set the frontiers to the possible. But within these limits society is free to choose priorities. To be sure, this is a very different perception of the economy than the earlier conception which regarded the system as a kind of natural phenomenon imposing its inevitable 'natural laws' which determine the fortunes of societies. Still the limits exist even when the state is free to intervene and this proved to be the new democracy's Achilles heel. Politicians want to be elected and court the voters' favour. They make pre-election promises, or pursue eve-of-election economic policies, which often overstep the limits. Sometimes when they are in government they also take opportunistic measures contrary to the long-run requirements of stable full-employment growth to put the public into a favourable mood. Time after time governments in the 'Keynesian era' created artificial pre-election booms when restraint would in the long-run have served their country better [Reijnders, 1988:132-52]. This, but not this alone, led to a constant rise in prices and wages – to 'demand-pull' or 'cost-push' inflation. To avoid this no government felt powerful enough; none had the strength to implement and sustain an incomes policy consistent with the share distribution of the gains from productivity improvements which would have been necessary for long-run growth without inflation. No government was able to convince labour for long to keep its wages down in line with productivity, or to persuade capital to desist from marking up prices excessively whenever the opportunity to do so arose [Brenner, 1983:94-115]. In fact even governments seldom kept their own expenditure in line although the reasons for this were frequently exogenous, motivated by political considerations. The Cold War and its less 'cold' manifestations, such as the hostilities in Korea and Viet-Nam, may serve as examples for such exogenous economically unwarranted government expenditures. The result was that government policies to influence levels of employment, national income, wages and prices by small changes in taxation or expenditures failed to contain inflation, although on the whole this fine tuning of the economic system successfully moderated fluctuations in national income and employment.

All in all the period between the end of World War II and the early 1970s – the era of Keynesian – regulated capitalism – witnessed a dramatic rise in productivity accompanied by an equally impressive rise in general living standards. Employment in agriculture continued to dwindle and employment in industry first rose and then fell while the demand for labour in the service occupations was markedly increasing. The share of the public and the 'not-for-profit' sector in the gross national product and in employment rose but the steep rise in productivity in the goods-producing sector was not matched in the service sector. This put an increasing strain on public finances because the share of services in central and local government employment was constantly increasing. The age and sex composition of employment was also changing. Young people joined the labour force later in life and more women sought full- and part-time remunerated work. The discrepancy between 'good' and well remunerated and 'bad' and poorly paid jobs widened.

Patterns of ownership and control of the means of production also altered. Management became increasingly separated from ownership and a new 'class' of salaried directors and technocrats came into existence whose interests were often not identical with those of the traditional capitalist owner-managers of businesses [Brenner, 1984:12-29; Galbraith, 1967:71-82]. State enterprises proliferated and so did multinational monster corporations directed by members of the 'new class' with long-term globe-embracing plans and with funds independent of the conventional financial institutions. Their capacity to shift investment and employment from one country to another, and their growing ability to influence political decisions, gradually eroded not only the link between saving and investment in one country, upon which the Keynesian instruments of economic regulation rest, but also the distributive powers of democracy. In conclusion, the old tenets of capitalism, alienation, private ownership, and the profit motive, continued to be the ruling economic paradigm but in a process of transformation toward a new social and economic order.

## Note

1. Technically, as long as the proportion of income saved is constant the *multiplier* will be

$$\Delta Y_t = \frac{\Delta I_t}{s}$$

[Where $\Delta Y_t$ stands for the addition to the national income in period t ; $\Delta I_t$ for the new investment in period $t$ and $s$ for the proportion of that income saved.]

and the *accelerator* will be

$$I_t = v(Y_t - Y_{t-1})$$

[Where $v$ is the normal capital–output ratio, i.e. a technological coefficient, and $Y_t - Y_{t-1}$ the income difference between the period $Y_t$ and the previous period $Y_{t-1}$ i.e. the additional income $\Delta Y$ in this period.]

If both equations are satisfied, then by substituting the second equation in the first, the following difference equation is obtained:

$$Y_t = \frac{v}{s}(Y_t - Y_{t-1})$$
$$Y_t = \frac{v}{v-s}Y_{t-1}$$

The value of the national income ($Y$) is expressed as a function of its own value in a previous period.

If a 'time-lag' is taken into account, as it ought to be, the acceleration equation should read

$$Y_t = (Y_{t-1} - Y_{t-2})$$

# 14.  'The Devil Watches all Opportunities'

In all its forms the labour movement was essentially a reaction to the social and economic evils that attended the rise and development of capitalism. Its strength lay in its opposition to exploitation, alienation, insecurity and poverty. Its weakness was its inability to offer a sufficiently attractive alternative before the economy had reached a level of productivity which could provide a 'bourgeois' living standard for everyone. Until this level of production efficiency was reached labour's alternative to capitalism could only mean a more equitable distribution of the cake but not plenty for all. It could reduce poverty at one end of society at the price of less affluence at the other end; it could provide distributive justice but not affluence.

Until the middle of the present century many people would have had to reduce their living standards before the poor could be better provided. Theoretically this was a possibility but politically and therefore practically it was not. Most people were not insensitive to the suffering of others, but their fear of becoming destitute themselves was stronger. In a world in which the accumulation of wealth seemed the only protection against privation it was not unreasonable to seek solutions individually rather than put one's trust in new-fangled doubtful collective promises of salvation.

By the middle of the present century technological progress in the industrially most advanced countries finally achieved the level of efficiency which could make 'bourgeois living standards' possible for all. But by this time the cultural legacy of capitalism had become too strong for Western society to grasp this possibility. In the same way as the mental legacy of the Middle Ages had persisted well into the capitalist era, and then had saved the goose that laid the golden eggs, so did the 'capitalist spirit' bequeath to late twentieth century society a state of mind which prevents (or at best delays) the coming of a safer and more equitable civilization. Uncertainty, and a particular kind of individualism had imposed themselves on Western culture and made material gain, profit, the major criterion of success.

That in the industrially advanced countries the fear of poverty and hunger could *in theory* be banished can easily be substantiated by a comparison between labour efficiency in the developed and in the underdeveloped countries, or between the levels of productivity in the developed countries themselves at 25-year intervals. In the United States 72 per cent of the labour force was engaged in farming in 1820, 63 per cent in 1850, 36 per cent in 1900, 12 per cent in 1950, but in 1975 only 4 per cent of the labour force supplied all the necessary food and materials of farm origin, and food surpluses rather than shortages became a cause for concern. At the current level of technology it requires in the United States no more than one man engaged in agriculture to produce all the necessary food and materials of farm origin to satisfy the needs of 25 persons [Ginzberg, 1976:26]; by comparison in Ghana two farmers can hardly produce enough to feed a family of five [Brenner, 1971:44-70]. In 1975 the percentage of people engaged in agriculture was estimated 40 in Latin America, 58 in Asia and 73 in Africa, but famines continue to recur.

A similar fall in the necessary labour input can also be observed in manufacturing. In spite of the rise in incomes, and the increasing number of items on which people can spend their money, the volume of employment in manufacturing has steadily declined. The real product per man-hour in the United States has grown since the beginning of this century more than fourfold. The rise in Western Europe and Japan was hardly less impressive.

In France, out of a total population of 38,451,000 in 1901, approximately 14,089,000 persons were engaged in agriculture, forestry, fishing, manufacturing, and in extractive and construction industries. 5,812,000 were employed in commerce, finance, transport, communications and other services. Out of a population of 41,000,000 in 1954, only 12,198,000 were employed in agriculture, forestry, fishing, manufacturing etc., and 7,068,000 in commerce, finance and transport. And out of a population of 46,500,000 in 1962, the number of people engaged in agriculture, forestry, fishing, construction and manufacturing had dwindled to only 11,333,000, while the number of persons engaged in commerce, finance and transport rose to 8,160,000 [Mitchell, 1975:20,155-6].

In West Germany in 1950, out of a population of 50,787,000, the number of people engaged in agriculture, forestry, fishing and manufacturing etc. was 15,046,000, and in commerce, finance, transport, etc. 8,032,000. One decade later, in 1961, out of a total population of 56,115,000, approximately 16,209,000 people were employed in agriculture, forestry, fishing, mineral extraction, construction and manufacturing, and 10,514,000 in commerce, finance, transport, communications and other services.

In the Netherlands 2,126,000 man-years were worked in 1958 in the primary and secondary sectors of the economy (agriculture, fishing, production of semi-finished products and food, drink, tobacco products, textiles, shoes, chemical goods, oil refining, public utilities, etc.) and 1,936,000 man-years in services. In 1970 the number of man-years in the primary and secondary sectors had increased to 2,201,000 and in services to 2,480,000. Even if the production-linked services, and the services in the public utilities, are included in the 'directly productive' statistics the relatively greater rise in employment in service occupations is obvious: it increased by 544,000 man-years while primary and secondary employment rose by only 75,000 [Central Bureau of Statistics, 1971:70].

In other words, relative to population accretion, in the industrialized countries everywhere, the number of people employed in the production of food and manufactured goods diminished while output and service employment increased [Mitchell, 1975:20,155-6]. It is of course true that the growing demand for labour in the service sector was a necessary concomitant of the increasingly specialized and intricate new mode of production, but this can hardly detract from the fact that at least in theory hunger and abject poverty can indeed be banished.

Keynes believed that 'if the State is able to determine the aggregate amount of resources devoted to augmenting the instruments (of production) and the basic rate of reward to those who own them, it will have accomplished all that is necessary' [Keynes, 1936:378]. He acknowledged the inequalities of wealth and income under capitalism and its failure to sustain full employment, but declared that 'these faults were diminishing, or that they served a social purpose.' His assessment depended, however, on a crucial change in the institutional structure of the system, namely on 'the acceptance of government spending as the motor of the system' [Heilbroner, 1990:1099]. Alvin Hansen added a historical dimension to the Keynesian framework 'by hitching it to a combination of Wicksellian long waves and a Spietoffian emphasis on filling up the 'bucket' of investment opportunities' [Heilbroner, 1990:1099]. The institutional changes materialized, but only partially engendered the result which Keynes expected.

The share of the government and of 'not-for-profit' employment (as opposed to employment in the capitalist private sector) has increased very considerably since the 1930s. Even in a country committed to free enterprise like the United States, 13,400,000 people (31.9 per cent) out of a total labour force of 84,700,000 were employed by government and 'not-for-profit' organizations in 1973. Of these 13,400,000, 7,100,000 were directly employed by the state and 5,000,000 by private firms working on government orders directly or indirectly and 1,500,000 by 'not-for-profit' organizations. The share of the combined output of the non-private sectors amounted to 338 billion dollars, which means 26.3 per cent of the national income [Ginzberg, 1976:26].

In the Netherlands the total volume of employment was 3,773,000 man-years in 1950, and 4,688,000 in 1974. Of this the state directly employed 392,000 in 1950 and 617,000 in 1974. While the overall labour force increased by 20 per cent, government employment increased by 58 per cent. The share of the government in employment rose from a little more than 10 per cent in 1950 to above 13 per cent in 1974. During the same period net investment (including stocks) increased from Fl. 3,127 million in 1950 to Fl. 29,480 million in 1974. Out of this the government share was Fl. 494 million in the former year and Fl. 5,680 million in the latter. Altogether, the share of the Dutch government in the country's fixed investment increased from 16 per cent in 1950 to almost 20 per cent in 1974 [Central Bureau of Statistics, 1975].

What Keynes failed to see was capitalism's cultural obduracy and exceptional capacity to internalize opposition. The growing share of the public sector, the increasing impact of 'non-profit-making' organizations on employment, the rising living standard and level of social security, impressive as it all was, tolled hardly the knell for the old social and economic system. The modifications smoothed the hard edges of capitalism, and for a time even gave it an almost human face, but did not eliminate its main socially debilitating elements. By virtue of the system's inner necessity, most activities continued to be subordinate to profit making, because without economic success few other objectives could be realized.

From the darkest days of pre-war capitalism, when competition had still ruled supreme and the fear of unemployment and destitution raised material wants above all others, an indelible legacy remained, namely the spirit of *competitive materialistic individualism*. Although the *objective* causes of that past era's privation were no longer of great relevance, this state of mind caused people to think and to behave as if the 'dark age of capitalism' had not waned. In spite of previously unmatched living standards for well-nigh everybody in the industrialized countries, and notwithstanding that the growth of productivity sufficed to increase the affluence of both capital and labour simultaneously, most people were unable to discard old fears and habits.

Everyone recognized that economic growth provided higher living standards, but few asked if this were true for all kinds of economic growth. Before long output statistics rather than humane values became the overriding measure of advancement. A person who has an elephant standing on his toes finds this the most pressing of his problems. He will devote his entire energy to remove the beast, and when it moves away the fear will linger on. For generations abject poverty had been such an 'elephant.' Economic growth removed it; but a society which was just emerging from a long history of destitution was ill prepared to recognize the full implications of the change. It was unable to appreciate that economic growth may lead in different directions. Unlike the pursuit of equity, the pursuit of growth seemed to everyone's advantage, though it was obvious that not everybody gained from it in equal measures. All rightly recognized that economic growth is a necessary condition for the achievement of higher living standards, but few perceived that it is only a *necessary* and not a sufficient condition, and that a stored surplus needs also to be fairly distributed.

The lingering climate of uncertainty and isolation, and the spirit of competitive materialistic individualism which accompanied it, penetrated almost all spheres of life. In science, von Neumann observed that *law* and *certainty* are not the same. He showed that 'causal laws are accumulations of laws of chance, which owe their success to the fact that they are admirable approximations of those cases where the laws of chance combine to give overwhelming likelihoods' [Bronowski, 1951:80-9]. He did not suggest that nature is 'lawless' but, together with the others who followed, he destroyed the belief that nature is governed by a mechanism which is a sequence of before and after and that there is a universal *now*, and not a *here* and *now* alone for each observer. As shown already Einstein, Planck and Heisenberg exorcized from nature the ghost of generalization and replaced the belief in the absolute by probability.

Similarly a person's future continued to be seen as neither teleologically nor strictly causally determined, but as moving within a calculable area of uncertainty. The limits of this freedom continued to be comparable to the earlier mentioned atoms in a stream of gas under pressure. On the average the atoms obey the pressure, but at any instant each individual atom may be moving across or against the stream. Given a degree of uncertainty, large events can be predicted and small ones cannot. In a society which allows individuals to find their places within the social structure on the basis of competitive ability, the 'small events' seem for an individual to matter most and not surprisingly receive most attention. Consequently the theory of the firm appeared more relevant than macro-economics. Those wishing to maintain the social order had no difficulty with allowing perfection *within* the system but they were hardly likely to encourage theories with general and long-run implications. They could be served by micro-economics but not by political economy; they could use a science which maintains that true knowledge is exclusively founded on sense experience, and therefore is concerned with particulars, with the 'small events,' but *not* with a global and historical perspective. The 'large events,' which might provide a clue to the future, were simply relegated to the world of mystics and utopians. People were discouraged from efforts to look into alternatives to equilibrium. No one wished to be reminded that organisms and species which could not foretell the future from the symptoms of the present and adapt to changing circumstances perished. Even Keynes did not always escape this mental trap: 'In the long run we are all dead' [Keynes, 1971,IV].

The point of all this is that the liberating diminution of economic fears in the industrialized countries during the 'Keynesian era' failed to be seen as such, because it was accompanied by a repudiation of some of the values which had previously been regarded as *absolute*. The question 'will it succeed?' increasingly replaced the question 'is it true?' and the question 'is it good for me?' replaced the question 'is it good?'. The criterion for judgments shifted. If there is no *absolute* then all is *relative*; and good becomes a matter of personal choice. What one feels to be good for oneself *is* good. People reason by analogy, and the loss of stable values was either a reflection of, or was reflected upon, the scientists' perception of society and the universe.

As long as economic growth was taken to be the automatic motor of change and change was taken to be identified with inevitable progress, economic growth was the focus of attention and by the end of the nineteenth century it was in the first place regarded as the product of scientific innovations. Before people became aware of the environmental hazards, they simply took for granted that any advancement of man's dominion over nature serves the public good. New discoveries were thought to add to man's ability to overcome the reticence of nature, to drive back the frontiers of ignorance, and therefore to improve the chances for a better life. This gave a special status to science and to scientists without regard by whom and with what they were engaged. Like economic growth itself, the scientists' achievements seemed to be guided by an 'invisible hand' which makes them socially neutral, to everyone's advantage and not detracting anything from one class of society to benefit another. In this light, scientists seemed to be 'above' all socially conflicting interests. The masses romanticized their work and believed them to be selfless servants of truth and human progress, but entrepreneurs recognized in them a useful tool to further their own material interest. They were assigned a social status above the one which suited them in a society which normally positioned people by their wealth. This general confidence in the redeeming power of science developed in the scientific community a sub-culture which for a time allowed many intellectuals to ignore the materialistic strains of the dominant profit culture which surrounded them. Many felt free to prefer the advancement of true knowledge to the pursuit of their personal material advantages. Not that there were no greedy scientists but they were not the ones who determined the scientists' image in the public eye. Many young people chose to study science, medicine, architecture and engineering, from a genuine desire to help mankind. Even those who studied for more pecuniary reasons, or to gain status or simply because their family expected them to study, were seldom able to escape the scientists' sub-culture and its set of values. For a while it seemed as if the profession of science imposed a kind of Hippocratic oath. Many scientists before the war genuinely believed that mankind's lot was their responsibility. It made many of them take up a public stand on ethical and moral issues where the Church had lost its influence. While socialists eulogized the dignity of labour and helped to preserve some of the humanitarian elements of early bourgeois culture, the scientific community sustained the values of the era of Enlightenment. Together they managed for some time to restrain capitalism's inherent tendency to subject all spheres of life to narrowly materialistic pseudo-Darwinism.

Before the war there was a difference between the European and the American intellectual elites. The latter were less socially influential and never seriously challenged the 'economic Darwinism' of the bourgeoisie. Europeans were accustomed to harbour in their midst minorities whose social position did not match their economic status. In Europe, aristocrats and artists enjoyed a social status which was far above their economic position, while even before the war, the ascendancy of the American bourgeoisie was more complete. Materialistic pragmatism was part of the 'American way of life'. American scientists were valued individually by their financial worth to their employers and were integrated into the system on its terms. Their European colleagues, at least until the war, retained a degree of independence and influence upon it. Motivated by competition, mainly among themselves, American scientists registered great achievements, especially where their work was of technological applicability, but they had little control over the direction of their work. More often than not they were more concerned with 'does it work?' and 'will it sell?' than 'is it true?' and 'is it socially desirable?' With less heed to their public responsibility than their European counterparts they left the decisions about *what* to research to the industrialists and politicians.

Again it must be emphasized that American scientists drove back the frontiers of ignorance and made magnificent contributions to society's better ability to satisfy needs and wants, but they left the decision what needs and wants to meet, and how they should be met, to the whim of the market. Since the war and often without realizing the social and cultural implications, European scientists also tacitly accepted the bourgeois notion that irrespective of disparity of incomes, price variations provide the indicator of desirability. Their efforts too were directed to where they were expected to render profit and not where they were best employed from society's point of view. Worse than that, the negative societal consequences of their work, for example the damage to the natural environment, were on the whole ignored. There were exceptions, but these were mainly in research financed by the state, and paradoxically, research motivated by military considerations.

In the light of the great technological achievements, and the rise in general living standards they engendered, all this may seem unimportant, but this is a delusion. Conquering nature, society lost its ability to control itself. The mechanism of incessant competition, which gave capitalism its positive achievements, deprived society of its freedom to make crucial choices about its collective long-term future. To be outpaced by someone else in a world ruled by competition is no vain fear. Consequently questions about the safety of nuclear power, for example, were pushed into the background. If American industry employs nuclear power and German industry does not, American products become relatively cheaper, and not only German industrialists but also workers suffer the economic consequences. Like the sorcerer's apprentice in the fairy-tale, capitalism releases forces which it cannot control.

Science is concerned with truth and capitalism makes truth subservient to expediency. Step by step the utilitarian climate estranged science from its liberating purpose and subjected it to the short-term desires of competitive commercial interests. But true science is not the blank record of facts. It is the search for order within the facts; it is 'not truth to fact, which can never be more than approximate, but the truth of the laws which we see within the facts' [Bronowski, 1951:134]. Alas, the discovery of these truths has little immediate market value, and so the scientific judgment, which selects from among the innumerable experiences what *matters* and what does not (and thereby influences our value system) is offered to the demon of commercial expediency. As Heisenberg said: although the philosophical background seldom influences the scientist's *answers* it usually determines his *questions*, and final understanding depends on this.

There were forces at work which by the middle of the twentieth century were pushing science and society in a particular direction. In the 1950s and early 1960s, scientists who departed from European universities for better remunerated employment in

American industry were conscious of their loss of status. They felt the need to 'justify' themselves by claiming that America offered better scientific equipment for research, which it did. By the 1970s, the scientific community was integrated in the capitalist system everywhere, and scientists no longer felt the need to deny that income differentials determined where they worked and to what purpose. This change was not lost on society. The scientist employed to discover a new flavour for a toothpaste which would give one firm a sales advantage over another could hardly retain the public image previously accorded to people believed to be dedicating their lives to mankind's struggle against sickness and want. Some people continued to respect learning, but on the whole, like the clergy and the aristocracy, the scientific community lost its moral influence. Unlike the Church, it not only lost its influence; it also shed an essential part of its value system.

In the nineteenth century a fragmented society encouraged individuals to find their position in the social hierarchy by competition. As more social needs came to light, which were not met by individuals' pursuit of their immediate interests, provisions were gradually made to correct the system where individualistic self-interest failed to meet them. The 'corrections' ranged from education and health care to state intervention in the entire economic system. Increasingly the promotion of economic growth, stability and equity became the legitimate responsibility of governments. At the same time industrial progress, which was raising living standards, imposed a previously unknown degree of complexity and specialization on the economic system. More and more the organization of society became crucial for the survival of individuals. More and more everyone's welfare came to depend upon everybody else fulfilling his task conscientiously, responsibly and on time. For more than two centuries in the past this 'discipline' had mainly been assured by fear. Employers feared their competitors and workers their employers. The fear accustomed people to a mode of conduct which, among other things, sanctioned the economic destruction of individuals by competition but not by highway robbery. Force of habit, which makes what has become customary appear to be self-evident, made the capitalist mode of conduct seem firmly anchored 'outside' man's will – in 'human nature'. Its rules appeared to be almost as firm as the Bible's 'thou shalt and thou shall not.' But improved social security diminished individuals' fear of destitution, and the ascent of relativism broke the custom's spell. Consequently, industrial discipline deteriorated. But without it industrial society is too specialized, complex and interrelated to survive. If there is nothing *absolute*, and *good* is a matter of *personal* choice, then, in a climate of short-sighted materialistic individualism, what one feels to be good for oneself *is* good. Therefore, with neither fear nor an extraneous moral sanction to assure work discipline, and without a sense of *social* responsibility to take their place, industrial society cannot for long sustain the comfortable living standard it provided. Thus capitalism has landed in a dilemma: in the absence of the old compulsive forces to obtain the necessary work discipline, it must either resort to force or procure social consensus. The former would imply the abolition of almost all the last century's achievements of the working class; and the latter a sufficiently equitable distribution of income and wealth to encourage social control for assuring diligence and responsibility in the production and distribution process. In other words, capitalism has reached a stage in which it is torn between two alternatives: to drift toward egalitarian democracy, or to revive some kind of fear and despotism.

It is of course by no means certain that religion really influenced man's conduct in the early phases of industrialization. Perhaps it had always been the 'here and now' which in the final analysis determined people's conduct. It is quite possible that in the eighteenth and nineteenth centuries the labouring poor were too near subsistence levels of existence to care much about religion, and that they simply were indifferent. But even so, it would be wrong not to acknowledge the influence of religion on the cultural climate in which industrial society developed. Durkheim believed that there was something eternal in religion which will survive industrial society. Weber thought that when the new order has come to maturity it will lose the ethical tenets which gave rise to it. Marx first followed Bauer, Strauss and

Feuerbach, but later concluded that religion must be understood as an institution within the totality of social existence. Einstein believed that 'everything that the human race has done and thought is concerned with the satisfaction of deeply felt needs and the assuagement of pain'. He thought that with primitive man it is above all fear that evokes religious notions but not fear alone. 'Social impulses... the desire of guidance, love, and support also prompts men to form the social or moral conception of God.' Sooner or later, he expected a higher development, which he called the cosmic religious feeling. 'The individual feels the futility of human desires and aims and the sublimity and marvelous order which reveal themselves both in nature and in the world of thought. Individual existence impresses him as a sort of prison and he wants to experience the universe as a single significant whole...' [Einstein, 1930]. Einstein was hoping for a religion ('with no dogma or a God conceived in man's image') which is communicated by art and science, and leading to a world in which man's ethical behaviour is based on sympathy, education and social ties and needs. Alas, as he himself admitted, there is little evidence for the spreading of such an ethical conception.

The realistic alternatives for the survival of industrial society seem to be either the replacement of individualistic rationality by social rationality, or the emergence of a new political system in which economic compulsion is replaced by legal coercion.

Post-war developments are pointing in both directions. The increasing participation of labour in the management of industries; the proliferation of action groups concerned with communal problems such as the use of nuclear energy and the environment in general, and the rising number of social services, seem to point toward a growth of social rationality. The proliferation of bureaucratic control over decision-making processes, ranging from who may study and where, when, and what, and state penetration into the most intimate spheres of individuals' lives seem to indicate that society is moving toward bureaucratic despotism.

'Periods of great social change are usually characterised by a decline in the authority of codes of morality and by greater dependence on experiment, expediency and rationality in conduct.'

They are accompanied 'by a deterioration in manners and by the frequent emergence of an uncontrolled egoism' [Ogburn, 1935:333]. When a culture changes gradually, by a slow process of trial and error, individuals adjust slowly and cohesion between them emerges. But it is doubtful whether the accelerated change in our age will allow society the time to adjust in such a constructive manner. Labour's failure to develop a counterculture of its own and its surrender to the brute materialism of the bourgeoisie; and the bourgeoisie's progressive abandonment of its own code of business conduct and failure to keep within the bounds of its own legality, may cause much greater dislocation than all earlier 'great social changes'. The 'uncontrolled egoism,' which in earlier periods affected only sections of society, and left the rest only marginally conscious of the developments, now penetrates all strata. Since the 1950s workers have exchanged the struggle against the principle of private ownership of means of production for the more pragmatic effort to gain a greater share in the fruits of capitalist production; and capitalists have abandoned the principle of trust, confidence, even the legality upon which their system rested, in favour of short-sighted egoism which has all but legitimized corruption.

When pre-industrial society, in which all human activities were treated as falling within a single scheme whose character is determined by God's chosen destiny, entered upon the path of industrialization, partial adherence to some of the old values was kept as an insurance lest there was an eternal justice after all. These rules were preached in church, passed on by parents to their children, and exalted in the books the pupils were told to read in school. When they lost their Godly credentials they had become simply self-evident. Though they could seldom stand up against the pressures of economic necessity and divert people from the path prescribed for them by economic fears, they could and did contain man's egoism within bounds beyond which society would have fallen into chaos. They were the anchor by which the ship of industrial growth, which floated on the current of individualistic utilitarianism, was held back before the whirlpool of socially self-destructive egoism. But the declining fear of destitution and the diminution of the impelling force of moral restraints have now combined with the lingering predominance of capitalist economic expediency, and constitute a danger for the future of society. It is this combination which puts in jeopardy the technological achievements of mankind so dearly paid for just at the point when they could liberate humanity form some ills which plagued it in the past.

These conflicts between the old and the new *values* are obvious. Young people are encouraged by the literature selected for them in schools and by the verbal admonitions of their teachers and their religious instructors (if they still go to church) to revere patently non-utilitarian values. They are told to be patriotic and compassionate, to respect human rights and dignity, to love fairness, truth and beauty. At the same time they are directed by the competitive reality surrounding them and by their parents' admonitions to follow a narrow utilitarian path. They are told to study or do the things which seem useful for their personal advancement and are most financially rewarding. The press photo taken in Paris during a demonstration in 1969 showing a student brandishing Marcuse's *One Dimensional Man* in one hand, and holding a banner reading 'We want it all, and we want it now' in the other, is a good illustration of this cultural predicament. For many the pursuit of wealth has become an almost sacred duty, a call on men to forge their destinies. But linked to the old ethical system utilitarianism cannot prevail, and without the link industrial capitalism cannot be sustained.

# 15.  Services and the Expanding Public Sector

The motive for investing in a free enterprise economy is profit. Profit is the difference between revenue and costs. New investment may be induced by an experienced or expected rise or change in demand for output, or by the desire to introduce cost-reducing innovations. When price competition is brisk it makes little difference whether it is expansion or changes in output, or the introduction of new cost-reducing innovations which predominates. The effect on income and employment will normally be positive. But when price competition is slack, when gains from cost-reducing investments are not passed on to consumers by price reductions, the consequences may be different. The increase in consumer demand generated by new investment may lag behind the increase in the volume of output and the chance of obtaining the expected profits in the marketplace will not materialize. If this happens, then to sustain profits, the emphasis in investment will increasingly be directed toward cost-reducing innovations. As a result the labour force required will decrease. National income may or may not rise, but its distribution will change. Profits of financially powerful and most innovating firms will continue to increase and the incomes of all others, including incomes from employment, will diminish. This means that without lively price competition to reduce prices in line with falling costs, consumers' total purchasing power will not suffice to clear the markets and unemployment will ensue. Before long the most powerful corporations will adjust their production targets downward to suit the shrinking market. To sustain profits they will concentrate even more on cost-reducing *process innovation* and *product innovation* will diminish further. But to maintain something close to full employment, the free enterprise system requires an adjustment of consumers' purchasing power in line with the progress of technological innovation. To clear consumer goods markets, earnings and transfer incomes must rise in line with investment and productivity. However this will hardly happen when prices are sticky and when the distribution of income between the different strata of society is drastically altered. If the share of the national income which goes to those who are able to save a large part of their earnings becomes disproportionately greater than the share of the national income which goes to those who consume most of their earnings, the system's self-correcting mechanism cannot come into its own.

Keynes did not believe that in a lasting depression low interest rates, or low wages, can revive investment and employment. In his opinion the key to a solution was the level of employment. He argued that if the government creates employment, effective demand will increase. The increasing demand will induce investment and hence revive employment in the private sector. By way of the *multiplier*, state revenue and private savings will also grow and the upward trend will become cumulative. His opponents regarded the rate of interest as the price of funds, which they assumed to react to the laws of supply and demand like the prices of all other goods in a competitive market. They believed that by pampering the rich by keeping wages and corporation taxes low, they would increase savings, reduce interest rates, restrain inflation, create new investment and raise the volume of employment. Since the 1930s economists have been arguing about the question whether the rate of interest determines investment, or the rate of interest is itself determined by effective demand. But the possibility that demand for funds may rise and continue rising together with and in spite of rising interest rates, as happened in the 1970s, was ignored or explained by causes which cannot be empirically substantiated.

Keynes's analysis referred to the situation in the 1930s, when unemployment was high and the rate of interest low. In the 1980s the situation was different. The new and crucial element became the rapidly changing incremental capital-output ratio, and the increasing price-fixing power of some major oligopolies. The point is that unemployment can increase without a fall in interest rates. This will occur if in a number of important industries a given investment produces a greater volume of output than an equivalent investment did before, and if advancing oligopoly in these industries hinders prices from falling in line with the fall in the unit cost of output. In such a situation demand for consumer goods will not increase sufficiently to clear the market, but profits will be sustained by the adjusting of output to the diminishing demand. Prices will remain at their old level and further cost reductions will be encouraged by the substitution of old by new and technologically more efficient equipment. The number of persons employed in the capital-producing industries will remain more or less the same, but the number of persons employed in the goods-producing industries will diminish. The scramble for investment funds to finance the cost-reducing new investment will raise interest rates in spite of high and rising labour unemployment.

In the past the rising productivity in agriculture was attended by an equivalent fall in the real prices of farm produce. The fall in food prices increased real incomes and people spent more on industrial goods. When the share of consumer income spent on industrial products rose, the demand for labour in industry made good the loss of jobs in agriculture. Then, when productivity in industry also rose, and competition reduced the prices of industrial products, and the demand for labour in this sector also began to flag, a growing demand for services made good the loss of jobs in industry. In this way, as long as competition was sufficiently powerful to pass on the benefits of technological progress to consumers, the diminution of the demand for labour in one sector of the economy gave rise to increased demand in others. Until the mid-1960s this was indeed what happened [Dettling, 1977:77]. The shifts in the demand for labour caused neither food shortages nor a deficiency of industrial products. On the contrary, there were indications in the 1960s that the markets for consumer goods in the rich countries were approaching saturation. For this, among other things, the conscious promotion of *false wants*, and the growing interest in Third World markets, may be regarded indicative. That some people in the rich countries did not possess the goods which were available can hardly be attributed to agriculture's and industry's inability to provide them, but to the persisting inequity of income distribution.

In the late 1960s affluence grew, and more people than ever before were able to purchase the goods they wanted and were still left with money to spend on services. The demand for services increased very markedly and led a number of social scientists to believe that the future of full employment lay in the expansion of the service sector. As several important services can hardly be improved by labour-time-reducing innovations this seemed a not unreasonable thought. In particular, services which require the simultaneous attendance of consumer and provider, like patients and doctors, pupils and teachers, patrons of restaurants and waiters, made it quite plausible. Again it appeared as if an 'invisible hand' were leading the economy toward full employment equilibrium. But it was an illusion. In many services, such as banking, insurance and even marketing, labour-time could be reduced: employment opportunities fell prey to the computer, and oligopolistic practices in some key industries prevented disposable real incomes from following the path experienced earlier. In the 1980s, the demand for investment funds increased and the demand for labour diminished. Workers previously employed in the replacement of depreciated capital were engaged in the substitution of less efficient by more efficient machinery, and workers who had earlier been employed in the production of additions to the capital stock to meet the growing demand for goods became redundant. Real incomes ceased to rise at the former pace; cost reductions were not fully passed on to consumers; work in innovation became more and more specialized, and demand for consumer goods and services no longer matched the rising productivity. Incentives to expand production dwindled, unemployment and the cost of social security rose, government revenue decreased, and corporations unremittingly discovered new ways to avoid taxation and to obtain government subsidies. The result was that unemployment and interest rates were high, and state budget deficits increased. In the belief that high interest rates and inflation were the product of excessive consumer spending, governments adopted various restrictive measures to increase savings by trying to curb wage increases and to reduce public expenditure. Consequently the rise in demand for consumer goods became too feeble to reverse investors' preference for process innovation, and product expansion all but ceased. At the same time governments' attempts to contain inflation by *tight money* made things even worse. It put an extra burden on small enterprises with few liquid reserves and forced them to abandon whatever plans for product innovation they might have had, and it obliged trading firms to reduce stocks to a minimum and raise prices to cover the high cost of borrowing.

Technological innovation, irrespective of whether it is *product-innovating* or *process-innovating* (labour-cost-reducing) gives rise to new employment. The advent of the automobile not only created jobs in the motor industry, and in the industries directly involved in car production, but also in the machine tool industry, in oil production and refining, in the construction of roads and garages, and in the services required to keep the new vehicles in good repair. As long as competition is brisk, what is true for *product innovations* is also true for *process innovations*. In the latter case the course of events may be less dramatic and direct than in the former (even the replacement of the old equipment may not require extra labour), but indirectly the reduction of the production costs of the final output will cause its price to fall and real consumer incomes to rise. The overall demand for goods will increase, and if the market for goods approaches saturation, part of the demand will shift to services. More money will become available for education, for recreation and for health care, and the loss of jobs in consumer goods production will create new employment opportunities in services. If at the same time some services are also affected by a labour-cost-reducing 'revolution,' as was recently the case in banks and supermarkets, this makes little difference as long as competition is brisk. In the long run, the innovations raise real income, boost demand and profits, and encourage further investment. But none of this will happen if business competition is ineffectual, if prices do not fall in line with productivity, and consumers' real income does not rise sufficiently to clear markets. Then, only an alternative to competition, namely state intervention, can restore employment by readjusting investment and consumer demand. This was precisely what in the 1980s most governments failed to do. Misinterpreting the causes of the high interest rates and inflation, and carried away by the unpopularity of their bureaucracy and earlier interventions, they restricted the money supply, dampened wage increases, and whenever they could reduced social security expenditure. The result was that income differentials deviated further and further from where full employment would have been restored.

Until the 1970s economic growth and full employment were on the whole sustained by entrepreneurs competing fairly vigorously for their relative shares of the markets; and capital and labour fighting a relentless tug-of-war for the fruits of innovation. Deviations from the path of growth with full employment were more or less effectively reduced by monetary and fiscal measures. Progressive taxation and social security provisions helped to maintain the balance between output and consumption even when *economic power* frustrated competition. But since the early 1970s competition has faltered and deviations from the full employment growth path have become cumulative. The price-fixing powers of oligopolies have increased while the strength of organized labour was diminishing. The self-correcting forces of the free market system weakened and governments failed to take the corrective measures which were necessary.

By adjusting output in line with the diminishing economic growth rates, monopolies and oligopolies kept prices up; and trade unions (which were presented by the media 'experts' as the main determinant of inflation) did not dare, nor enjoy enough support from their members, to make sufficiently high wage claims to match consumer demand to productivity. In short: the distribution of the national income between consumers and controllers of capital became lopsided in favour of the latter. Productivity continued to rise but real disposable incomes lagged behind. The surplus of income which should have become available to purchase more services did not materialize, and the new demand for labour in the service sector did not match the loss of jobs in industry.

In theory governments could have restored full employment and prosperity. By raising corporation taxes, to skim off oligopolistic profits, and investing the proceeds in the public sector, they could have improved their countries' infrastructure and expanded the collective services. Even a reduction of the length of the working week (without docking workers' wages) would have helped to offset part of the loss of jobs occasioned by the rising productivity of labour. The reasons why none of this was done were the fear of accelerating inflation, international trade complications, and most important of all, the effect of the cultural and social climate on the political oligarchy.

Scared of accelerating inflation, besieged by powerful persons who objected to public spending, governments misled the public by false analogies. Likening state expenditure to household budgeting, and public borrowing to private debts, and claiming that like a private household a state must always 'live within its means', and that high wages do not leave enough profit for investment, they convinced their citizens that low wages and cuts in social security will revive employment. To make this plausible some establishment economists even resurrected the *wage-fund theory*, or presented the *marginal productivity theory of employment* (which is a micro-economic theory) as if it were a macro-economic truth.

One reason why governments chose this line of action is that many successful politicians and economists tend to adopt the social and economic priorities of the higher echelons of the business community and of 'the technostructure'. Oblivious to the fact that unemployment is not only a matter of the next day's meal, but affects the redundant worker's entire existence (his or her social status, self-esteem, hopes and aspirations), the economic elite constantly repeated true and imaginary stories about the abuses of the social security system and reminded the public that no-one was actually dying of hunger in the European welfare states. And as high social, business and academic position gives access to television, radio and the press, while unemployment does not, the voice of economic advantage, being louder, was regularly mistaken for the voice of the masses [Galbraith, 1981:30]. The media picked up and broadcast the economic elite's ideas, and the economic elite listened and felt confirmed in its opinions.

The reason for the acceptance of the technostructure's scale of priorities by the rest of society lay in the cultural heritage from the long history of fear and poverty. With the rise of capitalism the fears of imaginary ghosts and demons which had plagued people in the Middle Ages were replaced by the real nightmare of unemployment and destitution. The new social safeguards evolved only gradually and the level of productivity required to satisfy the basic needs of all citizens was only attained in the industrialized countries by the middle of the twentieth century. But the old fears lingered on and continued to be transmitted from one generation to the next. Capitalism's competitive individualism imposed patterns of thought and conduct which made the acquisition of wealth a sign of social distinction in itself, provided of course that it was acquired by legal means. The pursuit of wealth ceased to be a compelling necessity for survival, but received social approbation, and having become habitual seemed part of *human nature*. Other status symbols, such as aristocratic and academic titles, yielded pride of place to wealth and riches became the yardstick by which an individual's position in society is measured. Goods not only secured the comforts they render but confirmed their owner's status.

The ranking of persons' social position by their property engendered a distinction between goods and services, and between private and collective goods and services in particular. Services are non-material or intangible goods. They are the 'output' of teachers, musicians, bankers, hairdressers and clergymen. On the whole they are not transferable but 'consumed' at the point of production. In a sense all work is service: some services render *utility* indirectly, through their contribution to the production of a tangible product, and others more directly. In this sense there is no difference between a worker on the Ford assembly line and a waiter in the McDonald's chain of restaurants. Whatever the source all remunerated work is added up in GNP statistics. But with regard to wealth as a status symbol, there is a difference. Goods can, and most services cannot, be stored and accumulated; and public goods and services add little to an individual's personal distinction. It is therefore hardly surprising that a society which assigns social status to the command of private property distinguishes between goods and services and between private and collective ownership. In such a society individuals feel happier when they acquire some good which they can call their own, than when they pay their rates and taxes to public authorities, even if the services they receive in exchange may be very considerable.

Even in the hardest of times, not many families would feed a grandparent who is living with them less than the other members of the household because he or she is no longer contributing to the budget. But in a recession many would be perfectly prepared to see old age pensions cut to lessen taxes. The reason for this is that a society accustomed to a culture which puts prime emphasis on the individualistic pursuit of economic security and wealth finds the link between taxation and the advantages received in return too remote and indirect. People socialized in an individualistic acquisitive society resent the feeling that they have insufficient control and supervision over the money paid to the state, and their resentment leads them to magnify beyond good reason each case of inefficiency in the use of government funds. They disregard the inefficiency and business failures in the private sector, the large profits sometimes earned by public corporations, but notice every mismanagement in the public sector. They confuse efficiency with profitability and forget that most state enterprises are not intended to maximize profits but to provide a public service. They overlook that many state enterprises render essential services to the public which are insufficiently profitable to attract private investment. They resent the rising cost of government and forget the great structural changes in industrial society which make more and more public services necessary. They simply turn a blind eye to the fact that developments like the dissolution of the traditional family transferred the responsibility for supporting the aged from the household to the state; that the progress of technology greatly increased the cost of education; and that the growing complexity of economic and social relations increased the need for national communication networks which are not only too expensive to be constructed by private enterprise but also increasingly costly to maintain. They regard the expenditure for protecting the public from epidemic diseases and from air and water pollution with suspicion, but accept increases in defence budgets simply because they have become accustomed to them.

The lack of rationality in all this is obvious. Even if all these needs could be met by private enterprise and even if private enterprise could meet them more efficiently, the share of the national income allocated to their satisfaction would continue to be high and rising. The aged and infirm would still have to be housed and fed; teachers would still want to be paid; roads and communication systems would still need to be constructed and maintained; and it would still be necessary to prevent epidemics and pollution. The real cause of the onslaught on governments' rising share in the national income is therefore not its cost but the distribution of the financial burden it imposes. It is the reflection of the struggle for the determination of who pays and who benefits. Progressive taxation, not the cost of the services provided by the state, is the crux of the matter. Those with most reason to object to high government expenditure are those who pay most taxes; those most dependent on government support are the poor who pay least. The middle income groups may sometimes receive more than their taxes' worth from the state and other times not, but they are persuaded by those with best access to television, radio and the press, and forget the fortuitousness of their economic position and of their future prospects. In short, the objection to government spending is in no more than the manifestation of the unwillingness of the rich to pay for sustaining the poor.

Another difficulty with creating more employment in the service sector is the legacy from times when productivity was still too low to assure an adequate supply of goods for all. This inheritance continues to cause many people to regard with suspicion all occupations which do not help to produce tangible products. In fact, however, the proliferation of services is inherent in the progress of technology. When subsistence farming was replaced by market production, the produce had to be processed, stored, graded, packed, transported and distributed. Similarly an entire range of new ancillary service occupations became necessary when manufacturing was replaced by industrial machine production. The point is that, irrespective of whether they provide services or contribute to agriculture and industry, the ratio of the number of persons producing the national output to the number of people sharing its 'consumption' is on the whole fairly stable. Taken together, the share of the *inactive* (children, old people and other persons who for one reason or another either do not seek or cannot find remunerated work) is normally about 65 per cent of the entire population.

Except for countries with high immigration quotas the ratio of the labour force to total population remained fairly stable up to the middle of this century. Since the middle of the century the share of the labour force in the population has declined in spite of the longer life expectancy. In the United States the share of the working population (above the age of ten years) was 33 per cent in 1850. It rose to 35 per cent by 1880; to 38 per cent by 1900; to 40 per cent by 1930; and to 43 in 1950. But in 1959 it fell back to 41 per cent and since then it has continually declined. It is difficult to say how much of the early rise in the share of the labour force in total population ought to be attributed to the age composition of immigrants, to changing work habits (for example, the greater demand for remunerated work by women) and to the steady reduction of the length of the working day, but the trend is clear. It is also difficult to establish precisely what caused the fall in the share of the working force in the fourth quarter of the century but longer schooling and early retirement certainly played a role.

In the beginning of the recent depression, there were few objective reasons why governments should not have increased public spending on services to maintain employment, but psychological impediments prevented such a course of action. Most people regard the construction of a road to a remote village a reasonable expenditure, but have doubts about subsidizing their national orchestra. They reckon that the number of concert lovers is much smaller than of road users. That the number of tax-payers who will *actually* use the road, namely the villagers and their guests, may well be smaller than the concert patrons remains unnoticed. This is because people are more used to public money being spent on 'tangible' and lasting assets, such as roads, than on services which are 'consumed' at the point of production like music. They fail to acknowledge that for the GNP it makes no difference whether the income added comes from a builder or a musician; the rate of economic growth is determined by the one precisely as the other.

To many people the terms *economic growth* and *technological progress* suggest more air- and water-polluting factories, more heaps of derelict cars and gadgets, and an earth increasingly covered by cement and asphalt. In other words, they mistake an increase in the volume of tangible products, and the advancement of technology, for economic growth. In fact economic growth and technological advancement are two different things. The one is the sum of all incomes earned or spent in a given period, and the other the means by which society gains the power to produce more with less human effort and resources. While the one determines the level of employment, the other may or may not cover the earth with ugly cement constructions or create milk lakes and butter mountains. The growth of the *national income* means no more than the statistical year-to-year increase in the real level of the national product measured in money. It reflects a combination of rising productivity with changes in the volume of employment. Productivity may even increase while economic growth diminishes. When cost reductions from rising productivity are not passed on to consumers, and consumers' purchasing power fails to rise sufficiently to encourage new investment, and consequently the volume of employment falls, *national income* may decline while productivity is rising. This actually happened in the Netherlands and in West Germany. In several years during the 1970s and 1980s the fall in the volume of employment exceeded the rise in labour productivity. Because productivity kept on improving the entire diminution in the rate of economic growth since the end of the 1960s may well be attributed to the high levels of unemployment. Therefore, to say, as politicians and some economists do, that full employment is restored when growth returns to the economy, is a tautology. If productivity continues rising, as it usually does, more employment *is* economic growth. Seen in this way, it makes no difference whether the revival of employment growth comes from the creation of more remunerated work in the production of goods or in the service sector. Ignoring frictional unemployment, and taking for granted that productivity in agriculture and industry suffices to produce the necessary volume of output to sustain the customary living standard, it makes little difference whether the rate of growth required to attain or sustain full employment is obtained from more steel production or from improvements in the health and education services. Apart from the need to maintain satisfactory international trade and payment balances real complications only arise in the sphere of income distribution.

The reason why even economists, who should know better, were impressed by the distinction between goods and services can perhaps be explained by a bias dating back to Adam Smith that mechanization, which is the key to productivity, has little or no role to play in services. Another reason may have been that as economic theory focused on the competitive market-place and many services are anchored in the public rather than the private sector, it seemed that they have little to contribute to the understanding of the economic system [Ginzberg, 1982:44]. But this alone can hardly account for the 'oversight'. In the mid-1970s more than 67 per cent of all employed in the United States were already working in the service sector and contributing 41 per cent to the country's GNP [Ginzberg, 1976:27-8]. The more likely reason for the 'oversight' is therefore that the recognition of the service sector's contribution to the economy, or the failure to recognize it, involves powerful real interests. If the service sector is no less productive than the other sectors, then the contribution of the public sector (30 per cent of employment and 25 per cent of GNP) which is mostly in services, must also be acknowledged. Public expenditure can hardly be written off as money 'wasted', and the entire indomitable campaign against 'excessive' taxes misses even a veneer of common sense. The real reason why many economists are indisposed to acknowledge the role of services comes from their sharing the ideological paradigm of those who wield economic and political power. The point is that with notable exceptions, economists adhere to the economic theories which reflect the opinions of a particular stratum of society, and that the policies they favour are tainted by this stratum's conception of the 'public good'.

In mid-eighteenth century France, when manufacture was stagnating, commerce lay in ruins, and landed interests had the upper hand, *physiocracy* flourished. Ignoring the catalytic nature of labour, the physiocrats proclaimed that no work other than farming was productive [Brenner, 1966:20-5]. When manufacture and foreign trade were on the ascent in early modern England, *mercantilism* flourished. Oblivious to the social implications of their theories mercantilist economists proclaimed that low wages lead to more employment and high profits encourage investment. Ignoring potential domestic markets, and also until close to the end of the era the distinction between *per capita* and total output, mercantilist economists provided the leading stratum of society with precisely the theory they wanted [Brenner, 1966:11-20]. From the mid-eighteenth to the mid-nineteenth century, the emphasis was on capital accumulation, the division of labour and the expansion of markets. Economists recognized labour as the source of *value* but ignored the worker's rights to the full fruit of their labour although they meticulously observed all other property rights. Sharing in the outlook of the upper class, classical economists simply accepted the social order as they found it. Many of them regarded poverty in the midst of riches deplorable but part of the natural order and therefore no legitimate cause for intervention. As Malthus said: 'the rich do not in reality possess the power of finding employment and maintenance for the poor, (and) the poor can (therefore) not possess the right to demand them' [Malthus, 1789:260]. Harmony and not equity was the objective to which the bourgeoisie aspired, and classical economics echoed this aspiration.

The structure of society, in its great features, will probably always remain unchanged. We have every reason to believe that it will always consist of a class of proprietors and a class of labourers; but the condition of each, and the proportion which they bear to each other, may be so altered as greatly to improve the harmony and beauty of the whole [Malthus, 1789:261-2].

Only David Ricardo deviated from the general consensus. He discovered that not always what is good for the rich is likewise advantageous for the poor; and he wondered if the world is really so harmonious as his contemporaries apparently believed [Ricardo, 1817:263-8].

By the middle of the nineteenth century, having attained social and economic power, the bourgeoisie was entering its first period of consolidation. As already stated its laws of 'dynamic stability' replaced the former 'laws of motion' and the study of the laws of equilibrium superseded the interest in growth. The classical economists' implicit theory of growth yielded its place to other theories designed to explain the economy in 'close analogy to statical mechanics... treating the Laws of Exchange as the Laws of Equilibrium of the lever' [Jevons, 1871:vi-vii]. With a vested interest in maintaining the existing order, liberal democracy adopted a conception which adjusted mobility to stability. It continued to accept mobility but only as running-in-place. It allowed individuals to determine their status in the social structure by their competitive ability, but only on the system's own terms, and as long as the system itself remained immutable. Progress became synonymous with accumulation of capital, advancement of cost-reducing technology and the spreading of trade and enterprise. Human beings became *labour power*, and nature a *factor of production*.

Henceforth the concern of the economics establishment was with the maximization of *utility*. Reflecting the pre-eminence of pecuniary values, quantification and exact methods of business accounting became its prime objective. The new conception disguised the inconsistency between the strict observance of property rights in general, and their non-observance with regard to workers' property rights in the fruit of their labour, and it deprived the Marxist opposition of its moral premise. If not *work* but *utility* was the source of value, then the ethical dilemma posed by the labour theory of value ceased to be relevant. Moreover, the new economics establishment claimed that judgments involving basic issues of fairness, justice and morality are beyond its special competence, and restricted economics to the study of 'the relation between ends and scarce means which have alternative uses'. The paradox that a society which is technologically capable of producing affluence endures widespread poverty could simply be excluded from economics as a science. Economics could be restricted to the micro level: to the theory of the firm and to the pricing of goods and factors of production in competitive markets.

The claim, of course, is not that establishment economists were deprived of humanity, but the questions they asked and the methodology they employed to answer them determined the strata of society they served. Pareto's later writings can serve as an example to illustrate the class content of the neoclassical approach [Brenner, 1982:25-9]. Ignoring the holistic nature of society and individuals' behavioural evolution, his work reflects the aspired reality of the bourgeoisie which having wrested hegemony from the aristocracy had little wish to share its power with the working class. Pareto's conception of inborn sentiments or 'residues' provided the necessary ideological relief for the bourgeoisie which had not yet shed the last remnants of Christian ethics and continued to feel uneasy about its self-centred utilitarian urges. In short, the neoclassical approach purged political economy of its social content and turned it into a set of purely systemic deductions which depend upon assumptions which at best cannot directly be checked and at their worst are plainly wrong.

To make reality fit the metaphor of an economic system striving toward equilibrium, *neoclassical* economists all but ignored monopolistic influences and the obvious imperfections of mobility of factors of production. To make economics more 'exact' and like the natural sciences, they excluded from their science all disequilibrating forces, namely technological innovation, population growth, changing attitudes and tastes. Focusing their attention on what they considered short-term processes, they disregarded the organic nature of society, overlooking that the entire system depends on the equilibrating tendencies of the *price mechanism* which is a *time*-consuming process of adjustments. They relegated economic growth to technology, and changing attitudes to sociology and psychology. They declared all change exogenous, studied its impact on the economic system but ignored the possibility of it being itself a product of the evolution of the economic system. They tacitly took for granted the existing social and property relations and adopted a methodology so burdened with qualifications, *ceteris paribus*, that its powers of prediction became extremely limited. In short, *neoclassical economics* did not, as Milton Friedman believes, provide the 'positive scientific knowledge that enables us to predict the consequences of a possible course of action' [Friedman, 1977:453], but a methodology which claims to be value-free but in fact implies the freezing of the capitalist system.

To be sure, prices do play a crucial role in the allocation of resources, but not in the way neoclassical economists erroneously assume. Capitalism is neither in a state of almost perfect competition nor is it gravitating toward harmony. Economists like Frisch, Tinbergen, Leontieff, Klein, Harrod, Domar, Kaldor, not to mention Kalecki and Joan Robinson, were aware of this but their notions of equilibrium only gained prominence later when the capitalist power structure was in disarray. The reason why in spite of all its weaknesses the neoclassical approach made proselytes was hardly its superior scientific status, but the illusion of objectivity it furnished and its apparent ability to meet scientists' deep-rooted urge to obtain precision by quantification.

In the post-war era capitalism was revised. This was the result of a combination of several developments. Capitalism attained a level of technology which made a general rise in living standards a realistic possibility. Moreover, the sustained improvement of productive efficiency allowed a wider spreading of affluence without causing an appreciable loss for the economic oligarchy. The rich no longer needed to share their wealth with the poor to raise living standards; they only had to be content with less than the entire additional wealth flowing from the rising productivity. In

addition, capitalism's manifest inability to extricate itself from the
depression of the 1930s, eventually compelled the capitalist
oligarchy to make concessions to the lower classes. Communism
appeared to be a real threat to the old order unless it was
amended. From a distance, even the Soviet system seemed to
many poor in the West less unattractive than the life of destitution
they endured in the Depression.

Another factor which contributed to the amelioration of
pre-war capitalism was the progress of political democracy. Before
the nineteenth century democracy had mainly been an instrument
employed by the bourgeoisie to wrest power from the aristocracy.
In the nineteenth century it became an instrument in the struggle
between various interests within the bourgeoisie itself [Brenner,
1969:145-70]. In the mid-twentieth century it was labour's main
weapon in its struggle for emancipation. The relationship between
political democracy and regulated or Keynesian capitalism is
complex. The reason for this is that labour's opposition to
capitalism did not so much arise out of a general or ideological
critique of the system, though elements of this were also present,
but from individuals' efforts to redress immediate ills and to
improve personal situations by concerted action with other persons
in similar positions. Therefore, the opposition did not constitute a
break with the system but a struggle within it by its own methods
and on its own terms. Individuals simply tried to protect or
improve their living conditions collectively, sometimes by direct
action on the shop-floor, and at other times indirectly by the ballot
box. It was the latter, which in the social and political climate
following the war, forced the Western oligarchies to accept the
Keynesian compromise, and led to the incorporation of economists
like Tinbergen into the economics establishment. Whether the
'Keynesian revolution' was the product of genuine reformist
notions or an attempt to forestall more profound revolutionary
tendencies, or both, is irrelevant. The point is that it formally
acknowledged people's *right* to work and to sustenance, and the
state's duty to ensure them. By this the 'Keynesian revolution' did
not deliver 'a final and fatal shock to the doctrine of the
automatic market mechanism and *laissez-faire*' but produced a

temporary truce filled in by the interventionist drift which increased the store of instruments for reducing unemployment and providing the collective goods and services, and the social security, which traditional capitalism had denied the working class. This truce, which lasted for as long as economic growth sufficed to increase both the share of capital and labour in the growing affluence, was well reflected in the revision of the old economic theories. Economists like Hansen, Samuelson and Hicks adopted some of Keynes's ideas and adapted them to form a 'neoclassical synthesis'. But in the 1970s, when economic growth abated and the improvement or sustaining of the affluence of one class implied a loss to the other, the truce came to an end. The capitalist oligarchy took the initiative to restore its lost hegemony, and within a decade it reversed the drift toward a more equitable and socially and economically secure society. Under new names the pre-war theories were revived and *monetarism, supply-side economics*, things like the *Laffer curve*, became part of the ruling economics paradigm. The dismantling of the social security provisions was hidden behind the aphorism '*deregulation*'.

The reason why the capitalist oligarchy was able to master this reversal was that in the 1970s democracy no longer was the same as it had been when it emerged victoriously from World War II. It looked the same, but it had lost its social and economic emancipating elan.

# 16.   The Demise of Democracy and Competition

Living conditions in the industrialized countries improved until the 1970s, and almost all classes shared in the fruits of growing productivity. In Western Europe the social security system seemed firmly established and served as a safety-net against poverty and destitution. But almost imperceptibly democracy was losing its emancipating powers, and in the 1980s the mesh of the safety-net was no longer tight enough to serve its intended purpose as well as it had done before.

There were several reasons for the erosion of democracy: the failure of education to keep up critical and normative traditions; the drift of the mass media of information from informing toward persuading the public, and the tenacity of the materialistic individualistic patterns of culture in spite of the changes in the structure and organization of industrial production and the new needs and risks which could only be met by socially responsible collective efforts.

The great success of positivism in the natural sciences led to a confusion of methodology with objectives in other fields of study. In literature the study of linguistics gradually replaced literary, ethical and aesthetic criticism. In sociology the study of methods and techniques for statistical analysis at the micro level reduced interest in dynamic macro processes. In economics the refinement of mathematical instruments replaced the integrated study of social and economic phenomena and focused attention on prices to nigh exclusion of income effects. In their effort to be 'scientific' many social scientists overlooked that even the doctrine that scientific work requires the exclusion of normative judgments is itself a

234

normative judgment, and confused *objectivity* with *non-involvement*. They did not see that a concept like economic efficiency is meaningless unless the meaning of the *best* allocation of resources is established, which is of course a normative issue.

Disregarding that all human action involves a normative choice, namely a decision to prefer one course of action to all others, social scientists were oblivious to the fact that focusing attention on the *is* implies either a normative choice to sustain the existing social order, or a very deterministic view which denies free choice altogether. Without questioning its logic or ethical values, most social scientists engaged in the perfection of the ruling system and abandoned the study of the dynamics of historical developments. Shedding tears about the impossibility of finding *absolute* criteria for deciding what is *good*, they declared themselves impotent to make value judgments and adopted a position of moral relativism. It left the determination of values to people asserting that 'there is no absolute universal ethics, that habits, values and principles differ everywhere,' and that one has to adjust, because 'all else is nonsense' [Dorsey, 1976]. Not visions of a more humane social reality but materialistic self-interest, only slightly mitigated by some lingering 'irrational' impulses, became the new foundation of democracy. Democracy ceased to reflect social conceptions and drifted toward becoming an institution for assessing the relative power of pressure groups vying to obtain material advantages at the expense of others.

Radio and television experienced a similar transformation. In theory they are excellent media for the promotion of democracy; they make the information accessible which is required to improve everyone's ability to make rational choices. In practice this is far from true. Television viewers receive programmes chosen according to the number of people tuning to them. This not only gives a particular slant to the selection of programmes but also determine the form of presenting information [Brenner, 1984:47-50]. The few discussions offered become popularity contests; points of view are 'sold' in a way which forces the public either to accept or reject them without adequate information about their often exceedingly intricate context.

As many people turn on their television the moment they come home, or listen to their radio driving a car or doing their housework, they are constantly subjected to the intellectual climate of the networks. The make-believe world of the 'soap operas' becomes so familiar to them that they can no longer distinguish reality from fiction. They are socialized into the world invented by public relations agents who have less concern for what they sell than that it sells. There are of course also excellent and informative programmes, but they are hardly the most popular. Consequently, radio and television offer neither a reflection of reality, nor true alternatives for democratic choice. Discussions on fundamental questions, for example whether greater profits for private industry can or cannot reduce unemployment are not offered. The establishment's point of view that high profits reduce unemployment is simply taken for granted. Viewers' freedom of choice is restricted to the alternatives of either wage cuts or reductions in social security expenditure to effectuate the profits. The possibility that the *income effect* of reduced wages, or of less government expenditure, on the volume of employment may outweigh the advantages from wage cuts, lower interest rates, or less taxation, is considered a matter settled by the 'experts' and best left out of the public discussion.

Altogether the public is gradually made into the passive consumer of ideas offered by people who are said to be more knowledgeable. In this way thinking is left to 'experts' who more often than not speak a language as unfamiliar as Latin to most listeners. Matters of work and working conditions are decided by trade union officials. Workers' solidarity is transformed into union discipline and class struggle – into the collective pursuit of narrowly defined materialistic self-interest. Conditions of work are normally determined by engineers who think only of machines and other technical problems which need to be solved. These designers, brought up in a business culture, do not consider conditions of work at all. Decisions about the quality of work are only taken to *correct* the negative effects of these technological designs [Manders, 1990:145-70]. In this climate of competitive individualistic utilitarianism the political cohesion of the working class is lost and democracy is divested of the progressive emancipating power which had created the Welfare State. In the 1980s it was so enfeebled that it lost the ability to sustain the state's distributive mechanism which for three decades had assured the distribution of the national product (between capital, labour and receivers of transfer earnings) in the proportions necessary for maintaining full employment when competition fails to perform this task.

What distinguished post-war capitalism from other systems was its ability to internalize most opposition. Treating labour as a factor of production whose price is determined by demand and supply in the market-place, and regarding trade unions as monopolists, comparable to some monopolistic – employers, it transformed class struggle into wage negotiations. It allowed labour to oppose inequity and deprivation but only on the system's own terms, that is as long as the system itself remained unchallenged. Similarly, liberal capitalism did not crash the cymbals of young people's discontent. It internalized them by making them into a part of the system [Brenner, 1984:166-8]. The Mao dress, long hair, protest songs, even 'subversive' literature, were not prohibited, but transformed. They were made into a fashion by the opportunity they offered to proprietors of expensive boutiques, elegant hairstylists, record companies, and publishers, to profit from the 'fad'. Finally, attention drifted from real issues to technicalities. Liberal capitalism did not reject Keynes but incorporated his ideas into a 'neoclassical synthesis' in a manner which reduced them to a 'special case' within the old paradigm.

But, not all opposition to the system could be internalized. Questioning the rationality of the system itself was placed beyond the pale. Whether the authors of this kind of criticism were preaching the ancient tenets of the Church or the egalitarian traditions of revolutionary socialism, they were subjected to the establishment's powers of 'repressive toleration'. No mass arrests or executions, but smear campaigns, against Churchmen like Gollwitzer, and *Berufsverbote*, against socially committed active people and teachers in particular, were equally effective. The bourgeois oligarchy, just like its communist counterpart in the

Eastern Bloc, discovered that compliant, unimaginative and socially uncommitted people can serve it best. Democracy remained intact, but the mechanisms which make it meaningful were gradually eroded [Noll, 1976; Nossiter, 1977; *Der Spiegel*, 1977].

There were other developments which also thwarted the recuperating powers of democracy. Vertical and horizontal integration of businesses, to achieve greater economies of scale and market control, led to a reorganization of society. It gave rise to what may be called *industrial feudalism* [Brenner, 1984:10-33]. New hierarchies developed, running downward from top and sub-managers, to heads of branches, departments, and sections, to skilled workers and unskilled labour at the bottom of the scale. Every 'rank' was assigned its own status, responsibilities and level of remuneration. But beside the appropriate wage or salary, each rank also received privileges (expense accounts, business vehicles, etc.) according to its status. The higher the rank, the greater the perks. This new-fangled feudalism spread in both the private and the public sector, and as enterprises grew and the state's share in a country's workforce increased, more and more people became part of it, and the old capitalist class distinctions waned. The 'personal nexus,' (whom one knows and whom one serves) rather than a person's capabilities became an overriding factor in an individual's advancement. A new vertically arrayed organizational relationship developed and replaced the old horizontal class allegiance. The members of the lower ranks in organizations 'protected' the higher because their positions depended on their superiors' status, and the members of the higher ranks 'protected' the ones below them, because holding higher responsibility any mistakes made by their inferiors would eventually be placed on their own doorstep. As a result hierarchical income differentials remained almost unopposed. People simply accepted them and found consolation in the illusion of their chances for eventual promotion. Some did not judge the differentials fair, but as long as general living standards were improving, they saw neither cause nor realistic chances of success for active opposition.

While people seldom questioned the equity of the institutionalized pay and status differences within their own organization, they did compare their incomes and perks with those received by similarly ranked employees in other businesses. As working conditions in large oligopolistic enterprises tended to be more favourable than in small firms struggling for survival in a competitive environment, employees in the more powerful corporations felt that they were working for a 'good master' and developed an *esprit de corps* which not only protected the firms against outside criticism but undermined all class cohesion. This new-fangled feudalism was not confined to the private sector but spilled over into almost all branches of public administration. This is hardly surprising considering that top bureaucrats resemble top business executives in the exercise of control over people, in social background, education and in life-style. There is of course a difference; the former are obliged to maximize profit and the latter to pursue socially desired objectives, but the difference is obliterated because business executives often find their way into government service, and top government servants into private enterprise [Brenner, 1984:21-2]. It is simply taken for granted that whoever does well in the private sector will do equally well in public service. The managerial class's paradigm imposes itself: whatever is good for a firm *ipso facto* is good for a nation – 'all else is nonsense'.

While democracy was losing its socially emancipating powers, the free market system was also losing its economically essential mechanism. Competition was rapidly degenerating. By the end of the 1970s even the establishment's professional economic literature widely acknowledged its demise [Marris & Mueller, 1980:32-63]. In some branches of the wholesale and retail trades price competition continued to play a role, but its influence on large-scale manufacturers became slight. When Japan re-entered world markets it seemed for a while as if international competition would take the place of the waning domestic market mechanism, but the growth of *multinationals* soon put an end to this illusion.

By the 1970s, if not earlier, the mechanisms which gave capitalism its vitality lost strength. Most essential supplies, from energy to grains and from electronic equipment to carrier services, were increasingly controlled by a small number of oligopolists [Morgan, 1979; Barnet, 1981; Bergsten, 1978; Hannah & Kay, 1977 and Sampson]. Entrepreneurs continued to be interested in innovation but mainly to reduce production costs – not prices. Where producers kept on vying for their respective market shares they did so more often than not by advertising and 'tied' services rather than price competition [Brenner, 1984:12-13]. More and more huge business conglomerates not only determined prices but also the structure of demand. The enormous cost of establishing new production plants made entrepreneurs wary of setting up competing ventures; and the amalgamation of firms into market-controlling conglomerates spread very rapidly. To exclude competitors' goods the giant conglomerates established their own sales organizations, or acquired the control of strategically located chains of stores and supermarkets. Having done this they were practically in a position to decide what the public 'wants'. As people can only choose between the goods offered to them, conglomerates with combined sales monopolies and goods-producing interests were able to adjust the assortment of goods offered for sale to suit their industrial establishments' convenience. Hence they became more concerned with changes in revenue from advertising than from price modifications. By this many of the large conglomerates were increasingly able to determine both the supply and the demand side of their markets. People remained free to choose but their choice was limited within the bounds of what the mighty offered them to choose from. Step by step capitalism was losing one prong of its two-pronged competitive mechanism, namely competition between firms, which had previously provided its 'restlessness' and progressive elan. In the 1980s it also lost the second prong, namely the 'competition' between capital and labour for the relative shares in the fruits of rising productivity.

The waning of the long-term growth mechanism had an important result. It was competition, which had previously obliged producers to innovate and to pass on the resultant cost reductions in lower prices to consumers. When competition diminished, effective demand ceased to increase sufficiently to keep investment, employment and consumption on the long-run upward path. In the 1970s, before the other kind of competition, namely between capital and labour, also faltered, increasing wage claims and social security payments still sustained consumer demand in line with the rising productivity, but with insufficient market competition to keep prices down, this type of competition had a drawback. The wage hikes, and the taxes to pay for the increasing social security cost, were passed on to consumers by continuously rising prices. And so, in spite of mounting productivity, it set in motion the familiar inflationary spiral.

Mistaking the symptoms of the problem for its causes, governments tried to curb inflation by monetary measures. The results were disastrous. Prices, wages and interest rates continued to rise and unemployment and the cost of social security soared. Producers adjusted their output targets downward in line with the lower rate of growth in consumer demand, and placed even greater emphasis than before on cost-reducing innovation. In the most powerful oligopolies rising productivity kept profits high enough to use internal resources for investment. The weaker firms, which had to borrow funds, were faced with increasingly severe liquidity problems. Many production plans were postponed and new ventures with long gestation periods were abandoned. Employment in the production of consumer goods diminished and work in the capital goods industry became more and more specialized and added frictional to structural unemployment. Finally increasing unemployment and high interest rates made traders careful when replenishing their stocks.

What governments failed to see or to concede was that there can be other reasons than an inflated money supply for raising the general level of prices. In fact there are at least two different types of price inflation of which one is and the other is not reversible by monetary measures. The former is caused by a surfeit of money [Friedman, 1956:3-21], and by disequilibria at the height of the business cycle, or the coincidental shortages of some essential resources. The latter, namely the inflation non-reversible by monetary measures, is the product of fundamental changes in the entire social and economic structure of society and in its

242 *The Rise and Fall of Capitalism*

cultural framework. This type of inflation continues until the dramatic developments which gave rise to it mature, the social and economic transformation is completed, and a new social environment becomes established [Brenner, 1983:94-113]. Something like this happened in the sixteenth century [Brenner, 1961:225-39]; in the twentieth it was happening again. Both types of inflation can be contained by restrictive monetary policies, but the long-run consequences for welfare and employment differ.

Confronted with a combination of unemployment and inflation or stagflation, many governments abandoned efforts to regulate the economy by the Keynesian instruments. They declared fiscal policies ineffective and sought refuge in a mixture of monetary measures with *supply-side* economics. Taking for granted the neoclassical postulate that saving equals investment, and reviving *Say's Law* which asserts that supply creates its own demand, they adopted policies designed to redistribute the national income to raise the share of profit. They believed that reduced consumer spending would contain inflation, and that increased savings would bring down interest rates and restore employment. In fact inflation became moderate but interest rates and unemployment remained high, and the unemployed became socially marginalized. Illiteracy, drug abuse and crime proliferated. In many towns entire districts became unsafe, and the humane achievements of the earlier post-war era were steadily eroded.

In theory investment is less restricted to current income than consumers' expenditure. Unlike the latter it is mainly funded out of financial reserves and money created by financial institutions. Potential investors can invest, and indeed often do so, when current earnings are low because factors of production are usually cheapest and readily obtainable in the trough phase of the business cycle. They may refrain from investing when incomes are buoyant because factors of production are too costly or they fear that the prosperity may not last much longer. Concerning the familiar business cycle all this is fairly true but when a recession is structural and not cyclical things are different. When the decline in the rate of growth of consumer expenditure is prolonged and unemployment is high, but wages and interest rates do not fall, potential investors are more apprehensive.

In the 1950s and 1960s when trade cycles oscillated about a rising secular trend of income, the relatively low factor costs during recessions induced potential investors to invest. A quarter of a century of economic growth, in which consumers' expenditure more than doubled and disposable income increased in line with productivity, generated a climate of confidence. It encouraged investment even during the recessions. Entrepreneurs believed in imminent recovery and that with recovery demand would exceed the level it had reached before the downturn. But in the 1970s, when demand ceased to increase in line with productivity, the climate changed. Confidence in long-term growth was lost and affected the behaviour of entrepreneurs. The various measures taken by the United States between 1968 and 1971 to increase exports and reduce imports; the extreme rise in oil prices between September 1973 and 1974, and the coming of *industrial feudalism*, combined to make entrepreneurs feel insecure about the future. They restricted investment to the replacement of depreciated capital, and where possible, replaced it by more labour-efficient equipment. Expansion almost ceased and the labour force previously engaged in the production of net additions to the stock of capital became redundant. The era of the *false wants* (when industry was inventing new products from electric toothbrushes to 'Silly-Putty' for the consumer market) came to an end and the era of the silicon chip, the robot and the other cost-reducing innovations, was beginning.

There were of course also cost-reducing innovations in the 1960s, but the main emphasis was on product expansion. In the 1970s the emphasis shifted. In the 1960s and most of the 1970s incomes had risen and consumers' share in the national income had increased in line with productivity. Consumer demand expanded and encouraged *product innovation*, but in the 1970s consumers' income ceased to rise in line with productivity. Oligopolies prevented prices from adjusting to real incomes and governments failed to increase their own expenditure to make good the loss of consumer demand. As a result of this investment was mainly directed toward cost-reducing *process innovation* and unemployment became chronic.

The point is that inflation was not caused by rising wages but by inflexible prices and high interest rates. Oligopoly prevented prices from falling in line with the mounting productivity and the resultant shortfall in demand for consumer goods encouraged cost-reducing *process innovation* to sustain the rate of profit. The demand for labour decreased and for investment funds increased. The scramble for funds raised interest rates and the rising cost of money was passed on to consumers in inflated prices. The rising prices engendered high wages in spite of mounting unemployment; and as unemployment increased government expenditure on social security also rose and pushed up interest rates and prices even further. The power of oligopolists increased and the profit margins in the competitive sectors, particularly in the retail trades, diminished and the financially least potent firms went out of business.

At first sight it seems as if all this could have been prevented by the application of Keynesian *fiscal* measures, a commensurate taxation of oligopolistic profits, and judicious government investment. But a closer study of the changes in the social and the economic structure of free enterprise society shows this to be a rash conclusion. Keynesian regulation requires considerable state control over consumption and investment as well as informed democracy to influence the leading politicians. By the 1980s the rise of multinationals and the demise of meaningful democracy had already reduced the power of the lower income groups to influence decisions by the ballot box, and the power of the state to control the flow of the economy by the Keynesian instruments.

A multinational is a corporation which derives a substantial proportion of its income from overseas activities. In most cases it is a large enterprise having a home base and wholly or partially-owned subsidiaries in other countries. Such corporations expand on an international scale to take advantage of vertical and horizontal economies of scale and to enjoy near monopoly status. By producing abroad they export jobs, transfer technology to foreign affiliates, erode trade unions' bargaining power, alter the distribution of the national income away from labour towards capital, draw off revenue from the national government, involve the state in the internal politics of other countries, manipulate foreign exchange markets and destabilize their currencies, and sometimes even subvert governments in both their home country and abroad to serve their purposes. Whether they do all this or not, they certainly introduce a break in the direct link between domestic saving and investment upon which the practicability of both Keynesian and non-Keynesian economic revival theories depend. Multinationals can accumulate savings in one country and invest them in another. This may give rise to new income by way of international trade, but it can also destroy entire sectors of domestic industry. In the words of the President of the Royal Shell Group, the 'only power' his multinational has is to decide if to invest and where to do so. Mr de Bruyne seems unaware that this is no small power, but in effect it is the power to invest with little regard for where the savings come from, that is the power to frustrate any efforts by national governments to regulate their economic system by the Keynesian instruments.

In the late 1970s and in the 1980s, while the Dutch government was pressing for wage moderation in order to allow enterprises to accumulate the savings necessary for investment to revive employment, capital exports from the Netherlands increased at an unprecedented rate. They were equal to the 'missing funds' which would have been necessary for domestic investment to maintain economic activity at an even level [Brenner, 1981:37]. While unemployment was rising in the Netherlands, the country became the greatest investor in the United States and its investments amounted to almost one-third of all other European investments there taken together. Not surprisingly, at the head of the list of foreign investors in the United States in this period were Royal Dutch Shell, Unilever and Philips [Crowe, 1978]. Given this power of the multinationals little room is left for either an automatic equilibrating mechanism, or an unamended Keynesian method, to restore full employment and prosperity in countries with an open economy.

All this does not imply that autarky is the solution; such a 'remedy' would be worse than the disease. But it does imply that low wages are *not* the key to full employment and economic recovery. It shows that, given the structure of present-day capitalism, the real cause of unemployment and prolonged recession in the later part of the twentieth century was and continues to be lack of effective competition between producers and insufficient government regulation of income distribution to adjust consumer demand in line with productivity.

Those who continue to believe in the self-regulating powers of the market deny the lack of competition or belittle the impact of the price-fixing powers of the giant corporations. They point to the many vociferous and usually genuine complaints of businessmen about the 'murderous' competition they are facing and the relatively small *formal* share monopolies and oligopolies have in income and employment [Shepherd, 1982:613-26]. The complaints about 'murderous' competition are true enough. They come mainly from small enterprises and the retail trade. But the floor below which prices cannot fall is not set by them. It is determined by the large producers who with a fair measure of success avoid price competition among themselves although they too sometimes feel threatened by their foreign equals but soon find ways to come to an accommodation with them. It therefore makes little difference whether monopolies or oligopolies employ a large or small share of the labour force; if they are strategically placed in the economy they restrict price competition to the trading profit margins and these have little influence on the general level of prices and the overall volume of production and employment.

If OPEC and 'The Seven Sisters' determine the price of oil, they indirectly also fix the floor prices for all oil-based products and services. The best manufacturers of such products will try to reduce the oil content of their output. For this reason it is less the size of the share monopolists or oligopolists hold in the market than the nature of the resources they control which determines their influence on prices. Measuring the market share or degree of concentration is therefore not enough to determine the strength of monopolistic influences. There are several chemical fertilizer suppliers trading in Europe, and there is no evidence of collusion or price agreements between them which would stand up in court. But in spite of open frontiers and considerable price differences there is no trade in chemical fertilizers between the member countries of the Common Market. The point is that market control is a matter of power and therefore too elusive to be measured by counting units of production. It depends on intangibles which neither figure in the economic textbooks [Brenner, 1984:169-76] nor fit into the established body of neoclassical economic theory [Eichner, 1976]. If more cars made in Japan are sold in the USA, it need not cause a loss of profits, but it will cause greater unemployment among American automobile workers. If part of the shares of an American producer of automobiles is exchanged for an equally profitable part of a Japanese producer's shares, the losses from the one are made good by the profits from the other. For the American shareholder it makes little difference whether Americans drive Fords or Toyotas, but the effect on the volume of employment in the American automobile industry is very different indeed. In this way, rather than competing, British Leyland came to an agreement with Honda; Germany's Volkswagen came to an agreement with Nissan, and Italy's Fiat joined Honda in building a Yamaha motor factory in the United States. In the mid-1970s, 84 Dutch enterprises were either directly or indirectly connected with each other through the multiplicity of the functions of members of their boards of directors, and 80 of the 84 had also close links with the government through the advisory functions of their top executives [Helmers et al., 1975].

The result of this was that capitalism lost the mechanism which had previously reconciled the micro-economic needs of individual enterprises with the system's long-term macro-economic progress. Following their immediate requirements, corporations continued their efforts to reduce wages, and dismissed employees as the demand for consumer goods and services was flagging. But their increasing power to sustain prices in spite of falling demand, and to keep profits up by reducing production costs with the help of labour-substituting technological equipment, deepened the division in society. The rich and the diminishing number of employed workers became more affluent, and the poor and growing number of unemployed became more and more disillusioned and destitute. Towns divided into the living quarters of the well-to-do and the ghettos of the poor. The former were protected by private security firms and well maintained at the residents' expense, and the latter were left only marginally policed because of inadequate public funds and became slums and breeding places for drug abuse and crime and spreading disenchantment with democracy. In theory all this could have been prevented by state intervention. But this would have involved a break with the mental heritage of capitalism and so capitalism became the victim of its inner logic.

Logically, and taken together, the *long-run* prosperity of most giant corporations would have been best served by allowing prices to fall so that consumers' real incomes and employment would continue to rise and induce further expansion. But the *short-term* advantages of low wages made this impracticable. It would have required a sense of historical perspective, and an agreement between the corporations to pursue a common policy. Managers whose entire life is fashioned by the belief in competitive environment and trained in a positivist tradition, can hardly be expected to develop a strong sense of history, or to abandon the practices which have become second nature to them. But determined political intervention might have been of help. The state could have skimmed off excessive profits and wages by taxation, and with the proceeds improved public services, increased welfare expenditure, expanded the infrastructure and even established its own enterprises to increase competition and reduce prices. But the demise of meaningful democracy, and the resultant decline of organized public pressure, emasculated politics and left the conduct of the state in the hands of leaders recruited from the same milieu as the managers of industry and with the same interests, prejudices and limitations.

Keynesian economics and the coming of the Welfare State hardly touched the individualistic profit-seeking mentality. This is unfortunate because this individualistic mentality could not cope any more with an economy which was becoming increasingly complex so that no part of it could adequately function in separation from all others: an irresponsible postman who fails to deliver the mail on time [AFP, 1977; ANP, 1978], or the failure of one worker to oil an essential machine component in a sensitive key industry, can cause production to be halted and hundreds, perhaps thousands, of workers to be idle for hours and even days. If for one reason or another, capitalists stop investing; if Arab states stop the flow of oil; if train drivers strike; if electricians refuse to man the power plants; in fact, if any strategically placed group of people refuses to fulfill its task or performs it erratically, the entire economic life of industrialized nations can be in jeopardy. A highly industrialized nation's affluence depends on the smooth operation of the system as a whole. Unless all its component parts drop in place in clockwork precision it falls into disarray. In the era of regulated capitalism this was beginning to happen. The mechanisms which kept the clockwork moving began to be erratic. The improvements in social security reduced the fear of destitution and deprived the system of its major instrument for the enforcement of work discipline; the rise of ologopolies and of multinational business conglomerates reduced competition and deprived the system of the mechanism by which income was distributed in line with rising productivity; and progressive taxation reduced entrepreneurs' opportunities to become rich in the customary manner and deprived the system of its genuine entrepreneurial elan.

Classical capitalism had always differentiated between legitimate and illegitimate means to acquire wealth. Hold-up men, extortionists, drug-traffickers, thieves, swindlers, embezzlers, forgers, and the rest of that ilk, were excluded from free enterprise society. But in the era of regulated capitalism the threshold of public disapprobation became lower. The transgressions became less distinguishable from the tolerated practices and more difficult to prosecute [Brenner, 1984:7-8]. Workers' fear of unemployment continued, but it was less compelling than it used to be. Absenteeism increased, tea-breaks lengthened, and a large number of workers defrauded the community by claiming unemployment benefits though they were working secretly. Similarly, many employers made use of the most clever stratagems to evade taxes and to deceive their customers and workers. At one time or another, almost everybody came face to face with these malpractices, so that many people gradually came to regard them as 'natural'. Consequently more and more people began to resent working responsibly and honestly for normal wages and to pay taxes and national insurance contributions. Dishonesty is of course no new phenomenon, but the blurring of the boundaries between what is and what is not acceptable was new. And coming at the time when the old efficiency-promoting mechanisms of capitalism were waning, the blurring of these boundaries took on an ominous significance. It threatened the entire fabric of society and reduced the prospect of replacing the individualistic economic mechanisms of capitalism by a system based on social responsibility [Brenner, 1984:12-17]. In fact it nurtured the social climate which ushered in and made widely acceptable the conservative reaction of the 1970s and 1980s.

When the old sense of propriety was waning and with it the hope that the free enterprise system could function without fear of destitution as its driving force, many people came to take it as 'self-evident' that without reasonable prospects for personal material advancement, without the fears associated with unemployment, and without the sense of propriety to make working men feel responsible for, and taking pride in, their work, the efficiency required to maintain high living standards cannot be sustained. They recognized that *individualism* and *competition*, the foundations of the capitalist system, by their internal logic were approaching a paradoxical conclusion: that *individualism*, having been released from the fetters of an older culture, was rapidly becoming short-sighted pure self-interest; and that *competition*, having 'competed' out of business most competitors, was becoming an illusion. But they did not consider new alternatives and fell prey to the Thatcherite delusions that some kind of idealized pre-Keynesian capitalism can be revived, and that the old capitalist mechanisms can somehow be restored.

In fact the old system continued to be dominant even in the era of regulated capitalism but the cracks in it were widening. Ownership of capital continued to confer great advantages but they seemed to be circumscribed by trade unions and the state. The owners of capital continued to invest but the spirit of genuine enterprise declined. They sought security rather than high profits and state subsidies rather than risky innovations. Work became less diligent and dutiful. Employees allowed more time to pass between leaving one post and finding another.

In conclusion, the organized struggle of labour on the system's own terms achieved in the industrialized capitalist countries for most people greater social security and higher living standards than any society ever knew before. But by its inner logic, capitalism led to an increasing concentration and accumulation of wealth. It gave rise to monopolistic or near-monopolistic business conglomerates, with world-wide connections, which increasingly determined both prices and the structure of demand, while the greater affluence and social security and the materialistic individualism which capitalism fosters, was eroding work discipline and the cultural restraints which are necessary to keep the wheels of the highly complex and interdependent economic system turning.

Yet, while the old system was drifting toward social and economic atrophy there were also signs of the emergence of a new social consciousness. The steadily increasing threats to everyone's survival called into life new oppositions. The Chernobyl disaster which made plain that national boundaries no longer offered protection from things done or left undone elsewhere convinced even the most hardened 'war-lords' that nuclear war would mean the end of everyone. The increasing pollution of air and water showed clearly that no one in society is safe without the state being powerful enough to overcome particular interests in order to impose protective restrictions. Thus, while the opposition which was based on the traditional contradictions was losing its force, a new form of opposition was beginning to emerge. It took the form of 'single-issue' groups, such as the women's liberation movement, the anti-nuclear movement, the Friends of the Earth and

Greenpeace. Each in its own way suggests the coming of an ethical revival. Finally, the collapse of the state capitalism which posed as communism in the Soviet Union, liberated socialism from the paralysing fetters of the Russian example, and gives the labour movement a new chance.

# 17.  Summary and Conclusions

Economic progress means a sustained rise in the product of labour per unit of time; an increase in the yield of produce per unit of land and materials; and the exploitation of previously unrecognized resources or the utilization of resources which for technological, economic, or other reasons had remained unexploited. The effect of economic progress is that it gives societies the opportunity to become more affluent and to augment their freedom of choice. Reduced labour-time enables them to choose between working less hours to satisfy customary wants or to work as long as before to satisfy additional wants. Increased yields from land and materials enable them to sustain a growing population, and provide them with the choice to increase the wealth of a few or to spread affluence to a greater number of people; to enjoy the fruits of the new surplus directly or to invest it in larger advantages to be enjoyed in the future. But economic progress does not depend on the availability of land and labour alone; it also requires capital and incentives.

Capital is the wealth used for the more efficient production of further wealth. It needs to be 'created' and can only be obtained at the cost of forgoing something else. No economic progress can ensue without people recognizing the possibility of improving their future by abstaining from consumption in order to transform the savings into productive investment. If people do not trust in the eventual advantages, or if the expected advantages seem too small, too remote or uncertain, economic progress will not materialize. Therefore, given the level of technology, the parameters determining growth are delineated simultaneously by the *ability* to save, which depends upon the size of the difference between the volume of output produced and the minimum of the output necessary for current consumption; and by people's *wish*, or propensity, to save and invest, which depends on income distribution, which means on the cultural, social and political environment.

The *ability* to save is a necessary condition but not sufficient. Incentives to turn savings into economically productive assets are equally required. But having an incentive to utilize part of the produce for the satisfaction of future wants involves foresight. Consequently two kinds of rationality come into conflict: a concrete rationality, relating to individuals, and an abstract rationality, relating to large aggregates. The fact that the fruits of investment need not accrue to those who save makes people who consume all they earn no less rational in their behaviour than others who act on the assumption that in the long run restricted consumption will be more beneficial to them because it provides the savings which can be turned into economic growth-producing assets. This paradox cannot be resolved outside its social and cultural context.

The evolution of capitalism has its roots in earlier periods. The accretion of population since the last quarter of the eleventh century made land in the settled regions of Europe scarce and labour abundant. This encouraged a more intensive and efficient use of land and set in motion a trickle of people into the incipient towns. In the fourteenth century the Black Death turned the abundance of labour into a labour shortage. Rents fell, wages rose, and cultivation was restricted to the relatively most fertile holdings. But the agricultural improvements which had gradually raised the per acre yield of land in the previous period were not eradicated.

In parts of northern Europe competition among landlords for the relatively diminished labour force, the disarray of the central political power, and the end of the supremacy of the heavy cavalry and its replacement by auxiliary peasant forces, put many farmers in an unprecedented position *vis-à-vis* the mighty. It not only enabled them to increase their income, but to resist attempts by their 'betters' to deprive them of this advantage by force. As a result farmers' wish to invest in improvements also increased.

Stimulated by the population's increased purchasing power the towns were beginning to transform. In the thirteenth century the growth of towns had mainly been founded on foreign trade and domestic demand for certain high-priced luxuries. After the Black Death the relatively greater affluence of the working population created a domestic market for popular commodities. The new types of activity required more labour, and as more labour came more and more town inhabitants could no longer produce their own food and had to exchange their products for victuals. Cash crops replaced traditional subsistence crops and before long instead of subsistence requirements, prices determined production decisions. In this way both the ability and the wish to invest came together. Commodities ceased to be exchanged for money in order to obtain other commodities, but money began to be exchanged for commodities to obtain more money.

Certain norms of conduct, the legacy of the Middle Ages, continued to exert a restraining influence on social and economic relations. The Guilds' urban oligarchy set standards of behaviour which caused the nouveaux riches to modify their greed. They imposed strict rules and applied social and economic pressure to prevent fraud and reinforced the old waning religious and moral taboos with legal regulations. These rules inspired nascent capitalism with a spirit of moderation and trustworthiness. Unable to assimilate to the landed aristocracy, which regarded work as demeaning, the new urban elite stressed the quality of workmanship and made this, rather than the pecuniary reward, the hallmark of its status.

In the 'Age of Reason' money-making continued to be 'vulgar' in the eyes of the landed aristocracy, but in the urban environment it ceased to be so as long as those engaged in it kept well within the rules. Almost unnoticed the society which for generations had known only hierarchic vertical links became horizontally aligned. Although employers continued for a very long time to regard themselves 'responsible' for their employees, the inequitable distribution of the fruits of production became increasingly visible and the new antagonistic relationship between employers and employees developed. Craftsmen, journeymen and other workers slowly found that they had more in common with each other than with their various employers and began forming semi-religious organizations.

In the new era of the mercantilist nation state, government became the corrective agent channelling citizens' self-interest to serve the 'public good'. As rulers' power hinged upon the wish of individuals to enrich themselves the state not only legitimized but actively assisted its citizens in their pursuit of wealth. As the acquisition of wealth and skills became subjected to the 'public good' they also became symbols of social distinction and gradually bestowed upon the bourgeoisie a special place within the social hierarchy.

The old moral dogmas continued to maintain their hold, but people aware of their ability to influence their fate by rational endeavours re-examined them from a rationalist point of view. In the place of the teachings of the Church came social pressure and the Law of the Land to restrain undue rapacity. Gradually the political institutions adjusted to the new requirements. Laws founded on reason acknowledged the right to self-preservation, which included the right to the preservation of one's property. Morality was released from its metaphysical mooring, and from the conception of attainment in a world hereafter, and was placed in the context of the search for rational arrangements to obtain a more satisfactory existence here on earth.

The changing perception of the universe also mirrored the difference between the old almost static social world of the Middle Ages. In the world in which people could rise from humble origins, the idea of a world in motion was more convincing than the mediaeval conception of the cosmos. Copernicus, Kepler and Galileo saw a universe in motion. Descartes, Hobbes, Spinoza and Leibniz saw that it was orderly and rationally comprehensible. Newton discovered the mechanism by which the motion is regulated. The universe in motion became with Newton a universe moved by gravitational pulls between masses which attracted one another, harmoniously held together in their particular places or orbits because they were postulated each in its right position in relation to the others.

Cultural obduracy, the tenacity of old beliefs and norms of conduct which only gradually adapted to the changing economic and social opportunities, continued to confine rapacity and exploitation within legally defined limits throughout the 'Age of Reason'. The great writers of the era combined the utilitarian–rational and the traditional–conservative tendencies, by founding moral values in what they took to be man's innate power of judgment. As the gap between desired material improvements and their attainment narrowed the norms of proper conduct, imparted to the young by their parents and teachers, continued to provide society with a degree of stability and continuity.

Nevertheless, with increasing social mobility the old conceptions of natural philosophy also lost ground to a new principle. Galileo not only substituted an earth in motion for the earth at rest, but also experimentation for scholasticism: founding his evidence on observations, he suggested that seeing is better than believing, and that nature can be grasped by everybody's reason.

Man's interest moved away from the old matters of doctrine, from questions concerned with the purpose of life, and shifted toward the art of getting a living. At the same time the advancement of technology was also supplying scientists with new and better instruments to work with. The understanding of the laws governing the universe began to be harnessed to the pursuit of the material ends of the increasingly acquisitive society.

In the second half of the eighteenth century the division of labour caused an increasing number of people to lose their own means of production. On the one hand it solved the adaptation problem, because peasants could almost immediately perform the tasks required by the new industries. On the other hand it reduced workers' power to obtain an equitable share of the welfare which the new technology had to offer. Desolation and fear of unemployment delayed workers' resistance to the injustices of the new-fangled order and left the bourgeoisie free to accumulate investment funds. Desolation and fear taught the urban working class industrial discipline, and the bourgeoisie learned the new role and power of money. The transformation of money from a medium of exchange into a self-expanding value ripened with the new spirit of acquisition. Profit became the purpose of production and the satisfaction of real wants the coincidental concomitant.

The dynamic force behind the rising economic power of the bourgeoisie was competition. It imposed on entrepreneurs an incessant search for technological innovations and improvement. But the falling production costs were neither passed on in full to the consumers nor did wages rise in line with productivity. Increasing profits, mainly from exports, provided the ability to expand investment, but did not commensurately improve the living standard of the workers. For several decades the rapid accretion of people in the urban centres accounted for this. Everything became 'pregnant with its contrary,' but with few exceptions violent widespread social confrontation was deferred.

Some workers whose skills gave them a separate position organized and managed from time to time to improve their living conditions. But for the majority organization was not only hindered by the hostile climate of the period in which the principle of freedom of competition became the idol of the social elite, but also by the positive legislation which forbade it. However, most important was the fact that workers were not yet ready to abandon the ancient habit of looking for protection and guidance from those hierarchically above them, and were more inclined to approach the 'captains of industry' individually, 'cap in hand,' than to make common cause with fellow workers.

In the eighteenth century realistic possibilities for material improvement were confined to a relatively small minority and so were the new conceptions of morality. But this minority was growing and setting the pace of social and economic change. The great majority of people had little truck with the new ideas and continued to hold on to the traditional beliefs and moral value judgments. This combination of an active and utilitarian bourgeoisie with a compliant and submissive working class facilitated the accumulation of capital which provided the initial investment in technological advancement, and industrialization was accelerating. The bourgeoisie was gaining power and status, and by the middle of the nineteenth century it attained its coveted social and economic position and entered upon a period of consolidation. Mobility continued to be accepted but only for individuals on the basis of relative competitive ability within the existing social order; change of the system as a whole ceased to be acceptable. The laws of motion became the laws of dynamic stability and the attention shifted from growth to the study of equilibrium.

In the second half of the nineteenth century the spirit of acquisition not only seized upon all economic phenomena but reached over into the entire sphere of human activities and relations. Accumulation of capital, cost-reducing technological innovation, and the spreading of trade, became *progress*. Human beings became 'labour power,' and nature a 'factor of production'. All individual activities were guided by the highest rationality, but the coordination of the system as a whole was left to a self-regulating mechanism founded upon a metaphysical trust in a natural order which supposedly leads man by an 'invisible hand,' through the study of his own advantage, to employ his resources where they were best employed to the benefit of all. There were spontaneous outbursts of discontent, but the alternatives to the system had not yet become apparent. The organizational efforts of labour were little more than collective attempts by individuals to redress the immediate evils they personally experienced. The number of people employed for wages was very rapidly increasing. Wage-workers acquired most characteristics of a social class but class consciousness developed only very slowly. In part this was due to the greater openness of the middle class than the aristocracy to entrants from 'below,' and partly because class consciousness to be effective requires to be both objective and subjective. The objective consciousness, that people are divided into the rich and the poor was clear enough; but the subjective consciousness which unites individuals was missing. In other words, the division produced class coherence, a common experience and life-style, but not 'class consciousness.' The conflicting interests of employers and workers remained on an individual level within the context of the market system – not class contradictions. There were buyers and sellers of labour trying to obtain the best bargain for themselves, and when workers found it useful and practicable to combine to improve their bargaining position they tried to do so as individuals and not as members of a class.

While industrial society was in its infancy, the development of workers' class consciousness was identified with life-style – with the culture of poverty. the division between 'us,' the poor, and 'them,' the rich, was rapidly dividing industrial societies into 'two nations.' This not only deprived the working class of the ability to recognize the objective causes of its distress but denied it the support of the lower strata of the middle class and intelligentsia who were objectively its allies.

When merchant capitalism became technological capitalism, labour separated into two camps: one increasingly inclined to abandon capitalism altogether, and another prepared to bargain with it on its own terms. The *revolutionary* stream took its inspiration from Marx's theory of dialectical and historical materialism, and the *neoclassical* (unionist) stream from the logic of capitalism itself.

Marx himself never escaped the values he inherited. He had no other values by which to judge the bourgeoisie except those to which it itself was paying lip-service. By converting Ricardo's *economic* labour value theory into an *ethical* issue involving a property right, he claimed for labour moral hegemony. Invoking the bourgeoisie's own conception of property rights, and applying it to work, he supplied the labour movement with the ammunition for fighting the bourgeoisie upon its own ethical premises. But before long the bourgeoisie learned to parry this assault by abandoning the labour value theory in favour of *utility* as the source of value.

The purpose of labour movements and trade unions in both camps was, and continues to be, the protection and improvement of workers' living conditions. But there were large differences of opinion within them. The left wing of the social democrats and communists denied the practicability of gradual reforms and chose for a political rather than an economic struggle. Anarcho-syndicalists believed that capitalism could last for a very long time because the pursuit of gain permeated society and provided each individual with an illusion of security of life and property. It can therefore only be destroyed from outside by acts unexplainable in terms of bourgeois reason – preferably by a *general strike*. The reformist wing of the socialist movement was convinced that persistent pressure on employers would eventually lead to a peaceful socialization of industry. Some converts to this policy even proposed to use union funds to create union industries in order to eliminate capitalism by its own means – that is by competition. On the moderate right of the movement were the non-revolutionary (neoclassical) unionists who preferred to work with and within the capitalist system. They were primarily concerned with the immediate wants of their members – with wage rates and working conditions. They did not relate to any particular vision of a future society but operated like capitalist business organizations to maximize their members' 'dividends.'

It may be said that the era of bourgeois consolidation in the nineteenth century provided both the *ability* and the *wish* which were necessary for economic progress. It created conditions facilitating the accumulation of funds, and it provided powerful mechanisms to stimulate investment and work discipline.

The Depression of the 1930s was of previously unknown severity. In Germany neither the bourgeoisie nor the left had a credible, immediately practicable, policy for its termination. The bourgeoisie was held responsible for the Depression but Germany's social-democrats and communists were unable to give to the working class the insight required to effect the 'leap' to socialism. With all the technological advancement that had taken place capitalism had in fact not yet reached a level of productivity capable of meeting simultaneously the required resources for investment and higher living standards.

Unlike the liberal bourgeoisie and the left, Hitler's *national socialists* did not have to contend with this reality. Instead of a solution they proffered *escapism*. In the place of rationality they offered mystic and in the place of individualism they proffered unconditional loyalty to their leader. Instead of economic welfare, which was difficult to attain, they preached new values.

They offered a myth popularized by ancient prejudices, which made the individual meaningless outside the nation. They did not promise to eliminate poverty and destitution but to make them acceptable.

In one respect they were successful where their parliamentary predecessors had failed. They provided employment. The means by which Hitler achieved this were simple. He forced labour to accept low wages, and skimmed off the savings to finance new employment in the production of weapons and war-related public works. He did not increase workers' welfare but spread poverty more evenly. In the end it led to war and destruction.

But neither *national socialism* nor true *socialism* could conquer without destroying first the bourgeoisie's social and cultural hegemony. Genuine socialist movements attacked the bourgeois values from a rational and materialistic point of view, giving prime place to welfare and the satisfaction of real wants; national socialism's onslaught on the bourgeoisie was directed against its liberal individualism.

While Nazism 'solved' the German unemployment problem by preparing for war and diverting workers' attention from their material reality, and while socialism had only a critique of the capitalist system but no convincing immediate solace to offer to its victims, a new type of capitalism was beginning to take shape in the United States. This modified capitalism also allocated to the state the task of sponsoring employment, but unlike Nazism it genuinely regarded the revival of the faltering economy as its prime objective. It considered neither war, nor the subjecting of labour to politically inspired wage restraint, practicable or even desirable means to this end.

In the United States the economic crisis shattered the illusion that American society was classless. Being more pragmatic than Europeans, American society and a large part of the American political establishment acknowledged that the old approach did not work, and that it was no longer sustainable in the face of an increasingly irate electorate, and drew conclusions. Both major parties put forward new ideas which, to say the least, gave the impression to the voters of being capable of solving their immediate problems. Thus, even if for no better reason than vote-catching, politicians came up with new ideas. Consequently, democracy, capitalism's own creation in the course of its struggle for ascendancy, made the repudiation of the old economic credos unavoidable.

The President who first identified with this new trend was Franklin Delano Roosevelt. His slogan 'A New Deal' caught the imagination of the masses and signalled the coming of a new approach. Government ceased to be a mere guardian of 'law and order,' and assumed responsibility for people's welfare. For several decades the ballot paper became a powerful instrument in the hands of the American working class for the improvement of its living standard. The New Deal was ushered in by a host of social and economic legislation funded by *deficit financing*, and the era of 'regulated capitalism' and 'Keynesian economics' was born.

Classical capitalism always asserted that its economic system tends toward a full-employment equilibrium. Wages may be 'sticky' and delay readjustment, but in the end all must turn out the way it should. The way to recovery from recessions was not in the actions of a government. Its task was, at most, to try to prevent trade unions from keeping wages up, reducing its own expenditure to keep the rate of interest down, and making private investment as attractive as possible.

In 1936 Keynes published his *General Theory* in which he argued that in no sophisticated economic system, in which money is used, would wages, prices and interest rates fall far enough and fast enough to restore full employment once a major fall in investment or increase in saving had occurred.

Unlike the socialists, Keynes had no quarrel with the profit motive, but he believed that profit was just as much dependent on high revenues as on low costs. If the level of *national income* is determined by the rate of investment and its multiplier, and capitalists can only be expected to invest when they may hope for a sufficiently large demand to sell their prospective output with profit, then in a long-lasting recession only an 'independent actor' – one who is *not* necessarily dependent on the expectation of profit – can offer solace. Such an 'independent actor' Keynes saw in the state.

With this Keynes not only sinned against the sacred principle of *laissez-faire*, but deprived the bourgeoisie of two of its most cherished idols, namely the idolatry of low wages and of low interest rates, and 'Victorian morality.' He transformed economics from a science in which man seemed to have been created to serve the economy into a discipline in which the welfare of the majority of citizens became the focus of attention. Keynes was not alone. There were others who arrived at similar conclusions, but in Western Europe no one was able to sway government policy before the war. In America there was less social and cultural obduracy, and Roosevelt's election campaigns provided the required publicity to make the public aware of alternatives.

The war shook Europeans out of their customary way of life and put an end to their inertia. The reformers on the left gained prestige. Industrialized Western Europe took a step to the left and once the principle of full employment was established as a political objective the objections to Keynes's call for state intervention were no longer sustainable.

But there was more to the Keynesian revolution than its practicability. It was part of a much wider revolution which was transforming man's conception of the universe and his place in it. Scientists' philosophical background does not influence their answers, but it does determine their *questions*, and final understanding can depend on this. For the classicists the capitalist economic system was 'given.' Man could do little more than to adjust to it. For Marx it was a social artifact which by an inner logic, and by growth of consciousness, transforms itself into another system. For Keynes it was a positive fact, but one which can be moulded to suit society's requirements.

The problem with regulating the economy was how and when the state must intervene. Regulated capitalism requires a distribution of the national income between consumption and investment so that, taking account of population accretion and technological advancement, demand neither exceeds output nor rises insufficiently to induce savers to turn their savings into investment. But this depends on a long-run trend which is elusive and beset by distortions in perspective and stochastic variations. Consequently Keynesian regulation in the post-war era did not eliminate the economic fluctuations but it substantially reduced their severity.

The dynamic element in capitalism was its two-pronged mechanism of competition: competition between entrepreneurs for their respective shares of the market, and competition between employers and workers for their shares in the fruits of production. Fearful of being driven out of business by more efficient competitors entrepreneurs were inexorably driven to search for and introduce technological and organizational improvements. Facing an increasingly well organized and powerful labour force they were pressed to introduce improvements which could help them raise output per worker sufficiently to compensate for rising wages while maintaining sufficient profits to finance innovations. This dual mechanism was not only the dynamic but also the progressive element in capitalism. It increased mankind's ascendancy over nature and gave it the power to produce the material affluence which most people in the capitalist countries actually enjoy. The fuel which kept this economic growth-producing mechanism going was fear of destitution.

For a long time, this fear enabled the bourgeoisie to put the emphasis mainly on one type of competition, namely between employers for their market shares. In the twentieth century this type of competition was gradually eroding through the growth of monopolies, monopsonies and oligopolies, but the second type of competition, namely competition between capitalists and organized labour, was slowly filling the gap. The combination of both types of competition, the competition between the capitalists themselves, which compels most of them to pass on in lower prices the gains from cost-reducing innovation, and the competition between capital and labour, which forces employers to share with labour through wage improvements the gains from innovation when monopolistic practices prevent prices from falling in line with cost reductions, became the mainstay of the growing welfare.

In theory this dual mechanism of competition should assure a fairly equitable distribution of the growing wealth. However in practice its distributive power was, and continues to be, bypassed through exports making good the deficiencies in domestic demand. But when exports cannot continue to expand, the state alone can fill the gap. It must skim off excessive savings by taxation and restore the domestic purchasing power by regulated spending. To be sure, this needs to be done judiciously and without detracting too much from the 'self-correcting' powers of the 'wealth effect'.

For a quarter of a century government intervention successfully reduced the inherent instability of capitalism and markedly diminished its disgraceful social consequences. In fact the Keynesian compromise between free enterprise and regulation did much more than that. For almost three decades it transformed state intervention from a tool for reducing mass unemployment into a purposefully employed instrument to promote the public's welfare. From a kind of 'fire brigade' coming to the system's aid when it needed to be saved, it became a device for attaining well defined social objectives. While the economics profession was squabbling about whether the Keynesian theory was general or only a special case, or trying to integrate Keynes into the old paradigm, the general public gave its own meaning to Keynesian economics. The public became convinced that within limits the state can mould the system to its wants. Next to full employment the public demanded from it, and obtained in many countries, health care, general and free education, pensions for the aged, free or heavily subsidized food for infants and so on, which became the foundations of the Welfare State.

With the new mood came a redistribution of the national income by increasingly progressive and heavier taxation. The period between the end of World War II and the early 1970s witnessed a dramatic rise in productivity accompanied by an equally impressive rise in the general standard of living. The demand for labour in the service occupations increased, the share of government and the 'not-for-profit' sector in employment and the national product rose and surpassed the share of private enterprise. The rich did not like it, but as long as most people consciously used their ballot papers to further their own interests, their opposition was muted. But the rapid growth of productivity in the goods-producing sector was not matched by the service sector, where most of the new state employment was, and put an increasing strain on public finances. Government policies to influence the levels of national income and employment by small changes in taxation or expenditures failed to contain inflation. And in the 1970s, when public consciousness also eroded and meaningful democracy was losing its vitality, the rich grasped their opportunity for the 'return match'. Armed with the Laffer curve, supply-side theories, and monetarism, they contested the Keynesian compromise with vengeance.

In the meantime, however, the social composition of the powerful altered. Management became increasingly separated from ownership and a new 'class' of salaried directors and technocrats came into existence whose interests were often not identical with those of the traditional capitalist owner-managers. Multinational monster corporations with independent funds and long-term globe-embracing plans and the capacity to shift investment and employment from one country to another became more numerous and powerful. Their increasing ability to circumvent government policies and to influence political decisions eroded not only the distributive powers of democracy but also the link between saving and investment upon which Keynesian economic regulation rests. Alienation, private ownership, and the profit motive – in short capitalism – continued to be the ruling economic paradigm, but the paradigm assumed a new form.

As the labour movement arose as a reaction to the social and economic evils which attended the rise of capitalism before the economy could provide an acceptable living standard for everyone, its main weakness was its inability to offer a sufficiently attractive alternative. But by the middle of the present century, when technological progress achieved this level of efficiency in the industrially most advanced countries, a particular kind of materialistic individualism had taken hold of society and came close to being regarded as part of 'human nature'. This powerful mental legacy of capitalism prevented labour from grasping the real possibility of change.

Keynes thought that the state should determine the aggregate amount of resources devoted to augmenting the means of production and fix the basic rate of reward for those who own them. He believed that the inequalities of wealth and income, and capitalism's failure to sustain full employment, were diminishing and sometimes even served a social purpose. What Keynes failed to see was capitalism's cultural obduracy and exceptional capacity to internalize opposition. Rising living standards, improved social security, the growing share of the public sector and the increasing impact of 'non-profit-making' organizations on employment, did not toll the knell for the old social and economic system. They smoothed the hard edges of capitalism but did not eliminate its main socially debilitating elements.

Moreover, the liberating diminution of economic fears in the Keynesian era was accompanied by a repudiation of some of the values which had previously been regarded as absolute. The triumph of competitive materialistic individualism meant that the question 'is it good for me?' replaced the question 'is it good?'. 'Good' became a matter of personal choice, and as people reason by analogy, the loss of stable values was a reflection of and reflected upon the scientists' perception of the universe. As a result the question 'will it succeed?' replaced the question 'is it true?' and capitalism replaced the traditional concern of science with truth and made truth subservient to expediency. This approach had an unfortunate result because economic growth provided higher living standards, and people regarded it as the product of scientific innovations. Consequently, before they became aware of the environmental hazards, they simply took for granted that all scientific advancement must serve the public good.

Scientists motivated by competition registered great achievements, especially where their work was of technological applicability, but they had little control over the direction their work was taking. Too often the decisions about what to research were left to industrialists and politicians. While society was conquering nature it lost the ability to control itself. In this way the mechanism of incessant competition, which gave capitalism its positive achievements, deprived society of its freedom to make crucial choices about its collective long-term future. Like the sorcerer's apprentice in the fairy tale, capitalism released forces it could not control.

Industrial progress imposes a previously unknown measure of complexity and specialization on the economic system. Everyone's welfare depends upon everybody else fulfilling his task diligently, responsibly and on time. In the past this discipline had mainly been assured by fear. Improved social security diminished individuals' fear of destitution and the ascent of the new morality of relativism broke the custom's spell. Consequently, industrial discipline deteriorated. Yet with neither fear nor the old extraneous moral sanction to assure work discipline, and without a new sense of social responsibility to take their place, industrial society cannot sustain for long the comfortable living standard it provides.

The motive for investing in a free enterprise economy is profit, and profit is the difference between revenue and cost. When price competition is brisk it makes no difference whether the objective of investment is the expansion of output or cost- reducing innovation. The effect of both will normally be positive for income and employment. But when price competition is slack and the gains from cost-reducing investments are not passed on to consumers the consequences may be different. Then, to sustain profits, the most powerful corporations will adjust their production targets downward to suit the shrinking market. The emphasis on cost-reducing innovations will lessen the demand for labour and unemployment will increase.

Keynes believed that government expenditure creates effective demand which induces investment, and therefore also employment, in the private sector. His opponents, who regarded the rate of interest as the crucial factor for investment and employment, assumed that pampering the rich by wage restraint and low corporation taxes would increase savings, reduce interest rates, and restrain inflation. They ignored the possibility that demand for funds may rise together with, and in spite of, rising interest rates.

With growing affluence in the late 1960s the demand for services increased. As several important services can hardly be improved by labour-time-reducing innovations, social scientists thought that the future of full employment lay in this increase. It was an illusion; and not only because they could not foresee that in many services employment opportunities would fall prey to the computer. But because unemployment and the cost of social security rose; corporations discovered new ways to avoid taxation and to obtain government subsidies, and government revenue decreased.

Until the 1970s economic growth and full employment were on the whole sustained by entrepreneurs competing fairly vigorously for their relative shares of the markets; and by capital and labour fighting a relentless tug-of-war for the fruits of innovation. Even when oligopoly frustrated competition, progressive taxation and social security provisions helped to maintain the balance between output and consumption. But since the early 1970s competition has faltered. The power of oligopolies to fix prices has increased and the strength of organized labour has diminished. Yet in spite of the weakening of the self-correcting forces of the market system, governments failed to take the corrective measures which were necessary. They neither raised corporation taxes to skim off oligopolistic profits, nor extended the public sector and collective services. The reasons for this were the new cultural and social climate, international trade complications, and the fear of accelerating inflation.

In a society in which social position is determined by property, a distinction between goods and services seems natural. In particular a society which assigns social status to the command of *private* property has little appreciation for collective ownership and public services. The main cause of the onslaught on governments' share in the national income is therefore not its cost but the reflection of the unwillingness of the rich to pay for sustaining the poor. Those with most reason to object to high government expenditure are those who pay most taxes; those most dependent on government support are the poor who pay least.

A real difficulty to accept the expansion of employment in the service sector is the legacy from times when productivity was too low to assure an adequate supply of goods for all. Though the proliferation of services is inherent in the progress of technology many people continue to regard occupations which do not help to produce tangible products with suspicion. Even economists continue to be biased. As they hold mechanization, which plays a minor role in services, to be the key to productivity, and focus their attention on the competitive market-place, while many services are in the public sector, they feel that services have little to contribute to economic theory. But the overriding reason for the 'oversight' is that they share the ideological paradigm of those who wield economic and political power. With notable exceptions, economists adhere to the economic theories which reflect the opinions of the social elite and favour policies tainted by its conception of the 'public good'. As a result, they 'helped' the government to misinterpret the causes of high interest rates and inflation, and found solutions in restricting the money supply, limiting wage increases, and reducing social security. Moreover, by using false analogies they succeeded in convincing the public that these measures would restore full employment.

One reason for this success was that in spite of the fact that in the second half of the twentieth century the social security system seemed firmly established, and that it really reduced poverty and destitution, democracy was almost imperceptibly losing its emancipating powers. The failure of education to keep up critical and normative traditions; the drift of the mass media from informing the public toward persuading it to accept 'given' attitudes, and the resulting tenacity of patterns of culture nurtured in the era of pre-regulated capitalism, undermined the post-war achievements of society. Worst of all, the confusion of objectivity with non-involvement left the determination of values to people who claimed that their own values were universal. By analogy class struggle was transformed into collective pursuit of narrowly defined materialistic self-interest and workers' solidarity was transformed into union discipline. In this climate of competitive individualistic utilitarianism democracy was divested of the progressive emancipating power which had been responsible for the creation of the Welfare State, and capitalism was able to internalize most opposition. Democracy remained formally intact, but the mechanisms which make it meaningful were gradually eroding.

This erosion was strengthened by the arrival of 'industrial feudalism'; the vertical and horizontal integration of businesses where new hierarchies developed, with each 'rank' being assigned its particular status, responsibilities, remuneration and privileges. This organization spread from the private to the public sector, and as the state's share in a country's work force increased, it took the place of the old social distinctions. Whom one knows and whom one serves became the overriding factor in an individual's advancement.

Entrepreneurs continued to be interested in innovation but mainly to reduce production costs. Where producers kept on vying for their respective market shares they did so by advertising and 'tied' services rather than competitive pricing. Large business conglomerates were increasingly able to determine both the supply and the demand side of their markets. Step by step capitalism lost its two-pronged competitive mechanism and its long-term growth potential. Competition, which had previously obliged producers to innovate and to pass on the resultant cost reductions to consumers, diminished. Effective demand ceased to grow, employment and consumption no longer kept the system on the long-run upward path. In the 1970s increasing wage claims and social security payments still sustained consumer demand in line with the rising productivity, but with insufficient market competition to keep prices down, this type of 'competition' caused wage hikes and corporation taxes to be passed on to consumers. Thus real competition between capital and labour also faltered. In spite of mounting productivity this set in motion the familiar inflationary spiral.

But governments continued to mistake the symptoms for their causes and tried to curb inflation by monetarist measures. The results were disastrous. Prices, wages and interest rates continued to rise and unemployment and the cost of social security soared. Confronted with unemployment and stagflation, many governments abandoned efforts to regulate the economy by the Keynesian instruments and sought refuge in a mixture of monetary measures and supply-side economics to raise the share of profit. They believed that reduced consumer spending would contain inflation; that increased savings would bring down interest rates and together they would restore employment. The possibility that inflation may have been caused by inflexible prices and high interest rates rather than by rising wages was ignored. Inflation really moderated but interest rates and unemployment remained high. The era of the silicon chip, the robot and the other cost-reducing innovations rendered unemployment chronic. The unemployed became socially marginalized. Illiteracy, drug abuse and crime proliferated and in many towns entire districts became unsafe.

It may seem that all this could have been prevented by taxation of oligopolistic profits and judicious government investment. But this kind of regulation requires considerable state control and informed democracy. By the 1980s governments were already too emasculated to be effective, and the power of multinationals to decide whether to invest and where to do so had become too strong to be curbed. Capitalism had lost the mechanism which previously reconciled the micro-economic needs of individual enterprises with the system's long-term macro-economic progress. As the demand for consumer goods and services was flagging, corporations continued their efforts to reduce wages, and dismissed more employees. But their increasing power to sustain prices in spite of falling demand, and to keep profits up by reducing production costs, deepened the divisions in society. The rich and the diminishing number of employed workers became more affluent, and the poor and a growing number of unemployed became destitute and disillusioned. Slums became not only breeding places for drug abuse and crime, but also of spreading disenchantment with democracy. Capitalism fell victim to its inner logic by leaving the conduct of the state in the hands of leaders recruited from the same milieu as the managers of industry and with the same interests, prejudices and limitations.

Fear of destitution had imposed a particular life-style on capitalist society. It encouraged an almost purely utilitarian valuation of people, objects and events and established the supremacy of business interests over all other spheres of life. As a result the means by which capitalism had obtained the objective capability to ameliorate mankind's lot subverted the values of society and gave them a direction inconsistent with the attainment of this end. Post-war democracy and the Welfare State were not allowed sufficient time to eliminate the mentality of a profit-seeking individual. But it reduced the compulsive power of capitalism's economic mechanism while the economy was becoming increasingly complex so that no part of it could function in separation from all others. The improvements in social security reduced the fear of destitution and deprived the system of its major instrument for the enforcement of work discipline. The rise of oligopolies and of multinational business conglomerates reduced competition and deprived the system of the mechanism by which income was distributed in line with rising productivity. Progressive taxation reduced entrepreneurs' opportunities to become rich in the customary manner and deprived the system of its genuine entrepreneurial elan. As a result of all this, not only the marginalized poor undermined the moral fabric of society but the threshold of public moral disapprobation became lower. The transgressions became less distinguishable from the tolerated practices and more difficult to prosecute. People increasingly ceased to work responsibly and honestly for normal wages and to pay taxes and national insurance contributions. The old sense of propriety was waning and with it hope that the system could function by free enterprise, but without fear of destitution as its driving force.

Individualism, having been released from the fetters of an older culture, was rapidly becoming short-sighted pure self-interest; and competition, having 'competed' out of business most competitors, was becoming an illusion. But society was not yet prepared to consider new alternatives and fell prey to Thatcherite delusions that some kind of idealized pre-Keynesian capitalism could restore the defunct capitalist mechanisms.

Yet time does not stand still. New risks, like the pollution of air and water which can only be prevented by collective efforts, revived the recognition that the individual pursuit of wealth can hardly solve society's most urgent problems. The collapse of state capitalism in the Soviet Union finally liberated Western socialism from the mentally paralysing fetters of the Russian hegemony over progressive revolutionary thought. Whether a new era of social responsibility is dawning, or a revival of feudalism and a reversion to the old distinction between rich and powerful and poor and voiceless is approaching, is impossible to predict. As Gellner says: 'No principle of distribution is either self-validating or self-enforcing', and the new forces which will lead the way are not yet visible.

In conclusion: capitalism's success was the product of a particular combination of new self-centred materialism, and patterns of culture inherited from an earlier era which prevented it from becoming self-destructive. But driven by the inner logic of its competitive economic mechanism it destroyed these modifying patterns of culture before society had time to develop new ones for sustaining it in its new form while keeping its progressive element. For this reason, capitalism may be doomed and society destined to revert to poverty in spite of its technological capability to produce affluence for all. The one redeeming hope which remains is that the failure of the recent attempts to restore its pre-war social and economic relations will be recognized and that people will become conscious of the fate awaiting them unless they start thinking in a new direction.

# Cited Literature

AFP [1977]
Reported in *de Volkskrant,* 6 December.

ANP [1978]
Reported in *Het Parool,* 13 September.

Ashton T.S. [1955]
*An Economic History of England: The 18th Century,*
Methnen & Co.Ltd., London.

Bakunin M.A. [1914]
*Oeuvres; fédéralisme, socialisme et antithéologisme;
lettres sur le patrictisme; dieu et l'état,* Paris, 1895.

Barnet R.J. [1981]
*Fünf Handelsriesen Kontrollieren den Getreidemarkt der
Welt,* Berlin.

Bayle P. [1935]
Quoted here from Hazard P. *The European Mind 1680-1715,*
Harmondsworth, Pelican ed., 1964.

Bentham J. [1789]
*Introduction to the Principles of Morals and
Legislation (Writings:* vol.IV) Edinburgh 1838-1843, London
University, 1970.

Berger J. [1972]
*Ways of Seeing,* Penguin, Harmondsworth.

Bergsten F.C. [1978]
*American Multinationals and American Interests,*
Brookings Institution, Washington D.C.

Bernstein E. [1898]
*Evolutionary Socialism.*

Block M. [1962]
*Feudal Society* (English translation L.A. Manyon), Routledge & Kegan Paul, London, 2nd edition.

Block M. [1953]
'Feudalism', *The Encyclopedia of Social Sciences,* vol.VI (first published in 1935), Macmillan, New York.

Bourne H.R. Fox [1876]
*Life of John Locke,* London.

Brenner Y.S. [1961]
'The Inflation of Prices in Early 16th Century England', *Economic History Review* XIV, No.2.

Brenner Y.S. [1966]
*Theories of Economic Development and Growth,* George Allen & Unwin, London.

Brenner Y.S. [1969]
*A Short History of Economic Progress,* Frank Cass, London.

Brenner Y.S. [1971]
*Agriculture and the Economic Development of Low Income Countries,* Mouton, The Hague & Paris.

Brenner Y.S., Spithoven A.H. & Weggelaar M.J. [1981]
*Bezuinigen is geen Werk,* Uitgeverij Intermediair, Amsterdam.

Brenner Y.S. [1982]
'Het Positivisme van Vilfredo Pareto', *Intermediair,* Amsterdam, 26 February.

Brenner Y.S. [1983]
'Sources of Inflation: Old and New' in Schmukler N. & Marcus E. (eds) *Inflation Through the Ages Economic, Social, Psychological and Historical Aspects,* Columbia University Press, New York.

Brenner Y.S. [1984]
*Capitalism, Competition and Economic Crisis,* Wheatsheaf, Szabo, Washington & Brighton.

Bridbury A.R. [1973]
'The Black Death', *Economic History Review,* XXVI, no.4.

Brinton C. [1967]
'Enlightenment' in *The Encyclopedia of Philosophy* (ed. Paul Edwards) Macmillan, London, New York, vol.II.

Bronowski J. [1951]
*The Common Sense of Science*, Heinemann, London.

Burke E. [1790]
*Reflections on the Revolution in France* in Lawrence F. & King W. (eds), London 1803-1827. Repr. London 1964, Everyman's Library.

Burke E. [1793]
*Correspondence of Edmund Burke* (ed. T.W. Copeland), Cambridge Univ. Press, Cambridge 1958-1965.

Butler J. [1726]
*Three Sermons upon Human Nature*, London.

Carlyle T. [1843]
'Past and Present', *Fraser's Magazine*, Boston.

Central Bureau of Statistics [1971]
*Statistisch Zakboek*, Staatsuitgeverij, 's-Gravenhage.

Central Bureau of Statistics [1975]
*75 Jaar Statistiek van Nederland,* 's-Gravenhage.

Chase R.X. [1979]
'Production Theory' in A.S. Eichner (ed.), *A Guide to Post-Keynesian Economics*, Sharpe, New York.

Cicero M.T. [51 BC]
*De Re Oublica* (Smith S.B. translation of 1929), quoted from Sabine G.H., Faber, London, 1967.

Cicero M.T. [date unknown]
*De Legibus* (Keyes translation), The Modern Library, N.Y., 1951.

Cole G.D. [1925-27]
*A Short History of the British Working Class Movement, 1789-1947*, London, 1948.

Colie, R.L. [1968]
*International Encyclopedia of Social Sciences* vol.XV (ed. D. Sills) Macmillan, New York.

Condillac de E.B. [1776]
*Le commerce et le gouvernement considérés relativement l'un à l'autre*, Paris.

Crowe, K.C. [1978]
*America for Sale*, Garden City.

Der Spiegel [1977]
'Der Ramponierte Rechtsstaat' *Der Spiegel*, 5 December, Hamburg.

Descartes [1637]
*Discourse on Method* (quoted here from Sutcliffe translation), Penguin, Harmondsworth, 1968.

Dettling u.a. [1977]
*Die Neue Soziale Frage und die Zukunft der Demokratie*, München-Wien (2nd edition).

Dobb M. [1937]
*Studies in the Development of Capitalism*, International Publishers, New York.

Domar E.D. [1946]
'Capital expansion, rate of growth and employment', *Econometrica*, vol.14, pp.137-47.

Domar E.D. [1947]
'Expansion and Employment', *The American Economic Review*, vol.37 (March) pp.34-55.

Dorsey of Golf-Oil [1976]
Reported in *Der Spiegel* (German news magazine) September, Hamburg.

Dugas R. & Costabel P. [1958]
'The Organisation of the Principles of Classical Mechanics' in Rene Taton (ed.), *A General History of Science* (English translation), vol.II, Thames & Hudson, London 1964.

Dumke R.H. [1986]
'Income Distribution and Industrialisation in Germany, 1850-1913' (Paper: Utrecht Symposium on Income & Wealth Distribution).

Durkheim E. [1893]
*De la division du travail social*, Paris.

Dutt C. ed. [1964]
*Fundamentals of Marxism-Leninism,* F.L.P.H., Moscow.

Eichner A.S. [1976]
*The Megacorp and Oligopoly,* Cambridge University Press, Cambridge.

Einstein A. [1930]
Article in *Berliner Tageblatt,* 11 November. Translated into English in *Ideas and Opinions,* New York 1954.

Einstein A. [1938]
*The Evolution of Physics* (quoted here from 7th edition), Simon & Schuster, New York 1967.

Elvin M. [1988]
'China as a Counterfactual' in Baechler J. et al. (eds), *Europe and the Rise of Capitalism,* Blackwell, Oxford.

Engels F. [1885]
*Anti-Duhring* - Herr Eugen Duhring's Revolution in Science (quoted here from International Publishers Edition New York, 1970).

Engels F. [1890]
Letter to J. Bloch of 21 September, *Correspondence,* Foreign Languages Publishing House, 1960, Moscow.

Freeman J. [1935]
*Introduction to an anthology of proletarian literature in the United States,* New York.

Friedman M. [1956]
'The Quantity Theory of Money: A Restatement', *Studies in the Quantity Theory of Money,* Chicago, pp.3-21.

Friedman M. [1977]
'Inflation and Unemployment', *Journal of Political Economy,* vol.85, no.3.

Galbraith J.K. [1967]
*The New Industrial State,* Signet Books, New York.

Galbraith J.K. [1981]
'The Conservative Onslaught', *New York Review of Books,* New York, 22 January.

Gellner E. [1988]
'Introduction', in Baechler J. et al. (eds) *Europe and the Rise of Capitalism*, Blackwell, Oxford.

Ginsberg M. [1934]
'Class', in *Encyclopedia of Social Sciences*, vol.III, Macmillan, London.

Ginzberg E. [1976]
'The Pluralistic Economy of the U.S.', *Scientific American*, December.

Ginzberg E. [1982]
'The Mechanization of Work', *Scientific American*, December.

Godwin W. [1946]
*Enquiry Concerning the Principle of Political Justice* (3rd edition, ed. F.E.L Priestley), Toronto.

Goody J. [1968]
*International Encyclopedia of Social Sciences*, vol. XVI (ed. D. Sills) Macmillan, New York.

Grotius H. [1625]
*De jure belli ac pacis.*

Hamberg D. [1961]
*Principles of a Growing Economy*, Norton & Company, New York.

Hannah L. & Kay J.A. [1977]
*Concentration of Modern Industry*, London.

Harrod R.F. [1939]
'An essay in dynamic theory', *Economic Journal*, vol.49, pp.14-33.

Heckscher E.F. [1955]
*Mercantilism* (2nd edition), Allen & Unwin, London.

Heilbroner R. [1990]
'Analysis and Vision in the History of Modern Economic Thought', *Journal of Economic Literature*, vol.XXVIII, September.

Heisenberg W. [1975]
'The Philosophical Background of Modern Physics', Dubrovnik lecture notes.

Helmers H.M. et al. [1975]
*Graven naar Macht*, Amsterdam.
Hirshleifer J. [1966]
*Disaster and Recovery: The Bleck Death in Western Europe*, Rand Corporation.
Hobbes T. [1651]
*Leviathan* (ed. M. Oakeshott, Oxford, 1947).
Hoffding H. [1900]
*A History of Modern Philosophy* (quoted here from Macmillan Dover 1955 edition) New York.
Hume D. [1739]
*Treatise of Human Nature*, pts I & II, London.
Hume D. [1740]
*Treatise of Human Nature*, pt III, Oxford Clarendon Press 1951, London.
Hume D. [1748]
*An Enquiry Concerning Human Understanding* (quoted here from C.W. Hendel edition), New York, 1955.
Hutcheson F. [1725]
*Inquiry into the Origins of Our Ideas of Beauty and Virtue*, London.
Hutcheson F. [1728]
*An Essay on the Nature and Conduct of Passions and Affections* (quoted from 1730 edition), London.
Jaffe W. [1979]
'The normative bias', *Quarterly Journal of Economics*, no.91, August.
James J.A. [1986]
'The Distribution of Wealth in Late Eighteenth-Century Britain' (Paper: Utrecht Symposium on Income and Wealth Distribution).
Jenkins F. [1870]
*The Graphic Representation of the Laws of Supply and Demand, and their Application to Labour.*
Jevons W.S. [1888]
*Theory of Political Economy* (3rd edition), London. First published in 1871.

Joad C.E.M. [1953]
'Herbert Spencer' in *Encyclopedia of Social Sciences,* vol.XIV (first published in 1935) New York.
Kahn, R.F. [1931]
'The Relation of Home Investment to Unemployment', *Economic Journal,* June.
Kaldor N. [1966]
'Alternative Studies of Distribution,' *Review of Economic Studies,* no.33, pp.309-19.
Kalecki M. [1966]
*Studies in the Theory of Business Cycles 1933-1939,* Augustus Kelley, New Jersey.
Kalecki M. [1971]
*Selected Essays on the Dynamics of the Capitalist Economy 1933-1970,* Cambridge University Press, Cambridge.
Kant I. [1781]
*Kritik der reinen Vernunft,* Riga 1781, Hamburg, Philosophische Bibliothek Bk 37a, 1976.
Kant I. [1785]
*Grundlegung zur Metaphysik der Sitten,* Riga (translation by T.K. Abbott), London 1873.
Keynes J.M. [1936]
*The General Theory of Employment Interest and Money* (quoted here from 1954 edition), Macmillan, London.
Keynes J.M. [1971]
'A Tract on Monetary Reform', *Collected Writings,* Macmillan, London.
Koo S.M. & Lee J.W. [1988]
'Trade-off between Economic Growth and Income Equality' in Y.S. Brenner et al., *The Theory of Income and Wealth Distribution,* Wheatsheaf & St Martin's, Sussex, New York.
Koyre A. and Taton R. eds [1964]
*A General History of Science,* vol.II (quoted from English translation), Thames and Hudson, London.

Kraus F. [1986]
'The Distribution of Pre-Tax Incomes in Western Europe: Trends and Structures' (Paper: Utrecht Symposium on Income and Wealth Distribution).

Kregel J.A. [1979]
'Income Distribution' in A.S. Eichner (ed.), *A Guide to Post-Keynesian Economics*, Macmillan, London.

Kropotkin P. [1902]
*Mutual Aid.*

Kuznets S. [1955]
'Economic Growth and Income Inequality', *American Economic Review*, no.45, March.

Kuznets S. [1959]
'Quantitative Aspects of the Economic Growth of Nations. IV. Distribution of National Income by Factor Shares', *Economic Development & Cultural Change*, no.7, April.

Kuznets S. [1963]
'Quantitative Aspects of the Economic Growth of Nations, VIII. Distribution of Income by Size', *Economic Development & Cultural Change*, no.12, October.

Landes D. [1976]
'The ubiquitous bourgeoisie', *Times Literary Supplement*, 4 June, London.

Landes D. [1969]
*Unbound Prometheus*, Cambridge University Press, Cambridge.

Laski H. [1934]
'What are the Social Sciences', in introduction to the *Encyclopedia of Social Sciences*, Macmillan, London.

Lee Won & Koo Suk Mo [1988]
'Trade-off between Economic Growth and Income Equality' in Y.S. Brenner et al. (eds) *The Theory of Income and Wealth Distribution*, Harvester & St Martin's, Sussex, New York.

Leibniz G.W. [1685]
*Discourse on Metaphysics* (quoted here from Hoffding, vol.I, pp.350-1).

Lenin V.I. [1917]
*Collected Works.* All quotations from Foreign Languages Publishing House, 1961 edition, Moscow.

Lenin V. I. [1917a]
*State and Revolution* (quoted here from Moscow Foreign Languages Publishing House, 1947 German edition, vol.II).

Lenin V. I. [1964]
'The Development of capitalism in Russia' (quoted here from Clemens Dutt, *Fundamentals of Marxism-Leninism*, Foreign Languages Publishing House, Moscow).

Lewontin R.C. [1968]
'Evolution' in *International Encyclopedia of Social Sciences*, vol. V (ed. D. Sills), Macmillan, New York.

Lindert P.H. [1986]
'The Comparative History of Wealth and Income Inequality' (Paper: Utrecht Symposium on Income and Wealth Distribution).

Lloyd A. [1957]
in Singer Ch., Holmyard E.J., Hall A.R. & Williams T., *A History of Technology*, vol.III, Oxford, Clarendon Press.

Locke J. [1689]
*Epistola de Tolerantia,* Gouda 1689 (William Popple translation, London 1689).

Locke J. [1690]
*An Essay Concerning Human Understanding* (quoted from Everyman edition, London, 1947).

Locke J. [1690a]
*Two Treatises of Government* (quoted from Peter Laslett's translation, Cambridge, 1960).

Luxemburg R. [1918]
'Leninism or Marxism' (reprinted in *Le populaire,* 1922 and quoted here from *The Russian Revolution & Leninism or Marxism,* Michigan University Press Ann Arbor, 1961), pp.68-72.

MacIntyre A. [1967]
*A Short History of Ethics,* Routledge and Kegan Paul, London.

Maddison A. [1982]
*Phases of Capitalist Development,* Oxford University Press, Oxford.

Malthus R.T. [1789]
*An Essay on the Principle of Population* (quoted here from Everyman edition of 1960 which is based Malthus's version of 1872).

Manders A.J.C. [1990]
*Sturing van Productie-Technology (Decision-making about Production Technology)* Dutch. Kerckebosch, Zeist.

Mandeville B. [1714]
*The Fable of the Bees: Or Private Vices, Publick Benefits* (quoted from F.B. Kaye, Clarendon edition, Oxford, 1824).

Marris R. & Mueller D.C. [1980]
'The Corporation, Competition, and the "Invisible Hand," *Journal of Economic Literature,* vol.xviii.

Marx K. & Engels F. [1848]
*The Communist Manifesto,* Werke (MEW) vol.4, Berlin 1959.

Marx K. & Engels F. [1958]
*Selected Works,* Foreign Languages Publishing House, Moscow.

Marx K. [1859]
*A Contribution to the Critique of Political Economy* (English edition), Lawrence and Wishart, 1971.

Marx K. [1972]
*Das Kapital,* vol.I., Dietz Verlag, Berlin.

Marx K. [1938]
*Critique of Gotha Programme* (revised translation, ed. C.P. Dutt) International Publishers, New York.

Matthews R.C.O. [1959]
*The Trade Cycle,* James Nisbet & Cambridge University Press, Cambridge.

Mitchell B.R. [1975]
*European Historical Statistics 1750-1970,* Macmillan, London.

Molière J.B.P. [1664]
*Tartuffe.*
Molière J.B.P. [1670]
*Le Bourgeois Gentilhomme.*
Monroe D.H. [1967]
'Jeremy Bentham' in *The Encyclopedia of Philosophy*, Macmillan, New York.
Moraze C. [1961]
'The Spirit of the Nineteenth Century' in Rene Taton (ed.), *Science in the Nineteenth Century*, vol.II (English translation) Thames & Hudson, London, 1964.
Morgan D. [1979]
*Merchants of Grain,* Viking Press.
Newton I. [1687]
*Philosophiea naturalis principia mathematica* (English translation, 1729).
Niebuhr R.H. [1953]
'Protestantism' in *Encyclopedia of Social Sciences*, vol.XII, (first published in 1935), Macmillan, New York.
Noll Prof. [1976]
*Die Weltwoche,* 24 November, Zurich.
Nossiter B.D. [1977]
'Outcasts of the Islands', *New York Review of Books,* no.14, April, New York.
Ogburn W.F. [1935]
'Social Change' in *Encyclopedia of Social Sciences* (first published in 1935), vol.III, p.335, New York.
Oman Sir Ch. [1936]
'War in the 15th Century', *Cambridge Mediaeval History*, vol.VIII, London.
Parson T. [1953]
*Encyclopedia of Social Sciences* (first published in 1935), New York.
Perlman M. [1968]
'Labour Unions', *International Encyclopedia of Social Sciences,* Macmillan, New York.

Phelps E.H. Brown & Hopkins S.V. [1956]
'Seven Centuries of Building Wages', *Economica,* November, Appendix B.

Pirenne H. [1925]
*Mediaeval Cities,* Princeton University Press, New York.

Pirenne H. [1936]
'The Low Countries'. *Cambridge Mediaeval History,* Cambridge.

Pirenne H. [1956]
*Economic and Social History of Mediaeval Europe,* Harcourt-Brace, New York.

Postan M.M. [1944]
'The Rise of the Money Economy', *Economic History Review,* no.14.

Postan M.M. [1952]
'The Trade of Mediaeval Europe: The North', *Cambridge Economic History of Europe,* vol.II, Cambridge.

Prawer J. [1965]
'La Noblesse et le régime féodal du royamme latin de Jerusalem', *Moyen Age.*

Proudhon P.J. [1876]
*What is Property?* (translated by B. Tucker), Princeton.

Ransom R.L. & Sutch R. [1986]
'The life-cycle transition: Wealth holding in America' (paper: Utrecht Symposium on Income and Wealth Distribution).

Reijnders J. [1988]
'Economic Stability and Political Expediency' in Y.S. Brenner et al., *The Theory of Income and Wealth Distribution,* Wheatsheaf/ St Martin's, Sussex & New York.

Reijnders J. [1990]
*Long Waves in Economic Development,* Edward Elgar, Aldershot.

Ricardo D. [1793]
*Correspondence* (in Bonar ed., 1887).

Ricardo D. [1896]
*Quarterly Journal of Economics* (The correspondence with McCulloch was edited by Hollander J.H. for the American Economic Association), Boston.

Ricardo D. [1817]
*The Principles of Political Economy and Taxation* (Quotations here from Pelican edition, Harmondsworth, 1971).

Robinson J. [1964]
*Economic Philosophy*, Penguin, Harmondsworth.

Robinson J. & Eatwell [1973]
*An Introduction to Modern Economics*, McGraw-Hill, London.

Rosenberg N. [1983]
*Inside the Black Box*, Cambridge University Press, Cambridge.

Rosenberg N. and Birdzell L.E. [1986]
*How the West Grew Rich*, Basic Books.

Rosenberg N. and Birdzell L.E. [1990]
'Science, Technology and the Western Miracle', *Scientific American*, November, pp.18-25.

Rousseau J-J. [1762]
*Emile* (quoted here from 1886 translation).

Rousseau J-J. [1762a]
*The Social Contract* (quoted here from Everyman edition, 1941, London).

Rousseau J-J. [1865-1870]
*Oeuvres complètes de J.-J. Rousseau*, vols.1-13, Paris.

Rousseau J-J. [1915]
*The Political Writings of Jean-Jacques Rousseau* (ed. C.E. Vaughem), Cambridge.

Runciman S. [1951-2;4]
*A History of the Crusades*, Cambridge.

Sabine G.H. [1961]
*A Short History of Political Theory* (3rd edition), George G. Harrap Co. Ltd., London.

Sampson A. [1983]
*The Money Lenders*, Harmondsworth, Middlesex, Penguin.

Sampson A. [1975]
*The Seven Sisters*, Hodder and Stoughton, London.

Samuelson P.A. [1939]
'Interaction between the Multiplier Analysis and the Principle of Acceleration', *Review of Economic Statistics*.

Scholliers P. [1986]
'Industrial Wage Differentials in 19th Century Belgium' (Paper: Utrecht Symposium on Income and Wealth Distribution).

Shaftesbury A.A.C. [1699]
*An Inquiry Concerning Virtue or Merit*, London.

Shaftesbury A.A.C. [1709]
*The Moralist: A Philosophical Rhapsody*, London.

Shepherd W.G. [1982]
'Causes of Increased Competition in the US Economy 1939-1980', *Review of Economics and Statistics*, vol.lxiv, no.4, November.

Silts D.L. (Ed) [19??]
*International Encyclopedia of the Social Sciences*, Macmillan, New York.

Singer Ch., Holmyard E.J., Hall A.R. and Williams T.I. (eds) [1956]
*A History of Technology*, vols II & III, Clarendon, Oxford.

Slicher van Bath H. [1963]
*The Agrarian History of Western Europe AD 500-1850*, Edward Arnold, London.

Smith Adam [1759]
*The Theory of Moral Sentiments* (quoted here from 2nd edition, 1790).

Smith Adam [1776]
*An Inquiry into the Nature and Causes of the Wealth of Nations* (quoted here from 5th edition edited by Edwin Cannan. Page numbers refer to Modern Library, Random House, New York, 1937).

Smith D. [1987]
*The Rise and Fall of Monetarism*, Pelican Books, Harmondsworth.

Soderberg J. [1986]
'Wage Differentials in Sweden 1725-1950' (Paper: Utrecht Symposium on Income and Wealth Distribution).

Sombart W. [1953]
'Capitalism' in *Encyclopedia of Social Sciences,* vol.III, Macmillan, New York (first published 1935).

Sorel G. [1908]
*Reflections on Violence* (translated by T.E. Hulme & J. Roth, 1914), New York.

Sorley W.R. [1912]
*The Cambridge History of English Literature,* London.

Spencer H. [1850]
*Social Statics.*

Spencer H. [1862]
*First Principles* (6th edition, 1937), London.

Spencer H. [1876-96]
*Principles of Sociology* (3 vols), London.

Stalin Joseph [1928]
Quoted here from Clemens Dutt translation. *Fundamentals of Marxism-Leninism* [1964], Foreign Languages Publishing House, Moscow.

Steuart J. [1767]
*Collected Works* (quoted from 1805 edition).

Stewart M. [1972]
*Keynes and After,* Pelican Books, Harmondsworth.

Supple B.E. [1957]
'Currency and Commerce in Early Seventeenth Century', *Economic History Review,* vol.X.

Swift J. [1729]
*Modest Proposal for Preventing the Children of Ireland from being a Burden to their Parents or Country and for making them beneficial to the Public* (quoted from Clarendon Press edition, Oxford, 1927).

Tawney R.H. [1922]
*The Agrarian Problem in the Sixteenth Century.*

Tawney R.H. [1926]
*Religion and the Rise of Capitalism* (quoted here from Penguin edition, West Drayton, 1948).

Underwood Faulkner H. [1963]
*American Economic History* (8th edition), Harper International, New York.

Van der Veen D.J. [1986]
'The Standard of Living of Working-Class Families in the Netherlands 1850-1920' (Paper: Utrecht Symposium on Income and Wealth Distribution).

Walker D.A. [1984]
'Is Walras's theory of general equilibrium a normative scheme?' *History of Political Economy*, vol.16:3.

Webb S. & Webb B. [1920]
*The History of Trade Unionism* (new edition), Longmans Green, London.

Weber M. [1925]
*Wirtschaft und Gesellschaft* (first published Tubingen 1922).

Weber M. [1930]
*The Protestant Ethic and the Spirit of Capitalism*, London. First published in *Archiv für Sozial Wissenschaft und Sozialpolitik*, 1904-5.

Wenlersse G. [1937]
*Encyclopedia of Social Sciences*, vol.V, 'Economics' (Physiocrats).

White L. [1962]
*Mediaeval Technology and Social Change*, New York.

Williamson J.G. [1986]
'Income Inequality in Britain during the Industrial Revolution: Accounting for the Kuznets Curve' (Paper: Utrecht Symposium on Income and Wealth Distribution).

# Name Index

# Subject Index

Ability
    to accelerate economic
        growth  91
Absenteeism  249
Abuse  19
Acceleration principle  187
Accident Insurance  143
Acclaim  11
Accounting and control  7
Accumulation  115
    and concentration of
        capital  10
    of capital  128, 259
Achievement  29
Acquisition  115
Acquisitive society  257
Action  11
    groups  183, 212
Advertising  240
Aesthetic criticism  234
Affluence  4, 16, 31, 119, 200
Age
    and sex composition of
        employment  193
    of Enlightenment  124
    of Reason  71, 72, 257
Aged and infirm  224
Aggregate
    expenditure  168
    purchasing power  168

Aggregates  8, 165
Agricultural
    Adjustment Act  165
    improvements  15
    trap  16
Agriculture  7
Alchemists  78
Alienated  8
Alienation  267
Alternative society  117
Altruism  81
Amalgamation  240
American way of life  208
Anarchism  132, 134
Anarcho
    -syndicalism  131, 132-135,
        139
    -syndicalist ideology  131
    -syndicalists  127, 260
Ancient rights  25
Aristocracy  29, 30, 107, 118, 255
    the scientific community  210
Aristocratic
    life-style  29
    privileges  84
Aristocrats  113, 208
Armed insurrection  129
Artists  111, 208
Arts  31
Ascetic

Revolution   136

Safety-net   234
Salvation   23
   hope of   20
Save   2, 9
   ability to   2, 5, 253, 254
   and invest, ability to   16
   wish or propensity to   2
Savers   171
Saving   99
   catalytic effect of   6
Savings   2
   optimal utilization of the   8
   potential and actual   7
   restrictive measures to
      increase   219
Say's Law   242
Scarcity   123, 124
Scepticism   101
Scholasticism   71, 181, 257
Schools   194
Science   32, 71, 78, 180
   and society   32
   constant progressive
      element in   96
   modern   180
Scientific
   advancement   268
   community   207
   discoveries   126
   innovations   268
   outlook   32
   perception of the universe
      32
   perceptions   32
   socialism   127, 128
Scientists   159, 207, 208, 257, 268
   greedy   207
Scientists'
   perception of society and the
      universe   206
   perception of the universe
      268

philosophical background
   264
Secularism   24
Self-
   employed   148
   evidence   101
   evident   98, 101, 210
   fulfilling prophecies   187
   interest   131, 274
   love   98
Sense of propriety   250
Sensuous impressions   32
Separation of tasks   90
Serfdom   27
Service sector's contribution to the
   economy   227
Service occupations
   ancillary   225
Services   2, 4, 168, 194, 215, 217,
   218, 223, 224, 227, 270, 271
   are non-material or intangible
      goods   222
   which are 'consumed' at the
      point of production   226
   which require the
      simultaneous attendance of
      consumer   218
Set of values
   absolute   73
Share of the government   203
Short-term processes   230
Sickness Insurance   143
Skills   3, 29, 258
Slavery   26
Slaves   3, 26, 118
Slothfulness   23
Small enterprises   219
Social
   and economy system   204,
      268
   behaviour   21
   class   259
   climate   270
   consciousness   163